COLOR, RACE, AND ENGLISH LANGUAGE TEACHING

SHADES OF MEANING

COLOR, RACE, AND ENGLISH LANGUAGE TEACHING

SHADES OF MEANING

Edited by

Andy Curtis
Queen's University

Mary Romney
Quinebaug Valley Community College

2006   LAWRENCE ERLBAUM ASSOCIATES, PUBLISHERS
        Mahwah, New Jersey   London

Copyright © 2006 by Lawrence Erlbaum Associates, Inc.
All rights reserved. No part of this book may be reproduced in any form, by photostat, microform, retrieval system, or any other means, without prior written permission of the publisher.

Lawrence Erlbaum Associates, Inc., Publishers
10 Industrial Avenue
Mahwah, New Jersey 07430
www.erlbaum.com

Cover design by Tomai Maridou

Library of Congress Cataloging-in-Publication Data

Color, race, and English language teaching : shades of meaning / edited by Andy Curtis, Mary Romney.
    p. cm.
Includes bibliographical references and index.
ISBN 0-8058-5659-5 (cloth : alk. paper)
ISBN 0-8058-5660-9 (pbk. : alk. paper)
1. English language—Study and teaching—Foreign speakers. 2. Educational anthropology—English-speaking countries. 3. Minority teachers—English-speaking countries. 4. English teachers. I. Curtis, Andy. II. Romney, Mary.
PE1128.A2C675 2006
428.0071'1—dc22   2005040161
                                                                                      CIP

Books published by Lawrence Erlbaum Associates are printed on acid-free paper, and their bindings are chosen for strength and durability.

Printed in the United States of America
10 9 8 7 6 5 4 3 2 1

I humbly and respectfully dedicate this book to my multicoloured family, scattered across the continents, whose shades of black, brown and yellow have given my life its meaning.

—*Andy Curtis*

*I dedicate this book to the memory of my parents,
Alice C. Romney and Lionel Romney,
who gave me my appreciation for language and languages.*

—*Mary Romney*

Contents

Foreword   ix

Preface   xi

1   A Brief Introduction to Critical Race Theory, Narrative Inquiry, and Educational Research   1
Andy Curtis

2   Dark Matter: Teaching and Learning Between Black and White   11
Andy Curtis

3   An Exceptional Voice: Working as a TESOL Professional of Color   23
Shondel Nero

4   Stories Through Perceptual Frames   37
Donna Fujimoto

5   My Journey Into Racial Awareness   49
Carmen T. Chacón

6   From Learning English in a Colony to Working as a Female TESOL Professional of Color: A Personal Odyssey   65
Angel M. Y. Lin

7	Perpetual Foreigners: Can an American Be an American? *Shelley Wong*	81
8	Becoming an English Native: An English TESOL Professional of Color's Experience *Carlos Islam*	93
9	Musings of a Black ESL Instructor *Marinus Stephan*	107
10	The World Away From Home *Gertrude Tinker Sachs*	121
11	English Teaching and Ethnic Origin *Anam K. Govardhan*	137
12	Not a Real American: Experiences of a Reluctant Ambassador *Mary Romney*	149
13	Out of the Safety Zone *Suhanthie Motha*	161
14	Confessions of an *Enraced* TESOL Professional *Ahmar Mahboob*	173
15	Conclusion *Mary Romney*	189
Author Index		199
Subject Index		203

Foreword

Kathleen M. Bailey[1]
Monterey Institute of International Studies, Graduate School of Language and Educational Linguistics

In 2001, I attended a colloquium entitled "Linguistic Perceptions of TESOL Professionals of Color" at the TESOL Convention in St. Louis, Missouri, along with my Master's student, Desma Johnson. She was a young teacher from Florida, and this was her first TESOL convention. I had nominated Desma and she had been selected for TESOL's Leadership Mentoring Program. This initiative was started by the TESOL Board of Directors to encourage more nonnative speakers of English, more primary and secondary school teachers, and more members of U.S. ethnic and racial minorities to prepare for and take on leadership roles in the Association. I invited Desma to go to the colloquium with me because it had been organized by friends of mine who were active in the International Black Professionals and Friends in TESOL Caucus. From my knowledge of them, I expected that the content of the program would be quite good.

What I did not expect was to be moved to tears by most of the speakers. I did not expect to learn about serious (often negative) youthful experiences that my friends and colleagues had had, apparently as a result of their race. I did not expect to be ashamed of what teachers had said and done to them, perhaps sometimes unknowingly, perhaps sometimes intentionally.

When the colloquium was over and the panelists were entertaining questions and comments from the audience, I asked Andy Curtis and Mary

---

[1]President, TESOL Association, 1998–1999.

Romney what they planned to do next with this information, this momentum. They looked at me, somewhat startled, I think, because their months-long effort of planning and organizing the colloquium had finally culminated in a successful multi-ethnic, multinational effort to discuss these sensitive issues in a recognized, prestigious forum. They thought they were done. (Andy didn't exactly say, "What do you mean, *next*, Bailey?" but that was what the look on his face conveyed.) I suggested that these ideas were important enough to be collected and distributed in print, and so the idea of a book was born.

Now, some years later, I hope that Mary and Andy are pleased with the outcome. I know that I am. The edited papers collected here depict the personal and professional experiences of 13 successful teachers, teacher educators, and researchers. These authors represent various countries and ethnicities. What they have in common is that they all consider themselves to be persons of color, and they are all working in some capacity in the TESOL profession. Also, they have all chosen to reflect on and share their (sometimes painful) experiences with a broad reading audience.

What struck me most as I read the manuscript was how often an event that originally lasted only minutes (or even seconds) had so profoundly influenced a child, an adolescent, or an adult; how just a few words could make a lasting impact on the hearer, whether for good or for ill. Reading about these authors' experiences made me search my memory: As a classmate, as a teacher, had I ever said anything terribly hurtful, or particularly encouraging, to someone different from me—another student or one of my own pupils?

My student, Desma, left the colloquium that day, happy that she had come and glad to be a part of an organization that was dealing with issues of race in the classroom. I left the colloquium happy to have been there, but a bit ashamed that, as an association, we were only beginning to address these matters. I am delighted that Andy and Mary took up the challenge to collect and edit these contributions, and to produce this beautifully coherent volume of stories. I hope that, as you read it, you will be as moved and as inspired as I have been by the authors' insights and candor.

There are many shades of meaning here, and these chapters bear reading and rereading. I urge you to share them with your students and your colleagues, in hopes that we can all enjoy greater equality and recognition through open discussions of diversity in our profession.

Preface

PURPOSE AND RATIONALE

The beginnings of this collection of personal-professional narratives go back several years, to the TESOL convention (Teaching English to Speakers of Other Languages) in St. Louis, Missouri, in March 2001. There, at a colloquium presentation, five of us—Mary Romney, Andy Curtis, Shelley Wong, Donna Fujimoto, and Gertrude Tinker Sachs—described incidents and events in our personal lives, as people of color, that had had a lasting impact on our professional lives, as TESOL professionals of color (Romney, Curtis, Wong, Fujimoto, & Sachs, 2001). The panel presentation was unexpectedly well attended by English language teaching professionals—both White and of color—and we found ourselves engaged in not only presenting our stories but also in hearing those of many others in the audience that day. After the presentation, Professor Kathleen Bailey, of the Monterey Institute of International Studies in California, suggested that this had been an unusual and important event in our field, and that we should consider collecting and gathering together such narratives from an international group of teachers, writers, and practitioner-researchers. Several long years later, we have completed this task.

In terms of similar sources available and being produced at that time, which became another incentive to put this collection together, there were three books. The first was Christine Pearson Casanave and Sandra Schecter's *On Becoming a Language Educator: Personal Essays on Professional*

Development (1997). In their preface, Casanave and Schecter stated the purpose of their book: "both readers and authors use the stories told here to view their own professional lives from fresh perspectives" as "they forge links between the concreteness and commonality of the narratives and the potentially profound meanings to be found in human experience" (p. xiii). Although the second section of the book addressed "identity dilemmas," which was especially relevant to us, we felt that a complete collection of narratives that examined particular aspects of identity was still needed.

Diane Belcher and Ulla Connor's *Reflections on Multiliterate Lives* (2001) presented "eighteen highly successful second-language users" who were asked to "outline in their own words their struggles and successes along the path to language learning" (p. 2). Just as Belcher and Connor's contributors focused on language learning, we felt that there was need for a similar focus on language teaching, especially in light of the fact that, although race did surface in the narratives of some of Belcher and Connor's contributors' accounts (e.g., Suresh Canagarajah's account of his undergraduate essay "on the evils of racism"; p. 27), color and race generally appeared only as asides or were in the background. However, in our own experiences, race and color were usually very much in the foreground.

A third important collection for us was Lilia Jacobs, Jose Cintron, and Cecil Canton's *The Politics of Survival in Academia: Narratives of Inequality, Resilience and Success* (2002), which presented 10 "narratives of struggle." This collection included narrative reflections on race, class, gender, and disability, sometimes in overlapping and multiple manifestations (e.g., Eugenia Cowan's account as a woman of color, a lesbian, and a middle-class Black person in the United States). However, we were still looking for a collection of narratives that combined aspects of all three of these—and many other—works, with a focus on race and color in English language teaching and learning.

ELICITING THE NARRATIVES

In this collection, we set out to address what appears to have been a largely overlooked area of experience within the field of English language teaching and learning: What does it mean to be a TESOL professional of color? In addressing this question, we invited TESOL professionals of color to write about their experiences, responding to two related questions:

1. As a person of color, can you identify one or more critical events or critical conditions in your personal or professional life that were or are the result of you being a person of color, which affect who you are now, what you do, and how you do it as a TESOL professional of color? The question was complex because the issue is complex. By *critical events*,

we meant moments, incidents, or other individual, isolated occurrences. By *critical conditions*, we meant persistent, permanent, or recurring situations or contexts. It is also worth noting that our use of *critical* here was in its common meaning (i.e., "of great importance"), and not in connection with *critical* as used in, for example, *critical race theory*.

2. What have you learned from these events or conditions that have had a bearing on your life as a TESOL professional of color? For responses to these questions, we sought contributions from TESOL professionals of African descent, Asian descent, and mixed-heritage people of Latin American descent, working in a variety of contexts in Africa, North America, Latin America, and Asia.

OVERVIEW

The 13 narratives are presented in the order in which the contributors are introduced as follows. Before the main narratives is a brief introduction to and overview of aspects of critical race theory, narrative inquiry, and educational research. After the narratives is a concluding chapter, in which the recurring themes of the narratives are identified in relation to some of the main issues facing TESOL professionals, as highlighted by the narratives. The introduction, overview, and concluding chapters are highly selective, because one of the challenges we faced—which we believe many busy English language teaching professionals face—was the relative inaccessibility of much of what we came across in much of the writing in these three areas. The studies often appeared to be written by full-time professional academics and scholars for a similar audience, rather than teachers who spend 20 hours per week in the classroom, plus 20 hours on top of that in preparation and marking.

An important, and somewhat unusual, feature of this collection is the focus questions that we have created for each chapter. We have tried to make these as unintrusive as possible, using numbers in the text to refer to questions at the end of each chapter. It is, of course, possible to read the narratives without referring to the questions, but in our own readings of the narratives of others we found ourselves asking questions that helped us go beyond an initial reading, enabling us to apply aspects of the narrative of another person's life to our own, creating a new, synthesized, experiential understanding.

Some of the contributors have chosen to refer to published studies within their narratives, others have chosen to use footnotes to give additional details, and a third group has chosen to give only the narrative, with minimal reference to external sources. After much consideration and consultation, we found that all three of these approaches to narrative have their strengths and weaknesses, so decided to include all of them, in the belief that they balance each other.

ABOUT THE CONTRIBUTORS

Notes on contributors are often listed at the end of edited collections. However, when the contributors are writing about themselves—about the struggles, challenges, and successes of their personal-professional lives—it is their lives that give the book its substance, form, and structure. Therefore, we prefer to open our volume with information about our contributors:

Andy Curtis, Ph.D., is an Englishman of Indian descent. He considers the impressions that specific incidents have made on him and his teaching. He further discusses assumptions underlying the reactions of some of his students, and ways in which recent world events have influenced some of the treatment he receives.

Shondel Nero, Ed.D., is from Guyana. She describes what it means to be perceived as an exception, and discusses the causes of exceptionality and its effects on relationships with students and colleagues and on the TESOL profession at large.

Donna Fujimoto, M.A., a Japanese American, explains how her life and work in Japan have been affected by two contrasting contexts, and how she is perceived in each one. She describes her movements between one kind of minority status and another, depending on which context she is in.

Carmen T. Chacón, Ph.D., from Venezuela, describes her transition from "color-blindness" to awareness of race and racial attitudes reflected in her native language. She discovered the relationship between race and nonnative English status through her experiences living and studying in the United States.

Angel M. Y. Lin, Ph.D., from Hong Kong, reveals the evolution of her relationship with the English language and then explains how her professional life has been affected by task segregation along gender and racial lines. She discusses the consequences of this for the entire profession.

Shelley Wong, Ed.D., a Chinese American, draws parallels between her family's history in the United States and her experience in the TESOL profession. She explains what history can teach about the future directions toward which she believes the TESOL profession needs to move.

Carlos Islam, M.A., is an Englishman of Bangladeshi and Spanish descent. He reflects on who is considered English and how this affects his sense of identity. He finds contrasts in how he is identified and accepted by students, colleagues, and society at large, depending on whether he is in England or abroad.

Marinus Stephan, Ph.D., is from Suriname. In his chapter, he details how the convergence of race and nonnativeness formed certain perceptions that affected the treatment he received from some of his students. He also describes his research on the relationship between race and student preferences for ESL instructors.

Gertrude Tinker Sachs, Ph.D., is from the Bahamas. Her 12-years of life and work in Hong Kong, as well as some of her experiences as a graduate student in Canada, are the subject of her chapter. She discusses racial attitudes in Hong Kong, their impact on her work, and on how she was treated.

Anam K. Govardhan, Ph.D., from India, chronicles his experience on three continents as a student and a teacher. He comments on both reactions to his "Indianness" in a variety of settings and what his experiences have indicated about the profession.

Mary Romney, M.Ed., an African American of Caribbean descent, discusses some of her experiences in Spain. She describes how perceptions of English and the effects of the popular culture have led to certain perceptions of both Black people and who "real" Americans are.

Suhanthie Motha, Ph.D., is an ethnic Tamil, born in Sri Lanka, who grew up in Australia. She observes that concern for the interests of one group can eclipse the real value of discussions about challenging issues. She takes a stand on where responsibility for advancing justice should lie, and expresses concern about the effects of role models and mentors on students at all levels.

Ahmar Mahboob, Ph.D., from Pakistan, grew up in that country and the United Arab Emirates. He coined a new term, *enraced*, in order to capture a range of concepts of race as he has experienced them in the TESOL profession. He uses the new term to relate his observations and describe his experiences as a student and a teacher.

—*Andy Curtis*
Mary Romney

ACKNOWLEDGMENTS

I would like to thank my husband, Philip Schaab, for his support for this and all my professional development. I thank Kathi Bailey for all her encouragement through the years. I appreciate all of those who had the faith in this project to see it to fruition, especially my wonderfull co-editor, Andy Curtis. I am also grateful to our editor, Naomi Silverman, and her staff. And I would like to express my deepest gratitude to all the contributors, who had the courage to share their narratives.

—*Mary Romney*

My heartfelt gratitude goes to my mentor, Kathi Bailey, for many years of support and guidance, and to a great co-editor, Mary Romney, for helping us always keep our eyes on the prize. Thank you to all our contributors for having the strength and courage to share their stories and to Naomi Silverman at Lawrence Erlbaum publishers for believing in this project when others did not. My most heartfelt thanks go to my beloved traveling companion on this life's long and challenging journey, Liying Cheng.

—*Andy Curtis*

A BRIEF NOTE ON THE USE OF DIFFERENT TYPES OF ENGLISH IN THIS COLLECTION

It is standard practice to adopt one type of language, in this case, English, throughout a book, most commonly what is referred to as "American English", "British English", etc. However, we are grateful to Lawrence Erlbaum for accepting our proposal to allow different types of English to be used by different contributors to this collection, as the voice of the writer is of central importance in narrative inquiry and the type of English used is reflected in the way that English is written.

REFERENCES

Belcher, D., & Connor, U. (Eds.). (2001). *Reflection on multiliterate lives*. New York: Multilingual Matters.
Casanave, C. P., & Schecter, S. R. (Eds.). (1997). *On becoming a language educator: Personal essays on professional development*. Mahwah, NJ: Lawrence Erlbaum Associates.
Jacobs, L., Cintron, J., & Canton, C. E. (2002). *The politics of survival in academia: Narratives of inequality, resilience and success*. Boulder, CO: Rowman & Littlefield.
Romney, M., Curtis, A., Wong, S., Fujimoto, D., & Sachs, G. T. (2001, March). Linguistic perceptions of TESOL professionals of color. Colloquium presented at *TESOL 2001: Gateway to the Future*, St. Louis, MO.

Chapter 1

A Brief Introduction to Critical Race Theory, Narrative Inquiry, and Educational Research

Andy Curtis
Queen's University

The notion of being able to give a brief introduction to critical race theory (CRT), not to mention its relationships to narrative inquiry and educational research, reminds me of a seemingly unrelated book I read years ago. It was entitled *Kierkegaard in a Nutshell* (Van de Weyer, 1997), and was part of the Philosophers of the Spirit series, which included discussions of Hildegard, Pascal, and Socrates. On the first page of the introduction, Van de Weyer noted that Kierkegaard "was not an easy writer; his arguments are complex, his logic often tortuous and prone to unexpected leaps, and his prose frequently repetitive" (p. 9). In the same way that Van de Weyer attempted to present a brief but clear overview and summary of a great deal of difficult and challenging work, I have attempted here to do the same with critical race theory and its relationships to narrative inquiry and educational research. However, Van de Weyer had 90 pages in which to accomplish his task, whereas I very much doubt that any reader of this book has the time to work their way through 90 pages of CRT, narrative inquiry, and educational research. I have, then, attempted to be as focused and as selective as possible, which will, by definition, lead to omissions. But in return, my goal is to present a more accessible and more manageable introduction to these areas than most that I have come across.

RACE

According to Larry Rowley (2004), "Writing at the turn of the 20th century, W. E. B. Du Bois argued that the defining social problem of the historical epoch know as the 'American Century' would be the issue of race (Du Bois, 1903)" (p. 15). Although this prophetic statement from Du Bois has proved to be true in many ways, as witnessed by the recent reopening of the scientific debate on race reactivated by the Human Genome Project (Abraham, 2005), it has by now become a global discussion and not just an American interest.

A small but effective example of the problems involved in attempting to define or even describe "race" was presented by Carol Lee (2003), in her editor's introduction to the American Educational Research Association's 2003 special issue of *Educational Researcher* on "Reconceptualizing Race and Ethnicity in Educational Research." Lee described the difficulties of naming the special issue: "I tried to move beyond this country's race-based classification scheme because to use any of the current terms inadvertently communicates the assumptions of privilege against which we argue" (p. 3). Apart from the fact that "race-based classification schemes" are no longer an issue only in America, Lee made some important points about the limits of language in describing people. She went on to write that had they deleted the word *race* from the title and "had we called this special issue *Reconceptualizing Ethnicity in Educational Research* many would have assumed that people of African descent, for example, were not the subject of our inquiry because people of African descent are not generally viewed as an ethnic group; they are identified solely as a racial group on the basis of color" (p. 3).

In relation to studies on the relationship between race and school achievement, Mica Pollock (2001) described race as "the hidden subject" (p. 9), in part because of the difficulties of language and nomenclature she encountered in the school where she worked as a teacher and researcher, a place where teachers talked about "helping black students without calling them 'black'" (p. 5). Displaying admirable honesty, Pollock concluded with some soul-searching autobiographical self-study:

> Those players who feel closest to racial patterns, it seems, often become most afraid of mentioning their existence. After two years around Columbus [school] as teacher and then researcher, I myself would hear a student coming late to class and anticipate she would be "black"; I regularly assumed that honor roll lists would largely display names that were either "Filipino" or "Chinese." (p. 9)

However, even when a concept is very difficult discuss or describe, it may still be a central aspect of the debate. Indeed, it may occupy that position in part because it is so difficult to define or discuss, as Henig, Hula, Orr, and Pedescleaux (2001) pointed out in their work, *The Color of School Reform*: "[R]ace plays an important confounding factor in the development of civic capacity. It would be foolish and counterproductive to overlook it" (p. 7).

In relation to race and educational research, Michelle Young and Jerry Rosiek (2000)—referring to the early work of Gillborn (1990), Sleeter (1992), Tatum (1992), and others—noted that "scholars in the field of education have focused on issues of race as critical to socially just and equitable education, educational practice, and educational policy for a number of years" (p. 39). Young and Rosiek went on to state that "more recently, a number of scholars have succeeded in moving the study of racial identity, including white racial identify, into educational discourse" (p. 39).

In terms of defining what "race" is and is not, an important publication was Lawrence Parker, Donna Deyhle, and Sofia Villena's *Race Is ... Race Isn't: Critical Race Theory and Qualitative Studies in Education* (1999). In this collection, the different contributors "capitalize[d] on the theme of counter-storytelling as a narrative structure that can be used in qualitative research methods to document subjugated accounts of reality" (Lopez, 2001, p. 31). The book drew on the experiences of Latino/Latina and Navajo communities in America, as well as those of First Nations and Korean American contributors. In the concluding chapter of *Race Is ... Race Isn't*, William Tate (1994) suggested that work in the area of race and critical race theory should "explore the lives, successes, marginalization, and oppression of people of color" (p. 268).

CRITICAL RACE THEORY

The complex, tripartite nature of critical race theory was captured in Richard Delgado and Jean Stefanic's (2001) commonly cited definition, which highlighted the relationships among the development of an academic-professional theory, attempts to bring about specific changes, and the people making those attempts: "The critical race theory (CRT) movement is a collection of activists and scholars interested in studying and transforming the relationships among race, racism, and power" (p. 2). In terms of the origins of CRT, according to Delgado and Stefanic (2001):

> Critical race theory sprang up in the mid-1970s, as a number of lawyers, activists, and legal scholars across the country realized ... that the heady advances of the civil rights era of the 1960s had stalled and, in many respects, were being rolled back. Realizing that new theories and strategies were needed to combat the subtler forms of racism that were gaining ground, early writers such as Derrick Bell, Alan Freeman, and Richard Delgado ... put their minds to the task. They were soon joined by others, and the group held its first conference at a convent outside Madison, Wisconsin, in the summer of 1989. (p. 2)

The rise of CRT was accompanied by the emergence of critical legal studies (CLS), in which legal scholars of color developed theories of race and racism that enabled them to "better understand how racial power can be produced even from within a liberal discourse that is relatively autonomous from organized vectors of racial power" (Crenshaw, Gotanda, Peller, & Thomas, 1995, p. xxv). As Sleeter and Delgado Bernal (2004) maintained, "although CRT began in legal studies, it has spread to other disciplines, including education" (p. 245), and since 1994 "scholars of color in the field of education have increasingly employed it [CRT] in their research and practice" (p. 245). This can be seen in the work of educational researchers such as Gloria Ladson-Billings, who in the title of her 1998 paper provocatively asked the question: "Just What Is Critical Race Theory and What's It Doing in a Nice Field Like Education?" The question may be especially relevant to the field of teaching English to speakers of other languages, or TESOL, because it could just as easily have been: Just what is critical race theory and what's it doing in a *very* nice field like teaching English as a second/foreign language (EFL/ESL)?

In recent years, CRT has grown into independent subfields. One such subfield is LatCrits, which combines Latino/Latina studies with CRT (e.g., Gutierrez, 2000). Another subfield is FemCrits, which is based on critical race feminist theory (e.g., Ng, Staton, & Scane, 1995). One of most recent developments is Tribal Crits, which combines Native American Studies and CRT (e.g., Brayboy, 2001).

In responding to the first part of her own question on what CRT is, Ladson-Billings gave an answer that may surprise some with its openness: "Critical race theory begins with the notion that racism is normal in American society. It departs from mainstream legal scholarship by sometimes employing storytelling" (p. 7). The last part of the response highlighted the importance of narrative inquiry, whereas the next part of her response identified one of the potential limitations of CRT, because it is in its relatively early stages: "Critical race theory's usefulness in understanding education inequity is in its infancy. It requires a critique of some of the civil rights era's most cherished legal victories and educational reform movements, such as multiculturalism" (p. 7; see also Ladson-Billings, 1999; Ladson-Billings & Tate, 1995; Rasool & Curtis, 2000).

Sleeter and Delgado Bernal cited William Tate's 1994 article, "From Inner city to Ivory Tower: Does my voice matter in the academy?" as "the first explicit use of CRT in education" (p. 245). However, Tate had published a paper a year earlier based on a "critical race analysis of the proposed national assessment in mathematics" (1993), contrasting advocacy and economics. What may have made Tate's 1994 paper a first was that it was an *autobiographical* paper, with the voice in the academy being his own.

In relation to the three main contributions that CRT can make to the development of multicultural education, Sleeter and Delgado Bernal (2004)

1. A BRIEF INTRODUCTION TO CRITICAL RACE THEORY

identified "the third, and potentially greatest, contribution of CRT is its justification and use of storytelling in legal analysis and scholarship" (p. 247). In terms of how this contribution is made, Sleeter and Delgado Bernal went on to explain that "because CRT scholars view experiential knowledge as strength, they draw explicitly on the lived experiences of people of color by including such methods as storytelling, family history, biographies" (p. 247; see also Van Manen, 1990, for more on researching lived experiences). Examples of this can be seen in the work of researchers such as Adalberto Aguirre (2000), who has combined "academic storytelling" with CRT to present aspects of affirmative action from a sociological perspective (see also Aguirre 1987, 1995).

Within CRT, rather than standard narrative inquiry, there is "counterstorytelling," popularized by Richard Delgado, which originated within critical legal studies at the end of the 1980s (see Delgado, 1989, 1993, 1999). According to Sleeter and Delgado Bernal (2004), "Counterstorytelling [all one word] is a methodological tool that allows one to tell the story of those experiences that are not often told (i.e., by those on the margins of society) and to analyze and challenge the stories of those in power" (p. 247). In relation to education and counterstorytelling, Sleeter and Delgado Bernal specified three main applications and potential benefits: "building community among those at the margins of society, putting a human and familiar face on educational theory and practice, and challenging the perceived wisdom about the schooling of students of color" (p. 247).

As is the case with all theories, especially those "in their infancy" (see Ladson-Billings, 1998), CRT does not provide all the answers and it is not complete, as "some critics of CRT argue that it is an essentialist paradigm based on race" (Sleeter & Delgado Bernal, 2004, p. 248). However, much of the criticism of CRT seems to come from its use of narrative inquiry, which is discussed next.

CRT AND NARRATIVE INQUIRY

In terms of brief incidents that might stay with you for some time after the event, Delgado and Stefanic (2001) offered four examples from inside and outside of class:

> Think of events that can occur in an ordinary day. A child raises her hand repeatedly in a fourth grade class; the teacher either recognizes her or does not. A shopper hands a cashier a five dollar bill to pay for a small item; the clerk either smiles, makes small talk, and deposits change in the shopper's hand or does not. A woman goes to a new car lot ready to buy; salespeople stand about talking to each other or all converge trying to help her. A jogger

in a park gives a brief acknowledgment to an approaching walker; the walker returns the greeting or walks by silently. (p. 1)

Delgado and Stefanic then asked the reader to consider four sets of responses to these four incidents based on their color. In the white-to-white situation:

> You are a white person—the child, the shopper, the jogger. The responses are all from white people and are all negative. Are you annoyed? Do you, for even a moment, think that maybe you are receiving this treatment because of your race? Or might you think that all these people are having a bad day? Next suppose that the responses are all from persons of color. Are you thrown off guard? Angry? Depressed? (p. 1)

Then, Delgado and Stefanic addressed color-to-white and two types of color-to-color response and processing:

> You are a person of color and these same things happen to you and the actors are all white. What is the first thing that comes to your mind? Do you immediately think that you might be treated in these ways because you are not white? If so, how do you feel? Angry? Downcast? Do you let it roll off your back? And if the responses come from fellow persons of color, then what do you think? Suppose the person of color is from a group other than your own? (p. 1)

Delgado and Stefanic next offered two possible explanations for these reactions: "Sometimes actions like these are mere rudeness or indifference. The merchant is in a hurry; the walker, lost in thought. *But at other times, race seems to play a part*" [emphasis added] (p. 1). It is this last line, although so tentatively expressed as to be seemingly innocuous, that is at the center of this collection of personal-professional narratives. We will leave the question of whether or not race *should* matter to those in critical legal studies. But for English language teaching professionals, the questions then become: If race does play a part in our work, what part does it play? If race plays a part, what effects does race have on students, teachers, and administrators in our field? If some of these effects may be negative, what can we do to minimize or even negate these detrimental effects?

As with all theories, there are proponents and opponents, the latter arguing against the use of narrative in CRT. For example, Simon (1999) questioned CRT researchers and writers who "relentlessly replace traditional scholarship with personal stories, which hardly represent common experiences. The proliferation of stories makes it impossible for others to debate" (1999, p. 3). However, the editors of this collection of English language teaching (ETL) narratives believe that there are some aspects of a common experience, which are identified and discussed in the concluding chapter of this volume. Although an individual experience is, by definition, unique, there are certain commonalities that make narrative inquiry a valid form of educational research. This notion is discussed in more detail in the following section.

NARRATIVE INQUIRY AND EDUCATIONAL RESEARCH

One of the first areas of education in which narrative inquiry became established was the study of curriculum development, popularized by researchers such as Michael Connelly, Jean Clandinin, and others in the late 1980s. In their book *Teachers as Curriculum Planners: Narratives of Experience* (1988), Connelly and Clandinin stated that "The process of making meaning of our curriculum, that is, of the narratives of our experience, is both difficult and rewarding. It, too, has a narrative in that narratives of experience may be studied, reflected on, and articulated in written form" (p. 11). The ongoing development of this approach is demonstrated by the fact that more than a decade later, Clandinin and Connelly were still pursuing and exploring this approach, in their book *Narrative Inquiry: Experience and Story in Qualitative Research* (2000).

An example of this use of narrative inquiry is Margaret Olson's study of Canadian curriculum development (2000), which she claimed showed "the pivotal role that teachers' narrative knowledge plays in how curriculum is lived in classrooms" (p. 169). In her study, Olson compared and contrasted traditional, paradigmatic course-of-study views with narrative views of curriculum, with the former characterized by directional and container metaphors in which "a curriculum is one written *for* students and teachers in the form of prepackaged documents and resources" (p. 170). Olson contrasted this with a view in which curriculum is "understood as narratively constructed and reconstructed through experience" (p. 170). According to Olson, with teachers and students as key stakeholders in the educational change process, a benefit of the narrative approach is that "the stories lived and told by students and teachers of what is important, relevant, meaningful, or problematic for them are valued" (p. 170). However, Olson was keen out to avoid an either-or dichotomy and instead suggested an "interweaving" of the two approaches.

In Sigrun Gudmundsdottir's study of "Narrative Structures in Curriculum" (1991), which focused on two high school social studies teachers working at a school in northern California, Gudmundsdottir stated that part of her underlying research hypothesis is that "Stories are part of our identity and our culture. We create stories about ourselves that we communicate in various ways to our colleagues. This self narrative enables us to construe who we are and where we are heading in our lives. At the cultural level, narratives give cohesion to shared beliefs" (p. 207). In taking this approach, Gudmundsdottir helped to identify some of the important relationships among narrative, culture, and community.

A good example of the intersection among CRT, narrative inquiry, and educational research—as well as an interesting example of work clearly influenced by CRT but that does not refer to it directly—is a short (six-page) but potentially important paper by Gillian Creese and Edith Ngene Kambere (2003), both at the University of British Columbia in Canada. Creese and Kambere reported on their work with African immigrant women recently arrived in Vancouver, exploring the perceptions and impact of what they referred to as an "African English" accent (p. 565). The title of their paper—*"What Colour Is Your English?"*—came from a comment made during one of their focus groups: "When you come here, you come from a continent or a country that was originally colonized by the British. You had your education, you were taught by the British. You speak your good English, but somehow they ask you 'What colour is your English?' (Focus Group, 1997)" (p. 565).

In discussing the responses of their participants, Creese and Kambere drew on the work of Ng (1990), who noted that "common-sense discourses construct people of colour as immigrants and immigrants as people of colour" (Creese & Kambere, 2003, p. 566). Although the work of researchers like Creese, Kambere, and Ng does not focus on English language teaching and learning, it is relevant to readers of this volume, because it deals with aspects of "(dis)entitlement in employment" in relation to accent, race, and "perceptions of language competency" (Creese & Kambere, p. 566), all of which appear in a number of the contributions in this volume. Creese and Kambere (2003) concluded, "According to our focus groups, African immigrant women experience language as a problem in their daily lives not because they have difficulty with expression or comprehension, but because their African English accents mark them as immigrant, African, Black women perceived to have low-English competency" (p. 571).

CONCLUSION

It is not, of course, possible to present anything like a comprehensive summary of the work carried out in the areas considered in this chapter, and this chapter has not attempted to do that. Instead, the purpose of this chapter was to provide a brief introduction to a number of areas—a thorough examination of each could easily be a book many times the size of this volume. However, because so many large books have already been written on each of these areas (race, critical race theory, and narrative inquiry), and because very few of the busy teachers we know have ever attempted to read any of those tomes, the aim of this chapter was to introduce the reader to some of the most often-cited studies, published by some of the most productive researchers and writers in these fields, and to present examples of some of their main ideas. It is important to note that it is possible for a reader to go through all of the narratives in this book without knowing anything about formal studies of race, critical race theory, or narrative inquiry, but our assumption is that knowing something about these ideas may have a positive impact on the way the narratives are read, responded to, and understood.

REFERENCES

Abraham, C. (2005, June 18). Race. *Globe and Mail: Globe Focus*, F1–F12.
Aguirre, A. (1987). An interpretative analysis of Chicano faculty in academe. *Social Science Journal, 24,* 71–81.
Aguirre, A. (1995). The status of minority faculty in academe. *Equity and Excellence in Education, 28,* 63–68.
Aguirre, A. (2000). Academic storytelling: A critical race theory story of affirmative action. *Sociological Perspectives, 43,* 319–339.
Brayboy, B. (2001, November). *Toward a tribal critical race theory.* Paper presented at the Association for the Study of Higher Education (ASHE) conference, Richmond, VA.
Clandinin, D. J., & Connelly, F. M. (2000). *Narrative inquiry: Experience and story in qualitative research.* San Francisco: Jossey-Bass.
Connelly, F. M., & Clandinin, D. J. (1988). *Teachers as curriculum planners: Narratives of experience.* New York: New York Teachers College Press.
Creese, G., & Kambere, E. N. (2003). What colour is your English? *The Canadian Review of Sociology and Anthropology, 40*(5), 565–573.
Crenshaw, K., Gotanda, N., Peller, G., & Thomas, K. (Eds.). (1995). *Critical race theory: The key writings that formed the movement.* New York: New York University Press.
Delgado, R. (1989). Storytelling for oppositionists and others: A plea for narrative. *Michigan Law Review, 87,* 2411–2441.
Delgado, R. (1993). On telling stories in school: A reply to Farber and Sherry. *Vanderbuilt Law Review, 46,* 665–676.
Delgado, R. (1999). *When equality ends: Stories about race and resistance.* Boulder, CO: Westview.
Delgado, R., & Stefanic, J. (Eds.). (2001). *Critical race theory: An introduction.* New York: New York University Press.
Gillborn, D. (1990). *Race, ethnicity and education: Teaching and learning in multi-ethnic schools.* London: Unwin Hyman.
Gudmundsdottir, S. (1991). Story-maker, story-teller: Narrative structures in curriculum. *Journal of Curriculum Studies, 23*(4), 207–218.
Gutierrez, G. (2000). Deconstructing Disney: Chicano/a children and critical race theory. *Aztlan, 25*(10), 7–46.
Henig, J., Hula, R., Orr, M., & Pedescleaux, D. (2001). *The color of school reform: Race, politics, and the challenge of urban education.* Princeton, NJ: Princeton University Press.
Ladson-Billings, G. (1998). Just what is critical race theory and what's it doing in a nice field like education? *International Journal of Qualitative Studies in Education, 11*(1), 7–24.
Ladson-Billings, G. (1999). Preparing teachers for diverse student populations: A critical race theory perspective. *Review of Research in Education, 24,* 211–247.
Ladson-Billings, G., & Tate, W. (1995). Toward a critical race theory of education. *Teachers College Record, 97,* 47–68.
Lee, C. D. (2003). Editor's introduction: Why we need to re-think race and ethnicity in educational research. *Educational Researcher, 32*(5), 3–5.
Lopez, G. R. (2001). Revisiting white racism in educational research: Critical race theory and the problem of method. *Educational Researcher, 30*(1), 29–33.
Ng, R. (1990). Immigrant women: The construction of a labour market category. *Canadian Journal of Women and the Law, 4*(1), 96–112.
Ng, R., Staton, P., & Scane, J. (Eds.). (1995). *Anti-racism, feminism, and critical approaches to education.* Westport, CT: Bergin & Garvey.

Olson, M. (2000). Curriculum as multistoried process. *Canadian Journal of Education, 25*(3), 169–187.

Parker, L., Deyhle, D., & Villena, S. (1999). *Race is ... race isn't: Critical race theory and qualitative studies in education*. Boulder, CO: Westview.

Pollock, M. (2001). How the question we ask most about race in education is the very question we most suppress. *Educational Researcher, 30*(9), 3–12.

Rasool, J., & Curtis, A. (2000). *Multicultural education in middle and secondary classrooms: Meeting the challenge of diversity and change*. Belmont, CA: Wadsworth/Thomson Learning.

Rowley, L. R. (2004). Dissecting the anatomy of African-American inequality: The impact of racial stigma and social origins on group status and college achievement. *Educational Researcher, 33*(4), 15–20.

Simon, T. W. (1999). Racist versus anti-Semites? Critical race theorists criticized. *Newsletter on Philosophy, Law, and the Black Experience, 98*(2), 1–11.

Sleeter, C. (1992). *Keepers of the American dream: A study of staff development and multicultural education*. London: Falmer.

Sleeter, C., & Delgado Bernal, D. (2004). Critical pedagogy, critical race theory, and antiracist education: Implications for multicultural education. In J. Banks & C. McGee-Banks (Eds.), *Handbook of research on multicultural education* (pp. 240–258). San Francisco: Wiley.

Tate, W. (1993). Advocacy versus economics: A critical race analysis of the proposed national assessment in mathematics. *Thresholds in Education, XIX*, 16–22.

Tate, W. (1994). From inner city to ivory tower: Does my voice matter in the academy? *Urban Education, 29*, 245–269.

Tatum, B. (1992). Talking about race, learning about racism. *Harvard Educational Review, 62*(1), 1–24.

Van de Weyer, R. (1997). *Kierkegaard in a nutshell*. London: Hodder and Stoughton.

Van Manen, M. (1990). *Researching Lived Experience: Humans science for an action sensitive pedagogy*. New York: State University of New York Press.

Young, M. D., & Rosiek, J. (2000). Interrogating whiteness. *Educational Researcher, 29*(2), 39–44.

Chapter **2**

Dark Matter: Teaching and Learning Between Black and White

Andy Curtis
Queen's University

The first two incidents I recount and reflect on in this chapter are one-offs from more than 30 years ago contrasted with one that occurred three times a few years ago. The third set of incidents occurred, as I write this, a few days ago, and is written with more verbatim dialogue, because the incidents are so fresh and clear in my mind. However, one of the things that all three retellings have in common is that all of the incidents lasted just a few minutes. The disproportional relationship between the brevity and the significance of these incidents highlights, I believe, the importance and the value of looking in close detail at apparently fleeting moments from our personal and professional lives, as well as those longer and more arduous events that occupy much greater periods of time (although not necessarily space).

> "Pity the English Child of the Dark"[1]
>
> My mother bore me in the southern wild,
>
> And I am black, but Oh! My soul is white!
>
> White as an angel is the English child,
>
> But I am black, as if bereav'd of light

It is 1969. I am 6 years old, sitting in a classroom in England, as I hear these words from William Blake's poem "The Little Black Boy" (1970). They are

---

[1] First verse of "The Little Black Boy" pp. 9–10, from *Songs of Innocence and Experience: Showing the Two Contrary States of the Human Soul, 1789–1794* by William Blake, edited by G. Keynes (Intro & Commentary; 1970). By permission of Oxford University Press.

read by our teacher, standing at the front of the class, during one of my first official English lessons. I feel very hot, and wonder if my redness can be seen by my classmates. My eyes fill up and start to sting, but I will not cry. I will not. I don't remember much about the rest of that short lesson, except something about Blake wanting Black and White people to live together peacefully. I remember references to "Black bodies and sun-burnt faces," but mostly I remember feeling sick in the pit of my stomach. An incident lasting perhaps 30 seconds, in a lesson of around 30 minutes, being recalled so vividly more than 30 years later. This raises many interesting questions, not least about the possible cause-effect relationships between distant memory and present moment.

As the only child of color in the classroom, and one of the very few in the school, this was my first in-class experience of the power of language—and my first experience of feeling ashamed because of the color of my skin, relative to that of my friends. The school had a reputation for racial intolerance, as did the surrounding area, which often manifested itself in acts of damage and destruction of buildings (e.g., graffiti) and sometimes of people, too. It's not possible to fully recall everything that happened in that lesson, at this distance, but my clear memory is that we did not use this poem to lead into a discussion of color or race issues, in which my opinion might have been sought as "an expert witness." Although this would undoubtedly have been difficult for us, it would certainly have been preferable to what I remember did happen, which was a half-hour on the grammar, spelling, and vocabulary of the poem.

The fact that I still remember this incident more than 30 years later is also an indication of the longevity of such memories. An interesting question to start with, then, is why does the memory of this incident stand out among so many other incidents in school during those years? One reason is its unexpectedness. It's hard to say what the teacher was thinking when she was designing her lesson plan, but this has often seemed to me like a clear example of a well-meaning teacher, perhaps trying to use language and literature to raise awareness of social issues, but failing to do so and perhaps even doing more harm than good in the process.

It is tempting to put such an incident down to uninformed decision making on the part of a local, Caucasian teacher, set it aside, and forget about it. Can there have been any benefit to the hundreds (possible thousands) of times I have rerun this scene in my head over the last 30 years? As it turns out, there may have been many, although I perhaps did not think of them in this way until sitting down to write this chapter, which highlights the importance of reflecting on past experiences in a way that requires "articulation outside of our selves." Such an articulation requires us to give form, substance, and structure to our thoughts and feelings so that we may share those with another person; in this case, through reflective narrative inquiry.

2. TEACHING AND LEARNING BETWEEN BLACK AND WHITE 13

Of all the definitions of "a lesson" with which I have worked, I have found most useful the idea of a lesson being a series of uncountable moment-to-moment decisions, negotiated (or not) between a teacher and a group of learners. It is quite possible that this incident as a 6-year-old was my first direct experience of the effect of a teacher's decision making on me as a learner and as an individual. I would like to think that I have always been aware of the need to explore the bases for the decisions we make as language teachers, especially if they can have a potentially negative impact on our learners. However, it is possible that this awareness—as with much of our adult consciousness—comes from some very early childhood experiences.

I have often thought of this incident in relation to Abraham Maslow's hierarchy of needs, and the importance of starting from a place in which the learners feels safe and secure. Although I was not in any danger in that classroom as a result of the chosen material and focus of the lesson, I do remember that there was more poetic name calling than usual in the playground during the morning break time immediately following that lesson. However, the main problem for me was the feeling of insecurity in the classroom that this event caused.

This teacher's choice of material has ultimately helped me to understand the importance of making the learners the basis of our decisions, rather than what we as teachers believe would be useful, effective, or interesting. The teaching and learning events in our classrooms will be none of those things if we do not base our decisions on what we know about our learners. For a long time, as an undergraduate student completing a teaching degree in England, I could not fully get my head around the notion of learner-centered approaches to teaching. But recalling this incident has helped me, in some small but important ways, to better understand this notion, not just as one theoretical approach among many, but also as daily practice that enables our learners to feel they are able to and want to contribute and share.

It is possible that the effects of such brief but powerful incidents "color" our experiences of formal teaching and learning in more ways than we can imagine. It is also possible that such negative and painful experiences may eventually lead to positive and productive long-term side effects, once the immediate pain has worn off—as long as the moments, incidents, and events are reflected on and processed in some structured and systematic way.

A CASE OF MISTAKEN IDENTITY

Fast forward to 1997. We are in Hong Kong, fresh from its momentous change of sovereignty and the end of more than a century and a half of British colonial presence—or occupation—depending on your point of view. It is the first day of classes in the new academic year at one of the country's main universities. Although I have been in Hong Kong for 1 year already, I only stayed at my first job for a year, so this is also the first week in my new position and a new location.

The course is entitled *Introduction to Academic Writing*, and like all our courses is taught as an optional, undergraduate, noncredit-bearing English enhancement course. The class is due to start at 9:30 a.m., and only around two thirds of the students are here at this time. (My first year in Hong Kong taught me that this was not unusual here, at the tertiary level, in part an effect of living, working, and studying in the most densely populated place on the planet, in terms of both cars and people.)

We attempt a few "false starts" to the lesson between 9:35 a.m. and 9:40 a.m., and begin in earnest at around 9:45 a.m., although I notice that we are, according to the list of students I've been given to expect, still one body short. At around 9:50 a.m., a student—the missing one, I assume—runs in, glances hastily around at the other students, and sits down. After hurriedly extracting books, paper, and pens from his bag, he then looks up at me. A second later, he mutters an apology, gathers up all his stuff, and without putting any of it back into his bag makes his exit as noisily as he did his entrance.

During all of this, I did not say a word, having trained myself not to compete with more interesting things going on in my classroom, such as the ringing tunes of cell phones. "Don't attempt to compete with the technology," I tell the student teachers with whom I work, "It's too powerful. It'll win every time, so wait." And so I wait for the student to settle down. However, his clamoring, clattering exit leaves me lost for words. I look around the room, and notice that a few students have what appear to be somewhat knowing looks on their faces, and I make a note to ask them about this later. "Who was that?" I ask. No one answers, so I continue the lesson.

We make a start and, to my great surprise, 10 minutes later, back comes the same student. No clamor or clatter this time; he looks as if his tail is firmly between he legs as he sidles in, mutters another apology in my general direction, and sits down. This time, he stays. I try to talk with him at the end of class about this behavior, but he has either anticipated this and decided not to take my question, or he's late again for something else. Either way, he leaves in too much of a hurry for me to speak with him.

I mention this incident over dinner with friends who do not work in the education system, but other than that, don't give it much thought. That is, until it happens again. And then again. By the end of the first week, this has happened three times, with three different students, in the first lesson of three different courses. As I say in my research methods course, "Once may be a random occurrence in the universe; twice may be a coincidence. But three times, that's a pattern; that's data."

I try to talk with each of the students in turn, as discreetly as I can, at either the beginning or end of the sessions in the following week, but all I get

2. TEACHING AND LEARNING BETWEEN BLACK AND WHITE   15

is more mumbled, eye-averted apologies. Eventually, I meet some of the other students on the courses, outside of class, in the cafeteria, having dinner. I ask them about this behavior and they too apologize on behalf of the other students. I tell them that I'm tired of hearing apologies, that I am not offended but would very much like to know more about reasons for the behavior. They give me an explanation, and then it seems so obvious that I'm wondering why I didn't think of it beforehand.

It turns out the sequence of events was surprisingly similar in all three instances. Each of the students, all of whom are known for being late for most things, went to the course notice board, checked the title of the course and the room, then ran to where they were supposed to be. On entering, they saw familiar peer student faces, assumed they were in the right place, sat down, and started to get their stuff out of their bags. However, once they'd done that and looked up to see me, they assumed then they were, in fact, in the wrong place. Because there are so many sections of each course, and the arrangements are erratic and inconsistent at the best of times, this seemed to them like the most likely possibility. Thus, they left to check the board again, only to find they had been right the first time, and so had to return. I later got to know one of the students who did this run-in/run-out/run-back-in routine well, or at least well enough for her to tell me that she was so embarrassed to walk back in that she had even gone to the general office to see if she might be transferred to another section of the same course, not because she thought there was a problem with me, but rather because she would rather have transferred than have had to walk back in.

The question still remained as to why, on seeing me, these three students had assumed they were in the wrong place. After talks with them and their friends, I was able to discover that they had formulated a series of statements that were true but had led them to a false conclusion, catching them in their own logical fallacy. First, they saw the name of the courses, all of which were run through the English language teaching unit of the university, and then the name of the teacher, marked as "Dr. Andy Curtis." They had then created a mental picture of whom they were expecting given these two details/parameters (i.e., having had their schema activated). The fact that I stopped talking from the moment they first stumbled into class until they grabbed their stuff and ran out again also meant that they did not hear me speaking English with a fairly strong, obvious, and I'm told easily noticeable British English accent. But it is possible that even had I talked whilst they went through their routine, they might not have been listening carefully enough, if at all, to pick up on such linguistic cues.

After more than 150 years of British presence in Hong Kong, several generations of Hong Kongers had grown up with images of who British people were and what they looked like, especially in education, and perhaps especially at the tertiary level, because most Hong Kong universities were founded by Christian missionaries. Part of this imagery has been a quite strong belief in the native-speaker fallacy in language teaching; that is, that a native speaker of the target language is inherently better for teaching and learning that language than is a nonnative speaker. The interesting thing for me was the fact that I did conform to the native-speaker norm in my use of English, but not in my appearance. For these three first-year undergraduates (and perhaps many others too), all of their experiences of English teachers, all of the images drawn on when such a concept was referred to via their activated schema, were either to local, Cantonese teachers, often using little English in their English classes, and/or middle-aged, White males and females, who appeared to be obviously recognizable as British from quite a distance.

How did this experience affect how I taught in that setting and others since then, as a TESOL professional of color? For one thing, I now realize the meaning of the cliché about first impressions counting in terms of a first meeting with students, and for that matter, staff. Although there are few places like Hong Kong left on earth in terms of postcolonial, ex-British-colony enclaves, our physical appearance even in noncolonial settings (if such exist) can still lead to all sorts of genuine confusion, if we do not appear as our students expect us to appear. Not that there is anything we can do or should wish to do about our appearance, but we can help the students (and staff) to explore where those expectations originate. We can help them go beyond the rational appreciation that what is on the outside is usually of little value in predicting what is on the inside, and really internalize this understanding as part of their beliefs and attitudes.

Since that time in Hong Kong, I now start courses with a question-and-answer session between the students and myself about myself, in which students are asked to work together to formulate questions about me in writing, which they can then put to me orally. I explain to them that I will let them know if there are any questions I do not wish to answer, and let them know why that is. Many teachers understandably shy away from such disclosure with their students at the very beginning of a course, preferring to wait until much later, and sometimes never engage in such disclosure in order to maintain "a safe distance." Others have told me that they feel it's simply too narcissistic. But my experience tells me that if the students are so busy wondering about their new teacher's color and linguistic, professional, and personal background, they are almost certainly not giving their full attention to the teaching and learning we are trying to achieve in class.

Initially, I did this Q-and-A session only with my EFL and ESL groups, which not only gave them practice with question formation, but also helped them understand what were and were not acceptable topics in British English culture (e.g., being asked "How much money do you make?" by a stranger is considered unacceptable). It also gave me valuable insights into what their expectations were based on appearances and where these expectations came from, as well as a chance to make that kind of behavior less common, or at least more informed.

A year after I left Hong Kong, I started teaching on a master's program at a graduate school in Vermont. I began my classes with the same kind of Q-and-A session, realizing that, as the only professor of color there, I was again different from the majority of the teaching staff in appearance, and that this difference had not gone unnoticed by my new students. In fact, I eventually discovered that it had been the subject of several discussions between the students prior to our first class together.

Over some years, I have also gathered small-scale data sets from students in different countries, asking them on our first meeting to write down a few adjectives to describe me. I project the request onto a screen or write it up on a board, so that the students don't hear me speak. I gather in the slips, commence teaching our first lesson together, and then have the students write a few more adjectives at the end of that lesson. I can match up most of the pre- and post-lesson slips by handwriting, but still preserve the anonymity of the respondents. I presented the results of some of these data sets at a TESOL Association affiliate conference. One of the most interesting findings has been that almost none of the hundreds of students with whom I've done this exercise have ever written anything like "We cannot write any adjectives to describe you, because we have never met you before."

First impressions will continue to count, whether we like it or not, and whether such impressions are misleading or not. Having first impressions may be a natural human failing, perhaps accentuated by the image-obsessed media and marketing cultures that too many of us have grown up in and been shaped by. Whatever the reason, I have learned from experiences such as those played out in my courses in Hong Kong and elsewhere that we need to find ways of addressing the causes and effects of such impressions and work through these with our students. In this manner, we can do whatever possible to alleviate some of the most harmful effects of these tendencies.

"STEP ASIDE, PLEASE SIR": THE NEW FACE OF RACIAL PROFILING

Time and place: Connecticut, Atlanta, Chicago, or any one of a number of other airports in America in October and November 2001. "Excuse me, Mr. Curtis," says the person at the check-in counter. I interject as gently as I can, "Er, it's actually *Dr.* Curtis." I have no idea what makes me think that this will make any difference, but hope springs eternal. Sure enough, however, it does not make any difference. "Yes"—which sounds uncannily like "yeah, whatever"—comes the reply to my interjection, as the clerk continues, "Can you please step to one side and see that gentleman over there?" I try feigning confusion and innocence. "Of course. Why?" I ask. "You have been randomly selected for an additional complete security check," says the person at the check-in counter. "Randomly selected by whom?" I ask. "The computer," replies the check-in clerk.

Three times out of four, I dutifully comply. But when this little scenario happens for the fourth time in four days, I lose it a little. "No," I respond. The check-in clerk seems more than slightly taken aback, and I watch her make eye contact with a military police officer, armed and in full combat dress, standing a few feet away. Her gaze returns to mine. "I'm sorry sir, if you don't comply with our new security measures, we cannot let you board." I find myself wondering if it takes much practice to be able to say "sir" with little or no civility or respect. "I'm perfectly willing to comply with your new security measures," I reply. "But as I'm the only person who's been pulled out of line, and as this is the fourth time in four days I've been pulled out, I find it impossible to believe that this is random." No reply. Blank look. So I continue. "In fact, if you give me a few numbers, I can show you that it's statistically impossible for this to have been random." It occurs to me that my knowledge of statistics is rustier than I thought, but that seems pretty academic by this point. Still no reply. Blanker look. One last go. "I don't blame you for doing this. If the situation were reversed I might well do to you what you're doing to me now. Just please don't insult my intelligence and tell me it's random." The armed military police officer saunters over. "Problem?" he asks, although it's not at all clear to whom, if anyone, his question is addressed. "No," I say, and dutifully walk over, with my carry on luggage, to the "gentleman" over there, who proceeds to take most of the stuff out of my case and spread it on the table in front of him.

For some reason, none of this searching is conducted behind a screen. This means that when I assume a crucifixion-type pose—back straight, arms outstretched, legs together (although I think they're supposed to be slightly apart)—and turn away from the person waving a metal detector over my body, I am met with a sea of faces. Passengers waiting to board this flight, and other passengers at nearby gates waiting to board other flights, are all looking at me with a whole range of expressions, from amusement to embarrassment to fear.

Eventually, the ritual over with, I slowly and carefully repack all my stuff and get ready to board the flight. Smiling brightly, the woman who takes the main part of my boarding pass says, "Have a good flight." I walk slowly down the tunnel in a bit of a daze, wondering at what just happened, and how the world has changed.

What has any of this to do with being a TESOL professional of color? Everything. Since September 11, 2001, not only has the fact of my color become even more of an issue, but the nature of the color—the brownness of

2. TEACHING AND LEARNING BETWEEN BLACK AND WHITE 19

my skin—has become a key distinguishing factor. Looking back on such incidents reminds me of the fact that those other things that might distinguish me—having a doctorate, publishing 70 papers, giving 100 presentations in 25 countries—do not show. They are invisible. I find myself thinking, "So, is this how our visiting scholars and postdoctoral researchers from around the world might be made to feel when they arrive here? That none of their accomplishments compares to their skin color?" We may have come far in our understanding of cultures and peoples other than our own, but how very far we have yet to go. My heart sinks at the potentially regressive fallout of September 11, 2001. However, hope springs eternal.

EARLY PERSONAL AND PROFESSIONAL HISTORY

My parents and grandparents were all from a small country at the northernmost tip of South America. Until the 1960s it was known as British Guiana, but since then has been renamed Guyana, marking its so-called "independence." As the name change indicates, it was a British colony for around 150 years, like India and Hong Kong. My great grandparents and their ancestors came from India, although where exactly seems to have been difficult to pinpoint. My parents came to England in the 1950s, like so many other British colonial migrants, looking for a better life, only to find that they had exchanged one kind of hardship in their homeland for another, more difficult, and more dangerous hardship far from home, family, and close friends.

My brother, my sister, and I were all born in England, with one of the interesting appearance-related results of this background being that my siblings and I all look far more Indian than anything else, so for our whole lives in England we were assumed to be Indian—by Indians and non-Indians alike. The confusion was sometimes compounded if we tried to clarify our backgrounds by saying that our parents were from South America, because we were then expected to speak Spanish, but Guyana was the only part of South America where Spanish appears not to have been spoken.

As children, we lived in a run-down part of the city of Birmingham, which had become a kind of Indian ghetto. When we were ready to start school, my parents moved the family to a "nice neighborhood" where there were no families of color. Unfortunately, our arrival was met with fear and anger by the local residents, who signed a petition against our family moving in. My mothers still lives there, and ours remains one of the only families of color on the street, even after all these years.

As first-generation migrants, our parents duly funneled us into vocationally relevant career paths, a process that, at that time, began in England at the tender and far-too-early age of 14. "Vocationally relevant" was taken by my parents—and the parents of many other first generation-migrants—to mean "science," so we were instructed to choose among the sciences as our main subjects. But we all drifted away from science, sooner or later; my brother to accounting, my sister to law, and I to education. However, I took longest to drift, having been awarded a scholarship by the local health authority to study medical science, specializing in clinical biochemistry. Eventually however, I plucked up enough courage to leave what was thought to be a comfortable and stable job in England's National Health Service to pursue "some vague interest," as my parents put it, in education.

Going from clinical biochemist to language teacher is even harder than it sounds, and I settled for completing a teaching degree as a first move, earning a bachelor's in education, which gave me qualified teacher status to teach design and technology to 11- to 16-year-olds in state schools in England. It did not take me (or the children in the schools where I did my teaching practice placements) long to realize that I would never be very good in this role, which left me free to pursue what might always have been my real interests—language and communication.

PRESENT SITUATION

In the fall of 2002, I rejoined Queen's University in Kingston, Ontario, Canada; this time as Director of the School of English, an IEP/EAP (intensive English/English for academic purposes) program that works each year with around 1,000 students from more than 30 countries. (As I describe later in this section, I had been previously employed at Queen's University as a Visiting Scholar.) I am also responsible for a staff of 35 to 40 full-time and part-time teaching and administrative support staff. Interestingly, in the context of this book, I am one of the only persons of color, one of the only non-Canadians and one of the only males at the school. The university itself ranks high, in the top 3 to 5 of around 50 universities in the country. Its only poor showing is in its cultural and linguistic diversity, because the typical first-year undergraduate intake is more than 95% Caucasian Canadian. Here, I am a minority in so many ways, and yet it is this personal, first-hand experience of what it means to be a minority and "a new Canadian," as people here call us, that has helped me on many occasions to identify with and connect with the experiences of our international students.

Before this, I was at the School for International Training (SIT) in Brattleboro, Vermont, which is a small graduate school set in a couple of hundred acres of beautiful rolling hillsides. The parent organization, World Learning, was founded in 1932 as the U.S. Experiment in International Living. As one of the first new faculty members in the Department of Language Teacher Education in nearly 10 years, and as the only faculty

2. TEACHING AND LEARNING BETWEEN BLACK AND WHITE

member of color, I was once again aware of the important role that TESOL professionals of color play in language education and in TESOL.

Before SIT, I spent a year in the Faculty of Education as a Visiting Scholar at Queen's University. The university has made efforts in recent years to try and diversify its student and teaching populations, but at the moment it still remains a largely White, middle-class institution. Some of the most interesting work I did whilst I was there the first time was with bachelor of education students who had come from relatively monolingual, monocultural, affluent socioeconomic backgrounds who were preparing to work in schools with highly mixed multicultural populations.

Perhaps the most formative years in my growth and development as a TESOL professional of color were my 5 years based in Hong Kong, which gave me the chance to work with language teachers and teacher educators in many countries, including mainland China, Taiwan, Thailand, Singapore, Malaysia, Japan, Indonesia, and elsewhere. I think of these years as "formative" in part because they came immediately after I completed my PhD; my thesis was on the linguistic and cultural experiences of international students completing graduate degrees at universities in England.

The 5 years I spent in Hong Kong were also formative, because this was the first time I had lived and worked for such a long period of time based in a non-English-speaking country. In spite of the British presence—or perhaps because of it—the local sense of identity (often summed up in the popular press as "we are Hong Kongers first, Chinese second, and British third,") was very strong. However, because the population of Hong Kong was, at that time, between 96% and 98% ethnic Chinese, I had in many ways exchanged being an outsider in England for being an outsider in Hong Kong. Although I did not think of it in this way at that time, I have noticed this pattern in others like myself, who seem to have spent so much time being at first marginalized, then doing whatever we needed to be accepted, and eventually realizing that being on the edges has its advantages as well as its difficulties. It is often much easier to see clearly from the edges than from the center.

My first year in Hong Kong was at the country's main teacher training institute. It was perhaps the most British colonial tertiary institute in the country at that time, apart from the University of Hong Kong, which was perhaps the jewel in the crown of British colonial education. Every day during my 5 years in Hong Kong I encountered responses to me based on my appearance. Some of these responses were positive, some were negative, but the vast majority were simply incorrect.

QUESTIONS

1. If you are reading these first four lines from Blake's poem for the first time, what is your initial reaction to them? How do you respond to the

notion of having Black skin, but a White soul? How would you respond to the notion that angels are White?
2. How were you made aware of your own race relative to the races of others?
3. Have you ever tried to raise your students' awareness of social issues? If, so, how have you done it? How does the way you raised your students' awareness compare with the way that Curtis' teacher did it? Which issues did you select, and why?
4. Consider possible reasons for students running into Curtis' class, then leaving, only to return. What could be causing this?
5. Have you been able to determine the extent to which you conform or don't conform to your students' expectations of what you should look like in relation to your nationality and/or ethnicity? If you don't conform to their expectations, what has been the result of this unexpected appearance?
6. Curtis writes that "First impressions will continue to count, whether we like it or not, and whether such impressions are misleading or not." Do you agree with this position? If so, why? If not, can you offer an alternative position on first impressions?
7. Have the terrorist attacks of September 11, 2001 affected you or your students in a way that is similar to Curtis' experience? If so, how? What do you see as some of the "potentially regressive fallout of September 11, 2001?"
8. Have you or your students ever been victims of racial profiling? If so, describe the incident(s). Have you ever unintentionally been guilty of racial profiling? If so, describe the incident(s).

REFERENCES

Blake, W. (1970). *Songs of innocence and experience: 1789–1794.* Oxford, UK: Oxford University Press.

Chapter 3

An Exceptional Voice: Working as a TESOL Professional of Color

Shondel Nero
St. John's University

During my first semester at the university where I currently teach, one of my White female graduate students (whom I will call Lisa) approached me at the end of the second class and said, in the course of a brief exchange, "You're the first Black teacher I've ever had in my whole life." Somewhat taken aback by the comment, I responded, "Really, tell me about that." Obviously unprepared for my retort, Lisa stumbled through an answer that went something like this: "Well ... you know ... it's just that ... I've lived all my life in New York City and I went to elementary school, high school, did a bachelor's degree, and now I'm doing my master's, and only now I have a Black teacher." To which I shot back, "Well, that's very telling, isn't it?"—a reply that I could see clearly made Lisa uncomfortable. Lisa promptly tried to exit our conversation as politely as possible. It was an unsettling moment for both of us.

    As I reflect on that critical moment, I wonder what was it about Lisa's initial comment that prompted my knee-jerk response, which went from defensive to hostile. Perhaps I was bothered by the direct reference to my race (the first such remark ever made to me), which, at the time, I might have erroneously interpreted as a putdown or a questioning of my legitimacy as a professor. Yet, it is unlikely that a student would choose to insult her professor for no apparent reason. It is, of course, entirely possible, more likely probable, that Lisa could have simply been making a statement of fact based

23

on her experience. However, the fact that I found it disconcerting when she called my attention to my race without my initiating the topic highlights one of the effects of living in a highly racialized society: When race is so pervasive in the culture, as it is in the United States, the most mundane reference to race can set off unexpected responses. Still, what was I to make of Lisa's comment that framed me as an exception? Was it intended as a compliment? If so, should I have simply accepted it in that vein? If not, what exactly was her intent? Was I bothered by the fact that the comment came from a White student? Or was it that she dared to voice what was likely the experience of many other students? That such vexing questions can emanate from what began as a casual teacher–student exchange speaks to the reality of working as a Black professional in higher education, and in the field of TESOL in particular.

The incident with Lisa raises a number of key issues that I address in three parts in this chapter. First, I discuss the issues related to being a professional of color, with particular emphasis on being a Black professional. Next, I examine the challenges faced by TESOL professionals of color.[1] Finally, based on my discussion, I make recommendations for increasing the number and enhancing the working conditions of TESOL professionals of color.

ON BEING A BLACK PROFESSIONAL

Lisa's comments underscored the reality of the small percentage of Black teachers at elementary and secondary levels, and of Black professors at the college level, evidenced by the fact that she never had a Black teacher until she met me. This scarcity of Black educators sends a number of dangerous messages to all students, such as (a) Blacks may not be capable of being teachers or professors, (b) students should not expect to see or have Black teachers or professors, and (c) Blacks themselves should not expect to be teachers because most teachers (at least in the United States) are White. These messages lead to what I call the *exception(al) syndrome* (i.e., Black professionals are constantly seen as both *exception* and *exceptional*). Furthermore, Black professionals must constantly deal with the often ambivalent response to their presence by students and colleagues alike.

---

[1]By TESOL professional of color, I am referring to any non-White professional working in the field of TESOL in any of the following ways: (a) teaching ESL from kindergarten to university level in both traditional school or college as well as nonschool settings, (b) Teacher training for current and prospective teachers in ESL and EFL contexts, (c) research and publishing on issues related to TESOL, (d) creating ESL teaching materials, (e) developing standards and assessment instruments for ESL/EFL practitioners, (f) developing ESL/EFL curriculum for all age levels, (g) creating and enacting TESOL language policies, and (h) advocating for language rights of English language learners.

The small percentage of Black educators in the United States has been well documented. According to the National Center for Education Statistics, about 7% of the teaching force is Black, compared to 17% of the student body. Articles by Wehrman (2002) in the *Detroit Press* and Dehn (2002) in the *Seattle Post*, respectively, lamented the dearth of Black teachers in the nation's schools. The shortage of Black professionals in TESOL is particularly glaring despite efforts to diversify the organization through recruitment, the creation of caucuses, and other initiatives. In New York City, for example (a city known for its racial/ethnic diversity, particularly among the school-age population), the percentage of Black teachers and professors is surprisingly low, and even more so in the field of TESOL. For many students and professionals alike (regardless of their racial/ethnic background), the shortage of Black educators often reinforces popular perceptions that Blacks aren't intellectually capable of being educators or engaging in other professional pursuits—perceptions that are grounded in racist notions of the inferiority of the non-European IQ, notably manifested in publications such as Hernstein and Murray's *The Bell Curve* (1994).

The dearth of Black educators also perpetuates a mode of nonexpectation. That is, most students (including Black students) do not expect to see or have a Black teacher or professor; hence, the presence of a Black educator becomes a surprise (as I was for Lisa), and therefore an exception. This nonexpectation then translates into a self-fulfilling prophecy, because many Blacks don't expect or aspire to become educators, guaranteeing a continued shortage of Blacks in education and a vicious cycle of nonexpectation and exceptions.

What does it mean to be an exception in a professional context? In my own experience, being the exception means attending to, and living with, a host of ambivalent (often contradictory) attitudes and expectations from students and colleagues alike. On the other hand, being the exception has afforded me a positive visibility and influence at the institutions where I've worked, which has certainly helped me to grow as a scholar.

First, in literal terms, the exception might mean "the first ..." (as exemplified by my being Lisa's first Black teacher) or it might mean "the only ..." (as I've gotten used to being the only Black faculty or committee member in any number of situations). Sorting out which part of my "exceptionality" is being foregrounded can be tricky business, however, because I am also female and an immigrant. Thus, I can just as easily be the first and/or only Black, female, or immigrant, depending on the situation.

Of course, living in a highly racialized society, my being Black is the part of my identity that is most often foregrounded in professional circles. For many Black students (and I've had relatively few of them in my many years of college teaching, given that I've taught ESL to mostly Russians, Asians, and Latinos), my presence has meant being a de facto mentor for them. At the university where I previously taught, many Black students, including ones who were not students of mine, would approach me and ask my advice on subjects in which I had little or no expertise. For example, once a Black female graduate student asked me to serve on her Master's thesis committee. Her thesis was on contemporary West Indian literature. When I referred her to a White colleague whose expertise was in this area (explaining that my training is in linguistics, not literature), she seemed reluctant to pursue it. I could only assume that she was desperately seeking a connection with me as a Black faculty member, which I can totally understand. This, however, puts an undue burden on Black faculty. Given that we are so few in number, we are asked to be all things to all Black students at all times. At the same time, many Black students have very high expectations of Black faculty because we are, in fact, expected to *represent the race*. Hence, we must always be *exceptional* lest we reinforce negative stereotypes of the race. But there is a cautionary note here. If Black faculty appear to participate too strongly in what is perceived as the White establishment, then we risk being ostracized by our communities, so we must constantly walk a fine line.

Many non-Black students, on the other hand, come with their own expectations of and attitudes toward Black faculty. For example, based on comments they made, I noted that a number of my Russian students held very negative stereotypes of African Americans and Blacks in general—stereotypes that were ingrained long before their arrival in the United States. In order for them to deal with me, then, as their Black professor, they often chose to foreground my *immigrant* identity; that is, because my being Black could not be helped, they tried to frame me as a *different* Black, an *immigrant* Black. They would do this by periodically engaging in what I call "America bashing," assuming that, as an immigrant, I would be sympathetic to their comments. On these occasions, I had to skillfully direct the conversation to a more reasoned dialogue.

Yet, my students of all racial/ethnic backgrounds are often fascinated by my being an immigrant. Although I do not discuss my childhood years in my home country, Guyana, very often in class, students have shown deep interest whenever I've done so. They are curious about life there, cultural practices, the language, the educational system, and the economic and political state of the country. I've used these occasions not only to provide answers to the students' questions, but also to talk about diversity, not only in racial/ethnic terms, but also in terms of ideas and world views. It is at these critical, teaching moments that I see the positive effects of my racial/cultural difference.

Still, most students, regardless of their racial/ethnic background, are simply surprised at having a Black professor. Thus, my sense is that they may (mostly covertly) question my competence or authority, exoticize me, or suspend judgment until they get to know me. Lisa's overt expression of surprise at my presence, then, was clearly an exception, perhaps naïvely so.

My interactions with colleagues and their response to my presence are just as varied. Although I can delineate some general patterns of experience with White colleagues as opposed to colleagues of color, it is important to note that these observations are not absolute, and I acknowledge "exceptions" to the rule as I allow for individual differences. Most White colleagues, indeed most people today, are aware that overt negative racial remarks would be considered unacceptable and can incur serious consequences. Hence, "race talk" has an interesting way of being coded, even when it's complimentary. White colleagues, therefore, often exhibit a range of sometimes overlapping responses, from being genuinely comfortable with colleagues of color, to being condescending (even if not intentionally), to being resentful of our presence. This is a delicate game. As Pollock (2001) noted, American culture is caught in a paradox of being race obsessed and not wanting to talk about race at the same time.

There are many White colleagues who are genuinely supportive of and comfortable with professionals of color. For those colleagues, affirmative action is not just a superficial experience in the "flavor of the month"—it is actually seen as necessary and desirable and an inevitable part of living in a multiracial/multiethnic society. These are the faculty for whom professionals of color are not mere exceptions but part and parcel of a diverse society. For other White colleagues, professionals of color like myself are *only* seen through the lens of affirmative action (often translated as quotas), and we can be viewed as (a) threats to the status quo, (b) nuisances taking up slots that would otherwise go to Whites, (c) less than qualified candidates who were chosen merely on the basis of affirmation action, or (d) all of the above. Most professionals of color learn to live with and respond to these perceptions in their own way. As a sidebar, I should note that affirmative action has certainly increased the presence of professionals of color in all fields, but the fact that we are still viewed as exceptions shows that we have a long way to go.

Colleagues of color participate in this delicate game, too. Given that there have been so few colleagues of color in the institutions where I've worked, I tend to know most if not all of them, and they in turn, have sought me out. Individually or collectively, we have served on various committees, bringing our diverse perspectives to shape policy, programs, and practice in positive and enriching ways. For example, at my current university, a committee was formed a few years ago with the explicit purpose of recruiting and retaining minority faculty. I immediately joined that committee because I thought it would be an empowering forum for faculty of color. Yet, some colleagues of color chose *not* to be part of this committee, lest they become perceived as being race obsessed or seeking special favors. A similar line of argument is used by colleagues of color who do not embrace affirmation action, because they feel that it undermines the legitimacy of their credentials. I have often responded to these colleagues by arguing that it is possible to be qualified *and* Black; one need not preclude the other. Thus, we choose to embrace and not embrace each other in racial terms selectively. Much of this I attribute to what I referred to earlier as the "exception(al) syndrome" within a highly racialized society; that is, we are constantly responding to being either *marginalized* or *exceptionalized* as we grapple with issues of power.

TESOL PROFESSIONALS OF COLOR

The marginalization of professionals of color is palpably manifested in the field of TESOL. The major reason for this, I believe, is the notion in our field that ultimate authority over the English language (especially language teaching) rests with so-called "native speakers," who are tacitly assumed to be White, and of a certain social class and education level. Widdowson (1994) eloquently decried this constructed "ownership" of the language by a self-selected group that largely excludes people of color, and further argued that this does not reflect current usage of English worldwide. As Brutt-Griffler (2002) observed, "English has become a world language to the extent that it has been stripped of any simplistic association with Anglo-American and Western culture. World English has emerged because its users have changed the language as they have spread it" (pp. vii–viii). Yet, the bulk of TESOL graduate programs, hiring, research, policy, and teaching methods and materials emanate from the United States and the United Kingdom in contexts run by mostly White professionals, even though English around the world is more widely used by people of color (Crystal, 1998).[2]

As a student in a prominent TESOL master's program during the late 1980s, I was one of a small number of students of color, and certainly one of the few Blacks. Other students of color were mostly Japanese or Chinese international students who were expected to return to their countries to teach English. I would often listen to those Asian students lamenting their plight as nonnative speakers of English trying to gain legitimacy as teachers of English, and I would think to myself, well *their* problem is understandable, but *I*, (who always thought of myself as a native speaker of English having been born and raised in a former British colony) should have no problem in terms of my "native speaker" competence. Little did I realize that my "nativeness" would be questioned in TESOL and other circles because I don't "look like" or "sound like" a perceived native speaker. This questioning is

---

[2]Crystal's research showed that of the 75 countries where English has historically had some "special status" as either the sole, dominant, or official language, only the United States, United Kingdom, Canada, Australia, and New Zealand have White majority populations.

often quite subtle. It comes out in comments such as "You speak English very well" or "Where did you learn English?"

There is a caveat here. These comments are usually made in the context of recognizing that I am an immigrant due to my non-American accent. In other words, if I were an *American* Black, my "Americanness" would legitimize me as a native speaker, albeit one who may not be given a high status in the native speaker hierarchy. The combination of my being immigrant *and* Black tends to create an assumption of nonnativeness, especially among White colleagues.

In my own research (Nero, 2000, 2001, 2002), I have pointed out the limitations of the "native/nonnative" speaker paradigm on which our field is premised, arguing that it perpetuates racist/classist assumptions about language, and simultaneously undermines the complexity of actual language use/users in the world. Given that English has globalized through colonialism, postcolonialism, and technology, millions of people worldwide (mostly of color) claim and use the language as their own. Brutt-Griffler (2002) contended that, for these people, English is "*their* language, an expression of their unique identity. It is theirs because they have *made* it so—through their lived experiences in the language that have gained expression in the way they use English" (p. vii). As a result, a variety of "Englishes" have emerged worldwide, used for a myriad of purposes, all equally valid from a linguistic point of view. My research has focused on speakers of Caribbean English, like myself, whose claim to being native speakers of English is often questioned by colleagues and students alike. In fact, the "nativeness" of most non-White speakers of English is often questioned, even when, as noted earlier, they are *not* the exception but the rule worldwide. There seems to be, then, a hierarchy of nativeness, socially constructed, that places people of color on the lower rungs and that privileges White speakers of English, mostly from the United States and England.

The privileging of White speakers of English in TESOL is nowhere more evident than in hiring practices. The experiences of the competence of non-White native speakers of English as well as nonnative speakers of all racial/ethnic backgrounds being questioned have been well documented (Amin, 1999; Braine, 1999; Liu, 1999). Many of them have been refused teaching positions by prospective employers. Race, of course, could not be publicly given as a reason for such refusal. Instead, "nativeness" might be used as a euphemistic explanation, because many employers have unwittingly conflated race, language, and nativeness. It is not uncommon, for example, to see advertisements in *The New York Times* for English teaching jobs overseas that read: "Wanted. Native Speakers of (British) English." I often wonder how would my British-born Black niece be treated if she showed up for an interview in response to such an ad. Where would her "Britishness" or "nativeness" be placed on the hierarchy?

The native/nonnative speaker paradigm also discriminates against speakers of other languages who have successfully learned English and are competent teachers (Liu, 1999). As noted earlier, many of my Asian peers in TESOL graduate programs encounter employment practices that question their legitimacy as nonnative-speaking teachers of English. These students often face such discrimination upon returning to their home countries, where, armed with their newly acquired TESOL degree, they may be rejected by an employer who would rather hire a White American or British "native speaker" even if he or she were not appropriately trained to teach English. Furthermore, these students would face the reality that the employer was merely reflecting the wishes of many of the students in those countries who would also rather have a White American or British teacher, regardless of his or her teaching credentials. Nonnative speaking teachers of English who choose to teach in the United States also encounter similar challenges.

The marginalization of professionals of color in TESOL through discriminatory employment practices or enactment of the native/nonnative speaker paradigm perpetuates the exception(al) syndrome. Either professionals of color are literally the exception in predominantly White-dominated TESOL Programs in North America and Europe where they're expected to be exceptional; or, in countries where professionals of color do, in fact, comprise the majority of English teachers, they are also expected to be exceptional.

WHAT CAN BE DONE?

First, in the short term, there must be a concerted effort to increase the number of professionals of color, through a variety of measures, so that we do not continue to be perceived as exceptions. Although affirmative action has made significant gains in redressing the dearth of professionals of color, it has done so more as a reward for *accomplished* professionals rather than a conduit for *potential* professionals of color. It seems to me that we need more programs for targeting students of color at an early age who show promise for professional careers. Once identified, these students should be given the requisite information, guidance, and exposure *prior* to their college years to inculcate in them the idea that professional careers are as much an option for them as such careers are for their White counterparts. At a recent meeting of Black professionals in TESOL, it was noted by one member that, as an undergraduate, she was not advised of the existence of TESOL as a discipline or organization, or, for that matter, of language teaching as a career option. Such information gaps can be remedied by increasing early awareness, and this is likely to improve the number of students of color who successfully complete college and graduate school.

Davidson and Foster-Johnson (2001) argued persuasively for ongoing mentoring for graduate students of color, in order to improve retention. A larger pool of successful graduate students of color would (a) diffuse their presence as exceptions, (b) lessen the burden to always be exceptional (i.e., a significant presence of students of color with a wide range of abilities would be the norm, just as for White students), and (c) provide a potentially greater pool of candidates for the professional world, which is the ultimate goal.

In the long term, changes in racist attitudes in the society as a whole would be necessary—a formidable challenge, given the history of the United States. We are caught in a double bind here. The demonstrated successes of professionals of color is but one way to defy perceptions of their intellectual inferiority; however, it is the existence of those very perceptions that often prevents people of color from gaining access to the professional world. Thus, the onus is on *everyone* in the society to challenge racial discrimination—both individual and institutional—on all levels through interaction, honest dialogue, legislation, and any other viable means.

For TESOL's part, one way to counter racial discrimination is to develop alternative models of language use that do not presume an inherent link among language, nativeness, and race, which invariably privileges White American and British speakers of English. This might signal a radical departure from the native/nonnative speaker paradigm alluded to earlier. Leung, Harris, and Rampton (1997) proposed an alternative model of language use premised on affiliation, heritage, and expertise, which more accurately reflects the multifaceted ways in which various groups relate to and use particular languages in the modern world. My own selective use of Caribbean English, American English, and British English reflects this phenomenon.

Canagarajah (1999) correctly pointed out that in several countries in Asia, for example, American and British varieties of English are neither relevant to, nor appropriate for, local needs. Residents of these countries have developed their own forms of English (e.g., Singlish [Singaporean English] or Hinglish [Hindi/English]), forms that are increasingly being used and recognized as English continues to globalize. As Widdowson (1994) noted, a language best serves its community to the extent that it is *appropriate*, not *appropriated*. This suggests giving greater latitude to professionals of color around the world—particularly in Africa, Asia, and the Caribbean—to determine and develop the language standards, curriculum, and use relevant to *their* contexts, instead of blindly adopting methods and materials from North America and Europe, which are often inappropriate for local needs.

TESOL can also counter racial discrimination by increasing the pool of professionals of color within our field and by improving their working conditions and the attitudes toward them. The creation of caucuses within

TESOL has been a step in the right direction, by giving greater voice to the needs and issues of the diverse groups within the organization. Noteworthy in this regard was the creation in 1992 of the International Black Professionals and Friends in TESOL (IBPFT), a caucus whose explicit purpose is to "promote and enhance the positive professional growth and development of TESOL members of African descent, and other minority members, by providing a forum for the discussion of pertinent issues" (IBPFT web site). One pertinent issue is the aforementioned discriminatory employment practices encountered by several TESOL professionals of color, practices that have been and continue to be challenged. Advocacy for increased employment and fair working conditions will ultimately prevent the marginalization of TESOL professionals of color.

POSTSCRIPT

In the years since Lisa's remark to me, I've had a chance to reflect on my reaction and on the implications of the remark. I've come to realize that my discomfort during our brief exchange seemed to be part of my own grappling with a racialized self, a process that continues, albeit with more insight and maturity. Lisa's remark also convinced me, as I've suggested throughout this chapter, of the need for more teachers of color like myself, which, in the long run, will prevent the kind of comment she made in the first place.

Personal/Professional History

I've always been hooked on language—any language, any aspect of language; its sounds, its structures, its use, its misuse, its great power, its inextricable link to culture. This interest has been fueled by my somewhat migratory lifestyle in my early years.

I was born and raised in Guyana, the only officially English-speaking, now independent, country on mainland South America—the linguistic classification a mere accident of a history of prolonged British colonization. I was fortunate to have had a sound education in my formative years (I really enjoyed going to school, especially high school). In school, I developed an early interest, really a fascination, with language immediately after my first year learning French, when I was ten years old. The following year, I began learning Spanish, and my life was set from there on. I went into the foreign language track in high school and pursued language study vigorously.

In those days, I dreamed of being a career diplomat. I liked the idea of jetsetting around the world at different postings as an ambassador of Guyana, and meeting people from diverse linguistic and cultural backgrounds. In fact, the year immediately after graduating from high school, I worked at

3. AN EXCEPTIONAL VOICE OF COLOR

the Ministry of Foreign Affairs in Guyana to get a taste of life in the foreign service. I learned a lot in that year—mainly that life in the foreign service is much more than exotic diplomatic parties and immunity from traffic tickets. It is fundamentally political. As a diplomat, you are a political representative of your country, regardless of its political or economic state. In that regard, Guyana left much to be desired at that time. So I moved on to Plan B.

In August 1981, at age 18, I moved to Montréal, Canada, to pursue a Bachelor's degree at Concordia University. I majored in French and Spanish (although French was clearly my preference). Montréal was cold ... way too cold for me. It was my first experience with winter, with coats, gloves, and boots. But I weathered the storm, so to speak. I loved studying French. In Guyana, I had studied mostly French from France. In Montréal, I was in Rene Levesque territory—I was learning Canadian French, Québecois, Joual, whatever you call it. I was often the only non-French Canadian in my classes, but I had fun and learned a lot. I made friends with other West Indian (Caribbean) students like myself who were away from home and having their first taste of freedom. I graduated with distinction from Concordia and then moved to New York City in 1984.

During my first 5 years in New York, I was still trying to find myself, although my interest in language never waned. I got a job as a reservations agent at Air Canada Airlines in the New York City office. I was booking flights by telephone for passengers traveling to and from Canada. I often worked at the "French Desk" and got to practice my French talking with French Canadian passengers. Air Canada was good for the travel opportunities. I did a fair amount of jetsetting while working there. But, of course, I couldn't imagine spending the rest of my life booking flights. Hence, while working at Air Canada, I pursued a master's degree in TESOL at Columbia University's Teachers College. It occurred to me that TESOL was a field in which I could engage my fascination with language and culture. I would get to teach English to immigrant students from all over the world in one classroom. After earning my master's in TESOL in 1990, I taught ESL and French at a public high school in East Harlem, New York City, for 1 year—a real learning experience for me, given that I had never been in an American (let alone inner-city) high school, except for a semester of student teaching.

Toward the end of that year, an opportunity arose to teach on tenure track at Long Island University (LIU), Brooklyn Campus in the English department, so off I went. I spent 7 years at LIU, from 1991 to 1998, teaching composition to ESL students, most of whom were Ukrainian or Russian Jewish students who migrated to the United States after the disintegration of the former Soviet Union. During that time I returned to Teachers College and pursued both another master's degree and a doctorate in applied linguistics.

In the early 1990s, while at LIU, a new phenomenon was developing. A growing number of West Indian students at the elementary, secondary, and college level (LIU included) were being placed into developmental or ESL writing classes (the latter placement surprising to many of the students because of their English-speaking classification and self-identification). As someone from the region, I wanted to understand this new phenomenon. My doctoral dissertation thus examined the linguistic and pedagogical issues and challenges of Caribbean Creole English speakers' acquisition of standard academic English. Interestingly, I've come full circle. After starting out in foreign language, the dissertation brought me back home, and that return has given me a deeper appreciation of the richness and vitality of Caribbean language. A revised version of the dissertation was published as a book under the title *Englishes in Contact: Anglophone Caribbean Students in an Urban College* (Nero, 2001).

These days (since 1998), I'm Associate Professor in the master's program in TESOL at St. John's University in Queens, New York. My current research agenda has been shaped by both the work I began during my doctoral dissertation and my own cultural background. The issues raised by the placement, performance, instruction, and assessment of Caribbean Creole English speakers are certainly instructive for teachers of speakers of various World Englishes or nonstandard dialects of English. Today, as educators confront increasing numbers of speakers of various "Englishes" around the world in their classrooms—such as speakers of Caribbean Creole English, African American Vernacular English, West African English, Indian English, and so forth—TESOL is challenged to revisit such notions as the "native speaker" and, indeed, the very definition of English itself. To this end, I've edited a book *Dialects, Englishes, Creoles and Education*, (Nero, 2006) which brings together a multiplicity of voices on the linguistic and educational issues of speakers of various "Englishes" around the world. My hope is that this collection will add a critical perspective to our understandings of the spread of English, the politics of language, dialects, linguistic identities, language attitudes, and their implications for pedagogy.

QUESTIONS

1. If you are a TESOL professional of color, how would you have responded to Lisa's comment at the end of the class? If you are a White TESOL professional, how would you have responded to Nero's reply?
2. If you have received all or part of your education in the United States, approximately what percentage of your teachers have been persons of color? Has your experience been similar to Lisa's? If you received most of your education in a country other than the United States, are there many members of ethnic/racial minority groups represented in the education profession? What effect does the presence or absence of ethnic/racial minority group members have on the educational environment of your country?

3. Nero discusses the concept of "exceptionality." How do you interpret this concept? Have you had experiences in a professional or academic context in which you felt that you were an exception? If so, describe them. If not, what do you think are some of the effects of exceptionality on professional and academic contexts?
4. Nero identifies three dangerous messages that may result from the scarcity of Black educators in the United States. Are there more such messages that may result from this kind of scarcity?
5. Nero identifies some of the positive effects of her racial/cultural difference. Can you identify other positive effects of such difference?
6. Nero refers to a "hierarchy of nativeness." How do you interpret this notion? Do you agree or disagree with it? Why?
7. What is your perception of the role of nativeness in English language teaching (ELT)? From the perspective of your own background, or from what you have observed, what has been your experience with nativeness/nonnativeness in ELT?

REFERENCES

Amin, N. (1999). Minority women teachers of ESL: Negotiating White English. In G. Braine (Ed.), *Non-native educators in English language teaching* (pp. 93–104). Mahwah, NJ: Lawrence Erlbaum Associates.

Braine, G. (Ed.). (1999). *Non-native educators in English language teaching*. Mahwah, NJ: Lawrence Erlbaum Associates.

Brutt-Griffler, J. (2002). *World English: A study of its development*. Clevedon, UK: Multilingual Matters.

Canagarajah, A. S. (1999). *Resisting linguistic imperialism in English teaching*. Oxford, UK: Oxford University Press.

Crystal, D. (1998). *English as a global language*. Cambridge, UK: Cambridge University Press.

Davidson, M., & Foster-Johnson, L. (2001). Mentoring in the preparation of graduate researchers of color. *Review of Educational Research, 71*(4), 549–574.

Dehn, R. (2002, March 15). Black teachers are hard to find. *Seattle Post*. Retrieved June 14, 2002, from http://seattlepi.nwsource.com/disciplinegap/61967_staff13.shtml

Hernstein, R., & Murray, C. (1994). *The bell curve*. New York: Free Press.

Leung, C., Harris, R., & Rampton, B. (1997). The idealised native speaker, reified ethnicities, and classroom realities. *TESOL Quarterly, 31*, 543–560.

Liu, J. (1999). Nonnative English-speaking professionals in TESOL. *TESOL Quarterly, 33*, 85–102.

Nero, S. (2000). The changing faces of English: A Caribbean perspective. *TESOL Quarterly, 34*(3), 483–510.

Nero, S. (2001). *Englishes in contact: Anglophone Caribbean students in an urban college*. Cresskill, NJ: Hampton.

Nero, S. (2002). Englishes, attitudes, education. *English Today, 18*(1), 53–56.

Nero, S. (Ed.). (2006). *Dialects, Englishes, Creoles and education*. Mahwah, NJ: Lawrence Erlbaum Associates.

Pollock, M. (2001). How the question we ask about race in education is the very question we most suppress. *Educational Researcher, 30*(9), 2–11.

Wehrman, J. (2002, February 18). Few black teachers in nation's classrooms. *Detroit News*. Retrieved June 14, 2002, from http://detnews.com/2002/schools/0202/24/a02-419591.htm

Widdowson, H. (1994). The ownership of English. *TESOL Quarterly, 28,* 377–392.

Chapter 4

Stories Through Perceptual Frames

Donna Fujimoto
Osaka Jogakuin College

SOME BACKGROUND

Everyone always comments on how difficult it must have been to move from the balmy climate of Hawaii, where I was born, to the frozen winters of Alaska, where my family moved when I was seven and where I graduated from high school. I always respond that making the adjustment was not a problem at all—children can take all kinds of changes in their stride. No one has ever stopped to ask me about the more difficult adjustment I had to make—losing my membership in a majority group and becoming a member of a minority. Going through that culture shock was much more challenging than adjusting to simple temperature changes.

It was not until many years later that I gained perspective in order to understand that experience. It was indeed similar to what people go through when they travel to a foreign country. I remember feeling shocked at the way the children at my school and neighborhood spoke. They talked a *lot*, and incessantly. They spoke with loud voices, and they grabbed your attention in almost theatrical ways: "Hey, kid!" "Looky here!" I was totally shocked that very young children called adults in the neighborhood by their first name, and I was completely floored when I heard a young child call her parents by their first names! In my own case, I rarely had the occasion to think about what my parents' given names were, and did not even know what my grandparents' given names were.

As I got older, making adjustments was more difficult. My next move was considerably more difficult as I moved from provincial Alaska to the much more sophisticated, fast-paced, and urbanized culture of northern California. That was in 1967 when I started university. It was almost like having to learn a whole new language—I had to pick up the northern California university student lingo, and my perspective had to change in order to be able to interact appropriately with my classmates. The most difficult hurdle I faced was participating in class discussions. My communication style placed me at a tremendous disadvantage. Even after I realized that I had to change my style of academic interaction in order to be taken seriously, I experienced great anguish, frustration, and frequent failures when I tried to make my voice heard in class. The other students had no idea that I was desperately trying to get a word in edgewise; they assumed from my demeanor that I had no opinion or hadn't read the assignments.

I adjusted well enough to graduate with honors, and I'm glad to say that I eventually gained some positive experiences in class discussions. While I was in university I became very interested in Japan, because I am a *sansei*—a third-generation Japanese American. The third-generation Japanese American generally does not speak Japanese, unlike the second-generation Japanese American. This is a direct result of World War II and its concentration camps. Understandably, Japanese Americans felt the need to demonstrate to other Americans that they were VERY American, and this meant downplaying their Japanese roots. Perhaps that is why I grew up feeling I was 100% American and never paid much attention to my Japanese heritage. That changed in university, where I wrote some academic papers about Japanese society and became active in an Asian American political group.

After graduating in 1971, I went to Japan because I wanted to see it with my own eyes and had become more curious about my own "roots." Not surprisingly, I experienced the real culture shock—one that profoundly shook my understanding of myself and the world. The experience of being totally immersed in a culture that operated so differently from my own forced me to see things differently, even when my first reaction was to simply shut my eyes. As I have explained to my friends many times since, the period of adjustment to Japan was on the two poles of extremes—very positive and exciting, but at the same time painfully difficult. Perhaps the most difficult part was suddenly being an illiterate adult, unable to perform even simple tasks, like read road signs and get where I needed to go, or read restaurant menus and order for myself. This is the same for any non-Japanese person, but it was very tough for me because Japanese people thought I should understand. Being in Japan offered me my first experience teaching English, and I have remained an EFL teacher to this day. I enjoyed the chance to teach people of all ages and from all walks of life, and it was my students who

4. STORIES THROUGH PERCEPTUAL FRAMES

gave me so many priceless lessons about seeing another culture with a new pair of eyes.

MINORITY STATUS

As I mentioned earlier, at age seven I moved from being a member of a majority group (Asian Americans in Hawaii) to membership in one of America's minority groups. There were often times that other children would make me realize that I was not like them. "Jap"—although it was not said to my face and not loudly enough that I could hear the rest of the sentence, it stung nevertheless. I tried to pretend that I had not heard, but the shame still came crashing through. One boy made the sound of machine gun fire and directed it in my direction when the class touched on World War II. That made me feel self-conscious and ashamed, and again I pretended that I didn't hear it. I just wanted to be someplace else. I got nervous because I was afraid that someone, maybe my teacher (I was sure she had heard and seen it all), might scold the boys who did those things because if she did, I wouldn't know what to say. I'd be too embarrassed. That was why I hated history classes when we had to study about World War II. I was always afraid that someone would ask me whether my parents were in the relocation camps (they weren't). I did not want people looking at me just because I was of Japanese heritage.

It was in Alaska that I had my first experience of discrimination from an adult. I must have been in junior high school when it happened. As a substitute teacher was speaking, she learned my name, and the woman suddenly changed completely—right before my eyes! She had assumed that I was an Inuit or Eskimo—an honest mistake, because our facial features are similar. When this woman saw my Japanese American name, her whole demeanor transformed in an instant! Where previously she had been stern and almost scowling, her face broke out in smiles, her eyes widened, and she leaned toward me in a friendly manner rather than the cold stance she had maintained seconds earlier. Even her tone of voice changed: From flat, authoritative, and scolding, it became slightly higher and she had a more lilting intonation pattern. I remember her complimenting me on my classwork. I thought, "How does she know? She doesn't even know me."

The substitute teacher's attitude was unconscious, but it was the sheer suddenness and the marked difference in her that made me take notice. I remember feeling relieved that I was not Eskimo. That experience, however, made me aware of how people's perceptions of others can have a profound difference in a person's life. It matters to which group one is seen to belong, and it matters where power lies. With this teacher's first perception of me, I could actually feel the weight of being smothered and judged negatively. I could feel the low expectations she had of me, and I could feel that she had already made judgments on what my background was and what my potential would be. When all that was magically lifted at her altered perception of me, I could feel my "self" rise up to be able to interact with her eye to eye. I felt validated and encouraged, and moving from an icy, dangerous place I was suddenly enveloped in a warm and friendly atmosphere. I knew that I would now be given assistance if I ever needed any help, and I felt approval for whatever I would attempt from then on with her.

The Asian American minority is constantly being judged with these two lenses. When they are compared to other minorities, they are seen as the "model minority." However, placed in competition with the mainstream group, there are still negative judgments made, most of them not so obvious. Power, both blatant and subtle, influences the lives of members of minority groups in the United States. It affects which neighborhoods they live in, which schools they attend, which professions they pursue, and how they participate in the community—not usually in attention-getting incidents of discrimination, but in the more imperceptible, subtle ways, as illustrated by the unknowing substitute teacher.

AN INVISIBLE MINORITY

Moving to Japan presented another interesting perceptual twist. Suddenly, I lost my membership in a distinct minority group and was thrust into membership of the majority group. I had little in common with this group's members at that time. My language, my values, my body language, even my way of dressing were all different. It was my face that dictated my entry into this group, and there was a clear pull welcoming me to belong. Barraged with uncountable cultural jolts on a daily basis, it was all I could do to keep my balance. As is common when thrust into unfamiliar territory, I dug in my heels and leaned heavily on my American cultural identity and values.

In small and large ways I was forced to examine and articulate the parts of me that were identifiable as American and the aspects that I had not perceived before but were part of my Japanese side. It was not something that I did consciously or systematically. Over time, however, I noticed how certain anecdotes and personal observations cropped up in my conversations with friends or in letters to family. In times of confusion or difficulty, I sometimes wrote things down in a notebook in an attempt to make sense of my experiences and emotional reactions. I wrote as if I were writing to a friend or to myself, describing events and then trying to explain them. When I was overwhelmed, I just wrote and, once my reflections were put on paper, I felt a therapeutic boost and went on with my life. I never filled an entire notebook, so among my forgotten belongings are lots of partially used notebooks or bits of paper stuck in notebooks.

I often participated in "venting" (or "bitching") sessions with other North Americans working in Japan. In retrospect, I was going through a

4. STORIES THROUGH PERCEPTUAL FRAMES

process of examining my inner and outer selves—retaining the parts that I truly identified with and sometimes painfully letting go of what had previously been dearly held views. The ability to let go when something is no longer needed was perhaps one of the hardest lessons I learned, but was also the best. This was crucial in order for me to begin to feel more comfortable with being a Japanese American in Japan.

Although at first glance I was perceived to be Japanese, beyond that things were not so simple. I was certainly the source of many Japanese people's discomfort and surprise when my language or behavior showed me to be an American. It would have been much easier if I could have been always relegated to the subgroup referred to as foreigners, or *gaijin* and *gaikokujin*.[1]

In general, *gaijin* who are Caucasian are allowed a rather wide latitude when it comes to acceptable or appropriate behavior. Because they are not Japanese, they are often excused from having to adhere to the social rules in Japan. An inappropriate misstep or egregious gaffe can be looked on as a curiosity. More often, many Japanese opt to use their blind eye, which protects everyone from being offended. For non-Japanese who have Asian features, the story can be quite different.

Because we do not fit the basic identifying requirements of membership in the *gaijin* group (i.e., blond hair [or other hues] and blue eyes [or other shades], along with other features), we do not automatically pass. Thus, if we had broken some Japanese norm of behavior inadvertently, it depended on the Japanese interacting with us whether we would be excused or negatively judged for not having common sense. It made a huge difference if the person had had experience outside Japan or not, had studied other languages or not, or had had previous experience with *Nikkei* (Japanese emigrants and their descendants) or not. However, even with people from this group, I still went through perceptual screenings that were not unlike the one to which the junior high substitute teacher had subjected me. Because I was constantly being perceived differently—and this time in a culture where the differences are extremely subtle and difficult for non-Japanese to read—I often felt pressure and doubts about what was the best way to behave in different situations.

PERCEPTUAL FRAMES

From the day I stepped onto Japanese soil, I most probably caused a great deal of discomfort for the Japanese by not understanding their perceptual frame of "a woman." Having been schooled in the all-American catechism

---

[1] In Japanese, *gaikokujin* directly translated means "a person from an outside country," and *gaijin* is a shortened version. Thus, it means a foreigner or anyone who is non-Japanese. The term *gaijin* is sometimes used in a pejorative sense, but not always.

of freedom and equality, I arrived in Japan with clear feminist views. I was not happy about being paid less than *gaijin* men who were younger and less experienced than I was. I was not pleased when I was informed outright, with no apologies, that I could not have the job because I was a woman. I was not amused when I was viewed not in my own right but as part of a set with my husband. As I mentioned earlier, my instinctual reaction was to fall back hard on my American identity, which meant that I complained and vented frustrations with other *gaijin* women and Japanese women friends. I clung all the harder to my American views.

After much venting and more scribblings in notebooks, it gradually dawned on me that the frustration I was feeling was greatest when I acted like an American woman (something totally natural to me). Life was smoother when I behaved more like my Japanese female friends (these were newly learned ways that I consciously tried out to go along with my less-than-perfect but valiant attempts at the Japanese language). I realized I was being placed in the perceptual frame of a Japanese woman, *not* an American woman! I realized I could do something about lessening the frictions if I simply changed my behavior.

Learning how to act to minimize the friction is not easy even now. However, accepting the fact that I will always be placed in one or the other perceptual frame helped me eliminate useless stress. Accepting the fact that I will not be able to change the Japanese system helps me put my actions in perspective. There are, of course, boundary lines that I find hard to stay within. Some of them are beyond my abilities.

At this point, I need to explain an experience that surprised me but also helped me make sense out of my negative experiences. I once taught a husband and wife as private students, but I taught them separately. The wife was bright, interested in many areas, and much more proficient than the husband, who spoke excruciatingly slowly and made very slow progress. One evening, I was invited to a fancy restaurant with the couple and two of the man's colleagues. The dinner was very nice, but I was totally confused because the wife hardly said a word in English and acted like she had no idea what was being said. Her facial expression and the lack of energy or light coming from her made her unrecognizable to me. It was as if she were a different woman. Even when I tried to bring her into the conversation, she spoke hesitantly and not even in complete sentences.

It was only much later I understood what had happened. In public, a Japanese woman must not overshadow her husband or even a male who is present. The husband's English level was so low that the wife had to downgrade herself to a total beginner in order for the dinner to go well. Because of her deliberate actions, no one's ego was bruised and the dinner went smoothly. It was the wife's drastic transformation that had alerted me. Since that time I have realized that I do not behave as she did in the presence of Japanese males. Even if I tried, I would not be able to transform myself anyway. My

4. STORIES THROUGH PERCEPTUAL FRAMES

ability in speaking English also does not please Japanese men, even perfect strangers! People assume that I am showing off by speaking English in public. In my case, I obviously cannot downgrade myself to a beginning level. However, I have learned that in very important situations, things will go more smoothly if I learn to use silences meaningfully.

Thus, as I worked in finding my way, after many years and usually unintentionally, I began to see some things quite differently. The boundary lines of what is acceptable and unacceptable behavior are drawn differently in Japan than what I had expected as an American. The difficult part is that if I try to articulate where those lines are to check to confirm my conclusions, Japanese people are so enmeshed in their own culture that they generally cannot understand what the point of my question is and cannot make an informed judgment. To make matters worse, there are always individuals in every culture who exceed boundaries without drawing undue attention or negative repercussions. I paid attention when I observed them, because they alerted me to the possibility of finding more invisible lines. I was involved in a real-life intricate puzzle, and when not too frustrated or depressed because of some bewildering experiences, I enjoyed reading books and research studies on Japanese society because these gave me chances to gain more solid footing.

It finally dawned on me that Japanese have many more "frames" than those that were in my own repertoire. I realized that the most effective way in learning how to operate successfully within these frames was to simply "be" a part of it and to "feel," rather than always try to put things into words or search for causes and effects. I credit the years of training in martial arts for helping me to see and move differently. Martial arts opened up an entire new world with rules, hierarchies, and tough training, both physically and mentally—a different way of "being," but only after constant repetition and concentration.

I came to realize that when one knows what is being framed and when one is considered to be a "member" of that arena, then it is no longer as important to know exactly where boundary lines are, because even when one crosses them it doesn't change one's status. Members, then, are allowed generous freedoms, even protections. The attitudes toward *gaijin* began to make a little more sense to me. Because I looked Japanese, my membership in that group was not as clear-cut—sometimes I was a member, sometimes not. Because the Japanese could not always place me properly, I often received disapproval. Thus, from being a member of a minority in the United States, I had moved into a majority group, but as an individual, I had become invisible!

PROFESSIONAL DISCRIMINATION

Invisibility has its advantages. I can go wherever I want without anyone noticing that a non-Japanese is present. It gives me an excellent vantage point from which to observe people, like an anthropologist in the field. Japanese people don't change the topic of their conversation when I walk in the room. They don't get nervous if they have to speak to me. They don't feel embarrassed and flustered when they see me. They expect that I have common sense and will not do anything embarrassing.

However, in other ways, it is a decided disadvantage. In the first year I was in Japan, I applied for a short-term, high-paying position to teach English. I was totally shocked when I was not even considered, but a French woman, who wanted to teach French and admitted openly to others that her English was not very good, got the job. In my second year in Japan, a friend encouraged me to apply for a job at her school, so I went for an interview. After the brief interview, I never heard back from the Japanese man who interviewed me—not a phone call or even a letter. I had not gotten the job. Several months later, my friend told me that she had been furious because she thought I was the most qualified of the people who were interviewed. She told me she thought it was because the Japanese man had felt threatened because I did not act in a self-effacing manner, even though he knew I was American. If I had been Caucasian, I would most probably have gotten the job, she confided. She is probably the only person (she is Caucasian) who has articulated this so matter of factly. Everyone knows that Caucasians have an advantage over Asians in such teaching positions, but they shy away from talking about it.

It is not just at the level of hiring—this issue also surfaces at the daily class level. From the first time I taught in Japan, I saw that many students were disappointed to get me as a teacher. This still happens today, but not as blatantly as what occurred in my next story. In my second year of teaching in 1972, I had a class of male doctors. Their level of English was already quite high, and I noticed that two students in particular seemed to be checking my credentials by asking a number of very obscure grammatical questions. I was able to give good explanations, and I instinctively knew I had better throw in a number of grammatical terms as well to sound more authoritative. About a year later, my boss told me, that after that first lesson, he had received a call from one of the doctors asking him for another teacher. My boss asked the student why and asked if I had done anything wrong. "No, the teacher didn't do anything wrong," the doctor responded, but he still requested a different teacher. Finally, after a bit more probing, the doctor said the other class members wanted a native speaker. My boss explained to him that I was indeed a native speaker and that I was trained. Still, the doctor persisted in his request. My boss finally informed the doctor that I was the native-speaking teacher that had been assigned to them, and if they could not accept those terms they would have to find a different school. I continued to teach that class for several years, and it was one of the best classes that I've ever had.

This happens to be one example where a perceptual frame was being used incorrectly and, because of the boss, the students were forced to realign their perceptual frame. But what about the many times when there is no defender to insist on the appropriate perceptual frame? Unfortunately, I have a feeling that there are more of these latter cases. This seems to be the all-too-common lot of Asian teachers teaching English in Japan.

Why should these doctors prefer a Caucasian? And why did they equate "native speaker" with Caucasian? Why does a non-Caucasian have to work harder to be accepted as a teacher of English—to be seen in the proper perceptual frame of a bonafide teacher?

IT'S IN THE DNA

Befu (1991), a Japanese anthropologist, addressed contemporary Japanese belief in Japanese uniqueness and cultural homogeneity. He explained that despite empirical evidence to show otherwise, the Japanese tend to believe that Japanese culture, language, and even spirit are genetically transmitted. Befu went on to illustrate how this genetic theory of language transmission works to the detriment of Japanese Americans being hired as English teachers, which he called a "blatant expression of reverse racism" (p. 37). Not only are they not hired in favor of the Caucasian teacher, but also "their biological background stigmatizes them and diminishes the authority of their credentials as teachers and experts on matters of Western culture and language" (p. 37).

This may explain why Japanese people expect that I should have an advantage in speaking the Japanese language over people who are not of Japanese heritage. I often have to explain that I did not grow up hearing or speaking Japanese at home, and I had to learn it as an adult. I make it a point to tell them that all of my schooling and socialization were in an English-speaking environment, so I am not much different than any other American raised in the United States. Sometimes they hear me, and sometimes they don't.

It is not only Japanese who are guilty of faulty conclusions. In many other countries (including and even more so in the United States), strangers have changed their speech directed to me, thinking they are speaking to a non-native English speaker. I find myself often speaking faster and throwing in native speakerese to push them to change their perceptual frame of me. Sometimes it works, and sometimes it doesn't. I have often been asked, "Where did you learn your English?" and "Your English is very good." My responses have varied depending on whether I want to cut the conversation short or not. It surprises me when I get this strange type of compliment at English language teaching conferences, where I expect that teachers of English should be more aware that native speakers of English come in many different colors. A person's DNA cannot predict the language(s) that he or she can use fluently.

THE COLOR ADVANTAGE

When I talk about some of these experiences, some friends say that they do not think of me as a person of color. I am always surprised and unhappy at this attitude because, in fact, it denies an important part of who I am. Being Japanese American has affected my experience as a teacher of EFL. It *does* make a difference!

I have a lot in common with my Japanese students. When I see them struggling to participate in a class discussion, I recognize the communication patterns that place them at a clear disadvantage. These patterns are the very same difficulties I had when I was in undergraduate school. Both my students and I were taught that we must listen carefully to what another person is saying, and we generally wait for a pause after the last sentence before we raise our hand to speak. We sometimes rehearse what we want to say in our head before speaking and, as a result, we are usually too late to make our point. We are not used to formulating our thoughts as we speak, which is important to do when grabbing and holding the floor. It is hard for us to believe that it is permissible to say something that has no meaning and adds nothing to the discussion. We do not realize that this tactic is often used as a means to indicate that we are engaged and eventually will have something to say. We have to try not to be too silent, otherwise we will be seen as unintelligent or uninterested. It is a hard habit to break because we are used to speaking out only when we have something important to say. Being on the quiet side is part of our comfort zone.

For my Japanese students class participation is made doubly hard, because they are always aware that what they say can affect other people negatively. If they disagree with someone, it may hurt his or her feelings if the comments are not made indirectly or in a friendly way. My Japanese students sometimes seem overly careful not to sound too knowledgeable or too much better than others in the group. These rules are different than mine. For my students, disagreeing with a teacher or proving him or her wrong is not a good idea. They are very surprised when I tell them I was taught to find weaknesses in the arguments of others in the class, even the teacher's, and to make my counterclaim strongly and clearly.

I had read in books that Japanese students should not and usually do not challenge the teacher's authority, but I really didn't understand this fully until an incident in one of my classes. I called the roll at the beginning of every class and, after several months, I noticed that whenever I called out one student's name, other students around him looked at each other and said things, but I didn't know what they were saying. It was practically at the end of the semester when this talking and these looks prompted me to stop the roll call and ask what the matter was. There was a long, awkward silence, but I decided to be patient and wait for an answer. There were more looks ex-

4. STORIES THROUGH PERCEPTUAL FRAMES 47

changed and more whispers. I remember repeating myself several times, asking the students if they could tell me what they had been whispering. I only got more whispering and more nervousness from the students.

Finally, after what seemed to be a very long time and I was feeling exasperated, one of the students said just a few words that made me piece the puzzle together myself. The student's last name that I called in the roll was wrong, because it was listed incorrectly in my roll book. I could not fathom why the students didn't just tell me at the beginning of the term rather than keep on whispering and sharing looks for practically the whole semester. When I expressed great surprise and asked them why no one had told me, they looked very startled and no one had an answer. I was bewildered and irritated that I had been referring to a student by the wrong name for such a long time. Just when I was feeling comfortable that I knew how to work with Japanese students, this incident totally threw me off balance. Since then, the only explanation that I have come up with that might fit was perhaps the students thought that my roll was written in Japanese, and they didn't want to make me lose face because I could not read Japanese names correctly. I still don't know for sure if this is correct.

I have a hundred more stories in which my own perceptions entangled with the realities of Japan. I have learned a great deal about Japan, but I have learned even more about my own culture and myself. I discovered which parts of me are American and which parts are distinctly Japanese. I moved from one minority or majority group to another. I realized that how I am perceived and how I perceive myself has a great deal to do with my face and also my own reactions. The concept I refer to as *perceptual frames* has helped me be able to cope—from my childhood experience of discrimination from the substitute teacher to this very day. As a teacher, I have to continue to work sensitively with students, colleagues, and administrators to demonstrate and insist on proper perceptual frames to use. For us teachers, telling our stories is one way to help others understand our perceptual frames. For me, it is no doubt my quest to learn more about Japan and the constant questioning of my identity that have significantly affected how I view my teaching and how I work with my students.

QUESTIONS

1. Fujimoto describes how she felt being in the minority in her Alaskan school. Have you ever been in a similar situation at any point in your education? If so, how did it make you feel? Have you had any students who you believe were self-conscious because of their minority status? If so, how did you address their feelings?
2. Have you ever been treated unfairly by a teacher because of your race? If so, describe the experience.

3. Have you had experiences similar to Fujimoto's (i.e., being a foreigner who is mistaken for a native)? If so, how was your experience similar to or different from Fujimoto's? How do you respond to the difference in treatment received by different foreigners in Japan, as described by Fujimoto?
4. Have you ever had the experience of being an invisible minority and/or a visible minority? If you have experienced both, how did the two experiences compare? If you have not had the experience, what advantages and disadvantages do you think each type of minority membership has, other than the ones described by Fujimoto?
5. Fujimoto describes how some of her students reacted when they saw that she was to be their teacher. Has this ever happened to you? If so, how did you respond? If not, how would you respond?
6. How would you respond to Fujimoto's question about preferences for Caucasian teachers (i.e., why should the doctors prefer a Caucasian teacher and why did they equate "native speaker" with Caucasian)? Why are there occasions, such as those Fujimoto describes, on which non-Caucasians have to work harder to be accepted as a teacher—to be seen in the perceptual frame of a bona fide teacher?

REFERENCES

Befu, H. (1991). Inside and outside. In B. Finkelstein, A. Imamura, & J. Tobin (Eds.), *Transcending stereotypes: Discovering Japanese culture and education* (pp. 32–39). Yarmouth, ME: Intercultural Press.

Chapter 5

My Journey Into Racial Awareness

Carmen T. Chacón
University of Los Andes, Táchira, Venezuela

BACKGROUND AND EDUCATION IN THE UNITED STATES

I was born and grew up in the west part of Venezuela, South America. In 1979, I earned a degree in education with a major in English. In 1980, I was awarded a scholarship to come to the United States to pursue a master's degree. I lived in Spokane, Washington, for a year, and then moved to Cheney, a smaller town about 45 minutes from Spokane, to finish my master's in college instruction with a minor in English as a second language (ESL). My memories are still fresh about those 2½ years I lived in Washington. I had a few American friends with whom I used to meet over the weekends, chatting and sharing superficial cultural topics about "foods, facts, and fiestas" about Venezuela. I guess we did not want to get into anything controversial or too sensitive that may have hurt feelings on each side. I think my cross-cultural learning experiences in Washington lacked multiculturalism. My life in Washington was a valuable intercultural opportunity to improve my English proficiency and gain a sense of efficacy in communicating with native speakers, as well as to learn from a culture that was different from mine.

However, from a multicultural critical perspective, as a professional of color in the U.S. higher education system, I did not perceive differences in race or gender. At that time, I took for granted color-blind realities; my dream was to visit the United States and improve my English and cultural knowledge. From a neutral linguistic perspective I recognize that this intercultural experience helped me with my English, but from a critical multicultural perspective, I lacked awareness of my racial self. As a result, I identified myself only as a Venezuelan in the United States. I don't remember encountering much diversity on the streets or at school in either Spokane or Cheney. All North Americans I ran into were White; I don't remember seeing African Americans or Latinos in Spokane or Cheney. I generally interacted with international students from Asia and a few from Africa, but the majority of people around me were White (I mean Caucasian, a term I was not familiar with back then). When I look back, I realize that unconsciously I perceived my race to be bound to nationality; at that time, I considered myself as a Venezuelan and classified my international classmates simply as Japanese, Chinese, Korean, Nigerian, or Americans. Despite the fact that I recognized skin color differences, I was color blind. In Venezuela, I identified myself with Whites, because in my country I would be described as White because of my fair skin color.

I had grown up listening to a homogeneous discourse without distinctions of race. Race was not something I was aware of until a few years ago, when I first began reflecting on its significance in the United States. It was during my years as a doctoral student at one of the largest universities in the United States that I started to consider my racial identity. The experience of being perceived as a student of color opened up my awareness of the role of race in the United States. As a result of that awareness, I started to question my long-held beliefs of color blindness in Venezuela, and I began noticing prejudices and stereotypes against dark-skinned people conveyed in our social practices. Now, I am conscious of stereotypes that disqualify people of color, particularly African Venezuelans. In my effort to examine our discursive practices, I have found messages (e.g., jokes, sayings) that portray African Venezuelans as inferior. Although we are all a mix of races (i.e., Spaniards, indigenous people, and Black Africans), the darkest-skinned people are the targets of prejudice and disqualifying linguistic discrimination.

Going back to my first trip to the United States, living and going to school in Washington State was an incredible learning experience, full of pleasant memories that I enjoyed for the most part (except for the winters, which were too cold and snowy for somebody coming from a tropical country). Academically, I gained expertise and confidence about my English speaking proficiency and sociolinguistic knowledge. Nonetheless, looking back on those times, I think that my cross-cultural experiences in Washington were in a way blind to issues of race, power, and language, because I don't remember being marginalized or looked down on because of my accent or skin color. Although most of my classmates were White, I did not feel excluded from the academic discourse; as an international student coming from a rich oil country, (I was viewed by everybody with respect. I was seen as an international graduate student pursuing a master's degree in a U.S. University and who planned to go back home. In a way, I was exotic because I was a foreigner, and there were not many around, except for the other international students. I remember being asked questions about how things were back home in Venezuela. For instance, I was often struck to hear the question, "Do you have TV back home?" As the time passed, I have come to realize that the question about TV showed lack of awareness about Venezuela's material wealth and development at that time.

As I mentioned before, in my memories there were no issues involving race, accent, or ethnicity while I lived in Washington. Or, perhaps, I didn't see them because they were not part of my assumptions or "figured world" (Holland, Lachicotte, Skinner, & Cain, 1998). Now, when I look back, I just can't believe how much I have changed my perceptions of myself and my understanding of the role of race and color in my own and others' intercultural encounters and relationships. In Washington, wherever I went, I was a Venezuelan—just a Venezuelan going to graduate school. Identifying myself as a Venezuelan was who I was and where I came from, or so I thought.

CONSTRUCTING AND REPRODUCING STEREOTYPES THROUGH LANGUAGE

After I completed my master's degree, I went back home with new knowledge and expertise to teach English, but still carrying with me many misconceptions about the "American culture" that were instilled in me as I grew up, and reinforced later by the education I received in my master's program. For example, I always thought about the United States as a country of a homogeneous culture and White population. Until recently, I was blind to the fact that multiculturalism and diversity are major characteristics of the North American society.

I grew up believing that a label saying "Made in the U.S.A." is the best product in our market, because we have the tendency to buy and consume products made in the United States in the belief that what comes from the United States is better than what we produce. I think that these assumptions are part of the hegemony of the U.S. power and leadership spread through media to the so-called "third world" nations. In addition to the impact exerted by U.S. TV programs and Hollywood movies, the formal education I received also contributed to perpetuate the western ethnocentrism inherited from colonial times. One common example is found in printed materials, such as textbooks, in which Americans appear as White and rich, whereas people of color are not generally included or are negatively portrayed. Popular magazines are another source of media misconceptions on the United States as a homogeneous culture. I learned the common generalization that North Americans are rich and wealthy. Regarding women, a common shared assumption is that the Barbie doll is a genuine representation of the beauty of the North American woman—blonde, slender, and blue eyed. In fact, this doll has become so popular among Venezuelan girls that a Barbie is often the first doll that little girls receive. Even more, Barbie is the stereotype that many men have in mind as the woman of their dreams, at least in terms of physical beauty.

The preceding generalizations and stereotypes about North Americans can be related to the English hegemony perpetuated by the spread of English as an international language (EIL): "English is the language of the USA, a major economic, political, and military force in the contemporary world" (Phillipson, 1992, p. 24). Thus, not surprisingly, people on the periphery (e.g., Venezuela) take for granted the legitimacy of the dominant ideas and images that come from the center, in this case the United States. In Phillipson's (1992) words, countries "are peripheral in the sense that norms for the language are regarded as flowing from the core English-speaking fountainheads" (p. 25).

The privilege of English as *lingua franca* is present worldwide through technology, business, commerce, research, and communication. The fact that meaning is constructed through language, and that language is the mediation tool of social interaction (Vygotsky, 1978), explains the relation of language, power, and social inequities. Through language we express our identity; how we perceive ourselves and how we perceive others are linguistic representations of who we are and from where we come. As Bronckart (1995) asserted, language is "communicative action," "the author of the world" (p. 81); it is the lens by which we see and interpret reality. This is how race and language bias and prejudices are reproduced in daily discursive practices. For instance, it is not uncommon to find racist language in daily discursive practices in Venezuela, such as when people say, *"merienda de negros"*—Black people gathering particularly for a meal—meaning that Blacks are noisy and rowdy; or when somebody says, *"trabajo como un(a) negro(a)"*—I work like a black—meaning that hard work is for Black people.

In my early years at the high school, I learned tenets that "English is an open window to success," and "English is the international language of business and trade"—essentially, that English is a key for professional success and prestige. These two pervasive assumptions have been perpetuated by the media and the education I received. They represent ethnocentric ideologies imposed on so-called "third world" countries through media and disempowering discourses of colonialism. From my own experience, I acknowledge the fact that it was not until my doctoral studies awoke my racial consciousness that I realized that language was used as a tool to reproduce social inequities that I had not really noticed before. After this eye-opening experience, I started to "see" and understand why my status as a Latina in

5. MY JOURNEY INTO RACIAL AWARENESS   53

the center is perceived as inferior not solely because of my race but also because I come from the periphery. I started to "see" that generalizations and stereotypes are rooted in the education we receive in the expanding circle (Kachru, 1992).

Over the years, media has been used as a powerful source that works to reinforce ethnocentrism and misconceptions about the United States. Not surprisingly, a majority of Venezuelans think of the United States as the paradise that Hollywood movies usually show worldwide. Portrayals of rich White Americans who live in beautiful houses, own luxurious cars, and earn good salaries are powerful images that impact us, and make many Venezuelans long to live in the United States. However, when it comes to people of color, the portrayals tend to be negative. A few years ago, my sister and niece came to the Midwestern United States to spend their vacation with me. At first, any time they got close to an African American male on the street, they could not help being worried about his proximity. It was not by chance, my niece and sister were afraid—the images we are used to watching on TV and in Hollywood movies are generally prejudiced against people of color. Whereas Whites are shown living in wealthy neighborhoods, people of color are usually portrayed as inhabitants of poor neighborhoods, and generally depicted as being violent and more likely to commit crimes. This unequal distribution of power among Whites and people of color reflects differences marked by race, class, and ethnicity. The discourse that tells that people of all races, genders, and social classes are treated as equals in the United States becomes a fallacy because of the existence of two realities that cannot come together: Whites and minorities. Media, for instance, makes a clear-cut difference between poor neighborhoods that are commonly inhabited by minorities and wealthy white neighborhoods.

MY SECOND JOURNEY: HOW MY SUBJECTIVITY AND RACIAL AWARENESS HAS EVOLVED

After going back home in 1982, I worked as an English as a Foreign Language (EFL) teacher at a high school and then, after a few years, as a teacher educator at the University of Los Andes. Sixteen years later, in 1998, I came to the United States for the second time to pursue my doctoral studies in a large university of the Midwest. I lived there for 5 years. During those years my commonly held assumptions started to puzzle me. Between my second and third years as a doctoral student, I began to struggle with my racial identity. At the age of 44, I found myself reflecting on "who I am" and "where I come from." The answers "I am Carmen and I come from Venezuela" were not enough to help me understand why I was perceived as different in my daily encounters with the "American culture." The first time I listened to a graduate African American student talk about *who we are* and *where we come from*—in a multicultural class during my first year as a doctoral student—her arguments made no sense to me. I believe it was because race, ethnicity, and power were not part of my "figured world" yet.

In the poststructuralists' view, subjectivity represents a site of struggle where, as individuals, we deconstruct discursive practices through which race, gender, and power are exercised (Weedon, 1997). Up to 1998, for me, teaching English was merely interpreted in terms of applied linguistics (phonology, grammar, lexicon) because I was not aware that discursive practices carry out ideological representations of power and social inequities. It was not until my second journey to the United States, in 1998, that I began to question many issues that I had taken for granted during my first sojourn there. The first thing I started to realize was that I was seen and treated as a minority, a minority with an accent. In the academic community, I felt excluded and neglected by the ethnocentric behavior that often dominates in mainstream classes. I experienced feelings of despair in many cases, when my comments in group discussions were ignored by my American classmates; I was haunted by thoughts of lack of confidence and wondered if I was ignored simply because I was an outsider.

Minority in TESOL: My Experience as a Graduate Student

In my academic cross-cultural learning, I experienced feelings of exclusion and marginalization from the academic community. I empathized with other international students from Japan, Taiwan, Korea, and China who, like me, were trying to fit into the academic discourse in mainstream classrooms. I felt hopeless as I realized that the discourse was dominated by White students, while we foreign students just sat and listened. I felt neglected by that ethnocentric behavior, and I still wonder if international graduates' expertise does not count in mainstream classes. I am afraid my answer is that, in my experience, such expertise still does not count (as much as it should). During my years as a doctoral student in mainstream classes, I sometimes dared to jump into a class discussion, but I did not notice that my native classmates had much interest in listening to what I had to say as a nonnative English speaker (NNES). Being ignored in discussions dominated by native speakers and centered in the United States, has made me aware that the education we receive in U.S. teacher education programs lacks relevance for our foreign contexts. I also have to say that, fortunately, not all classes are alike. Two particular courses had a profound impact on my subjectivity as an NNES. I talk about them for the remainder of this section.

The first course, called "Infusing Global Perspectives In Education" was designed for K–12 American teachers. The instructor, Dr. Merry Merryfield, hired me and other international students to act as cultural consultants (CCs)

5. MY JOURNEY INTO RACIAL AWARENESS

in that class. As a CC, my mission was to interact and share my personal views and experiences with American teachers regarding issues of global interconnectedness, perspective consciousness, and experiential learning. For me, that course was a powerful cross-cultural learning experience and represented a space in which my voice could be heard. As a CC, I had a major role in the class because, perhaps for the first time, my American classmates were interested in listening to what I had to say because their goal was to exchange experiences with CCs. The instructor's whole idea of having CCs was also important, because it helped the native English speakers (NES) in the class to see the NNES teachers as an asset and as a resource.

A particular incident in one of those exchanges was critical for me. An American student teacher asked the CCs if we were going back home or staying in the United States after graduating from our programs. A CC from India raised her hand and talked about her plan to finish her master's degree and go back to India. She expressed feelings of marginalization and isolation, but above all, she said, "I would rather be a first-class citizen in India than a second-class citizen in the U.S." I was astonished to hear her saying what many times I had also thought but never dared to speak aloud. I thought about my own status as a minority in the United States; I saw race and language as marks for the individual's status. I came to the realization that, as a TESOL professional, I need to be aware of the interconnectedness of race, language, and power in order to understand who I am and from where I come.

The second course that had a profound impact on my subjectivity (who I am) was an elective seminar for nonnative English-speaking teachers (NNESTs) taught by Dr. Keiko Samimy, which I took during my third year as a doctoral student. The seminar unveiled hidden assumptions behind the teaching of English as an international language that I had reproduced as an EFL teacher for so many years. As an EFL teacher, my commitment was to help students develop communicative competence in English. All those years, I thought I was teaching English from a neutral and apolitical perspective, isolated from the sociopolitical factors that surround the spread of EIL.

During the NNESTs seminar, I read the works of scholars (e.g. Amin, 1997; Braine, 1999; Kachru, 1992; Pennycook, 1994; Phillipson, 1992; Tang, 1997) and engaged in a dialogic critical reflection with other NNESTs from the periphery. Struggling in the reconstruction of my subjectivity (Weedon, 1997), and deconstructing discursive practices that conveyed messages of oppression and disempowering discourses of colonialism, helped me to fully see power relationships of language, race, and status that explain social inequity in the world. As a result of this process of questioning and reflecting about myself, I started to rethink my teaching practices and self-representation in TESOL.

Interconnectedness of Race and Accent

One of the first things most people notice when I speak English is my accent. It is not uncommon for me to hear the questions, "Where are you from?" "Are you Mexican?" I am used to comments like "Your accent sounds nice." During my second journey as a graduate student in the United States, I got used to hearing the phrase "Can you say that again?" Often, some people looked at me in a puzzled way, without saying a word, which made me feel worse than I did when having to repeat things to make myself understood. Many times, I thought to myself, "this person has a monolingual ear." For me, a monolingual ear means somebody who belongs to a homogeneous group affiliation, and who is not used to diversity or who is not willing to understand accents other than his or her own—or the so-called "Standard American English." The following anecdote illustrates part of my point about the monolingual ear, and how accent is attached to geography. When I had lived in the Midwest for around 3 months, I had a conversation with an acquaintance about my feelings of despair as a newcomer. I was struck to hear his story. He told me, "People here are not used to diversity. Twenty years ago, when I first came I was considered and treated as a foreigner." "But you are an American," I replied. With a big smile in his face, he said, "Yes, that's what I am trying to tell you. I am from Kentucky!"

My experiences during my second trip to the United States made me realize that accent and race go together. I noticed that accent is perceived according to the region from where we come. In this sense, having a British accent is not the same as speaking English with a Spanish accent, particularly if one is identified as Latino(a). In my case, coming from the periphery, I think my accent is not perceived with the same privileges of someone coming from Australia or Great Britain.

At first, I used to feel very uncomfortable about my accent; I wanted to sound coherent and be understood as standard rather than different. Later, as my critical awareness developed, I realized that my accent is part of who I am. That is why it is important to note that how we interpret the world, the "figured world" (Holland et al., 1998), informs our reactions to events. I found this to be true for me. As an NNES teacher, my views about accent started to change as I challenged and deconstructed myths related to nativeness. This self-reflective process led me to uncover the interconnectedness of race, language, and power. In the next section, I deconstruct my assumptions as a Venezuelan struggling with her subjectivity.

Racial Consciousness

In the reconstruction of my subjectivity, I have challenged my own assumptions about race. In my country, I never thought of myself as being "different." There, I am a Venezuelan. As mentioned before, we come from a mix of Africans, Spaniards, and indigenous people that gave birth to the *mestizo*.[1] In my experience, skin color is not as much of an issue for Venezuelans as it is for Americans. Social class prejudices are more important than skin color; however, I recognize that the standards of beauty I grew up with favored the lighter shades of skin as best. Hence, as I started questioning my beliefs, I noticed the linguistic racism hidden in our discursive practices. Now, I do recognize the existence of prejudices against people not only for their social class, but also for their dark skin.

Despite the fact that it is common to find from the lightest to the darkest shades of skin within the same family, as is the case in my family, the lightest tend to prevail in our standards of beauty. My niece, for instance, has very dark skin, as opposed to her brother, whose skin is light. She was in first grade the day she came home with tears in her eyes and asked her mother: "Mom, why is my brother White and I am not?" A few days later, her mother found out that the principal at my niece's school used to call her *"mi negrita,"*[2] which in my context is not necessarily rude or offensive. Nonetheless, for my niece the fact that her classmates started calling her *"negrita"* obviously caused discomfort to her; she did not like to be perceived as *"negrita."* Until now, I had not realized that my niece's anecdote reveals that beliefs that lighter shades of skin color are better involve racial prejudices that I had not previously questioned. I realize that although in my context racism is not apparently considered an issue that affects children in schools, in reality, it does, as my niece's anecdote shows. Some authors (Montañez, 1993) have explained that, in Venezuela, prejudices against people whose skin is not light are rooted in the colonization, because Spaniards were considered superior whereas Africans slaves and indigenous people were seen as inferior. Montañez goes on to argue that, paradoxically, the *mestizo*, in our country, is "endoracist" (p. 114) because *mestizos* highlight the white in their race, but tend to reject the African mix in their veins.[3] This endoracism is unconsciously perpetuated in our daily practices. On the one hand, the educational system helps reproduce prejudices against the original cultures in Venezuela. On the other hand, those prejudices are reinforced through negative images and stereotypes spread by the media.

Discourse structures are not free or transparent, but instead are the medium to express power and oppression. However, this is an issue that I have

---

[1] According to the *Oxford Spanish Dictionary*, *mestizo* refers to a person of mixed race. In Venezuela, *mestizo* means a mix of Spaniards, Black Africans, and indigenous people.

[2] In Spanish, the suffix *-ita* and *-ito* are attached to nouns to make their diminutive form, such in the case of *negra/negrita*, and it can be used in a loving or pejorative form depending on the context and intonation used by the speaker.

[3] According to Montañez (1993), endoracism is a phenomenon by which *mestizos* accept white physical features but reject the nonwhite (African, indigenous) physical features of themselves and others.

begun to think about recently. Now, I wonder about the education Venezuelan children receive and the necessary curriculum changes conducive to help them develop a critical awareness of cultural bias and racial prejudices so that they are better prepared for the future. I also think that it is essential to promote changes in the curricula of teacher education programs in order to prepare EFL teachers to challenge and transform hegemonic cultural discourses that reproduce social inequities.

Living in the United States made me aware of racial identity as I dealt for the first time with race categorizations such as Caucasian, Hispanic, White non-Hispanic, African American, Asian American, and so forth. I think that these categorizations are not merely linguistic signs, but are also social representations that involve prejudices and stereotypes based on race, skin color, and language. I always identify myself as a Venezuelan in terms of nationality, but after reflecting on the intersections of race, language, and power, I became aware of my multiple identities as a woman, a Venezuelan, a Latina, a teacher, a mother, and a minority in the United States. I believe that my experience living in the United States was invaluable. During the years of my doctoral studies, I looked at and lived experiences through the lens of race; it became clear to me who I am in terms of racial self-identification. For the first time, I felt what is like to be perceived as "the other," as both an ethnic and racial minority. Now, as a professional of color, I feel affiliated with those who suffer from color prejudice and social discrimination. It's been a struggle for me to reconcile the views about Hispanics/Latinos as different from those about White non-Hispanics. As a Venezuelan Latina, mother, wife, teacher, and teacher educator, I cannot be indifferent to the reproduction of the dominant common-sense assumption that language is neutral, and therefore, my role is just to teach English in its linguistic components. Language is not neutral (Pennycook, 1994; Weedon 1997); it is the tool to express ideology and discursive practices that are exercised under social, political, economical, and historical circumstances. Slowly I have learned this, and now I find myself struggling with issues of race, language, and privilege not only in my classroom but also in my community with colleagues, friends, and relatives.

LANGUAGE AND RACE RELATIONS

Reading about the "native speaker fallacy" (Phillipson, 1992), I found my voice represented by NNESTs, who experience considerable struggles against prejudices to establish their credibility and to receive fair hiring opportunities in the United States and sometimes in their own countries because of race and language issues. The reality is that there are millions of nonnative teachers inside and outside the United States in search of credibility from those holding administrative positions at schools and universities who believe in the native speaker fallacy. In Venezuela, as well as in some other countries, academic institutions and people in general hold the belief that the native speaker is more competent to teach English than is the nonnative.

Over the last decades, technology and globalization have contributed to increase the spread of EIL; the power of English as a *lingua franca* has dominated all areas of human knowledge. An ongoing debate around the role of EIL questions the apolitical neutrality (Pennycook, 1994; Phillipson, 1992) of EIL. I think that being aware of issues involved in the power relationships around EIL has helped me, as a TESOL professional, to empower myself and my students to use English to express "voice." Although it is true that English serves as the medium of global communication, this is not the only reason why people all over the world learn it. There are political and economic factors that result from the United States imposing its language and its power in the world. Thus, interpreting the spread of EIL from a purely linguistic standpoint without looking at these political implications contributes to perpetuate social inequities.

Over the years, the native speaker fallacy has been grounded and reproduced in the education that most nonnative EFL teachers receive. I myself, as a nonnative teacher, have been educated in the belief that teaching EIL is an apolitical, transparent activity. After reflecting on who I am and where I come from, I have become aware that the distinction between native and nonnative speakers of English goes beyond a simplistic difference, but instead is imbued with ideological and political motivations. I still remember the obsession of some of my English teachers who insisted on having us sound like native speakers. I was never aware of my strengths as a nonnative speaker of English, only my weaknesses. My preservice English teacher education focused on mastery of linguistics (grammar, lexicon, syntax, phonology, and morphology) contributing to the views that for so long I had held about the neutrality of EIL. I was not exposed to world Englishes or courses related to identity, ideology, power, and language. It was not until I experienced multiculturalism and diversity during my second journey into the United States as a doctoral student that I started to debunk the common myths about the Standard American English and the neutrality of EIL.

Part of this situation, as I have written elsewhere (Chacón, 2000; Chacón, Alvarez, Brutt-Griffler, & Samimy, 2003), results from the fact that my initial education was predominantly rooted in behaviorism and structuralism, in which language acquisition is seen as an external behavior. Thus, emphasizing nativelike pronunciation and fostering "idealized" Standard English pronunciation were major goals in learning English. The "idealized" Standard American English is a myth, because native speakers also have an accent depending on the region from where they come (Lippi-Green, 1997). It is important to note that although speakers from Australia, Canada, Great Britain, and the United States have different accents within their own regions, those accents are not perceived as negative or disqualifying when compared with the accents of NNEST from periphery countries. Our story is different. The accents of Singaporean English, Puerto Rican English, Indian English, and the English of other people from the periphery like me carry ideological and political bias that may be used to exclude us as English speakers.

The distinction among the world Englishes (Kachru, 1992) shows the relationship among prestige, power, and language. Why is it that American English or British English has more prestige than do the other Englishes in the world? Definitely, this is not a coincidence. Why is it that immigrants are considered as "the other" as "culturally and linguistically inferior" (Rockhill & Tomic, 1995, p. xi)? Race determines which variety of English is prestigious. Labels such as "third world," "at risk," and "LEP" (limited English proficiency), among others, are generally used to categorize people as inferior or limited in their abilities.

**AWAKENED AWARENESS:
HOW IT HAS AFFECTED MY TEACHING**

During my two sojourns in the United States, I learned powerful lessons and gained a great number of insights through cross-cultural learning. I have struggled with my subjectivity in a multiplicity of roles as a woman, a mother, a nonnative English teacher, an educator, a Latina, a Venezuelan, and a minority in the United States. My journey into racial awareness has affected my professional life in several ways. First, I believe I have developed a critical understanding of who I am; this critical understanding has helped me open my awareness of how I see myself and those with whom I share racial classification, as well as those I perceive as being outside my race. Second, as a teacher educator and an EFL teacher myself, I have reflected on my role and actions in the past that led me to question my long-held beliefs on issues of race blindness and social injustice. For instance, I am now aware of discursive practices that in my own context convey messages of exclusion and discrimination against race, class, and gender; it is not only a matter of being "the other" but also of being aware of social injustice exercised through race and power in our own settings.

Regarding my identity as an EFL teacher, I feel empowered because I am conscious of my strengths as an NNES. Thus, I see myself compelled to reeducate my students and colleagues by helping them develop a critical awareness about our strengths as nonnative speakers. Also, in our role as TESOL professionals, I believe we can no longer be passive consumers of center ideology and reproducers of social inequity. We have to debunk pervasive assumptions about linguistic racism. Hence, I am positive that we

5. MY JOURNEY INTO RACIAL AWARENESS

need to transform the TESOL curriculum in teacher education. I believe it is critical to incorporate the political into the teaching of English to help prospective teachers challenge taken-for-granted assumptions and long-held beliefs about race and language. The incidents and experiences I have narrated in this chapter illustrate how education and media affected my conceptions, or "figured world," using language for the maintenance of dominant ideologies that generally come from the center to the periphery.

Currently, I am in the process of incorporating a critical praxis into my teaching by having my students question prejudices about racism and unveil relations of language, race, and power as they approach them in daily social practices and textbooks and media, particularly on TV and in films. In addition, in 2003, with a colleague, I conducted an elective seminar for NNESTs in order to help student teachers develop a critical awareness of their role as TESOL professionals. As a teacher educator and an NNES, I have the responsibility of empowering student teachers (Chacón & Alvarez, 2001), helping them to deconstruct linguistic racism and nativeness. Prospective EFL teachers need to be exposed to world Englishes. Nonnative Englishes comprise 30% to 40% of English spoken in the world, but have not generally been seriously considered by linguists, except for studies on contrastive analysis (Kachru, 1992).

Finally, as a teacher educator I am also concerned about the education and hidden racism in Venezuela. What can be done to prepare Venezuelan children to deal with racial prejudices and social inequity in their future? I believe that incorporating critical literacy and multiculturalism into our educational system would help create a critical conscious awareness about social injustice. Furthermore, English teacher education programs should address social inequities and foster prospective EFL teachers' empowerment through English.

In sum, during my journey into racial awareness, I have struggled and continue to struggle with my subjectivity. In my personal life, as a TESOL professional I believe I can play a major role as an agent of transformation by taking actions in and out of my classroom to dismantle the pervasive racism spread through language. As a TESOL professional and teacher educator, I am committed to helping student teachers develop a racial consciousness to struggle against social injustice and inequities. Debunking disempowering discourses in the teaching of EIL will lead teachers to construct and reconstruct their subjectivities as TESOL professionals on both personal and institutional levels.

QUESTIONS

1. Chacón describes herself as "color blind," with respect to race. How do you respond to the notion of color blindness?

2. Chacón identifies discriminatory discursive practices in her language. Are there any in your language? How do you identify them? How did you become aware of them? Are you aware of any in English?
3. As a result of its economic and politic presence, the United States holds a unique place in the minds of many people throughout the world. If you have taught EFL outside the United States, did you know what your students' perceptions of the United States were? If you have taught ESL in the United States, did you know what your students' perceptions of the United States were before they arrived, and how those perceptions compared to their perceptions after living there? Have the perceptions of your students been affected by the popular media? How do Chacón's descriptions of impressions created by the popular media and textbooks compare to your own experience or that of your students?
4. Chacón describes some of the difficulties she encountered in classrooms as an international student. If you have been an international student (in any country) studying with natives, have you had any experiences similar to Chacón's? If you have not been an international student, what do you think faculty and other students could do to help international students to not feel isolated?
5. Chacón states the need to be aware of "the interconnectedness of race, language, and power in order to understand" who she is and from where she comes. What is your understanding of how race, language, and power are interconnected in terms of your identity?
6. Chacón describes the effects of different contexts on her feelings about herself. Have you ever had the experience of feeling different about your racial identity in different contexts? If so, what was the cause of your feelings? What was different about the contexts? If not, have you ever felt "different" in different contexts for a reason other than race? If so, what were the bases of these differences?
7. Chacón sees a role for world Englishes and nonnative Englishes in teacher education. Do you agree? If not, why not? If so, what should be the role of these Englishes in teacher education?
8. Chacón believes that teacher education programs should address social inequity. Do you agree? If not, why not? If so, how should they address it?

REFERENCES

Amin, N. (1997). Race and the identity of the nonnative ESL teacher. *TESOL Quarterly, 31,* 580–583.
Braine, G. (Ed.). (1999). *Non-native educators in English language teaching.* Mahwah, NJ: Lawrence Erlbaum Associates.

Bronckart, J. (1995). Theories of action, speech, natural language, and discourse. In J. V. Wertsch, P. del Rio, & A. Alvarez (Eds.), *Sociocultural studies of mind* (pp. 75–91). New York: Cambridge University Press.

Chacón, C. (2000). Reflections from the classroom: Empowering NNESTs. *NNEST Newsletter, 2*(2), 11.Chacón, C., & Alvarez, L. (2001, February/March). *Critical pedagogy and empowerment in teacher education.* Paper presented at the 35th TESOL Annual Convention, St. Louis, MO.

Chacón, C., Alvarez, L., Brutt-Griffler, J., & Samimy, K. K. (2003). Dialogues around "Revisiting the colonial in the postcolonial: Critical praxis for nonnative-English-speaking teachers in a TESOL program," by Janina Brutt-Griffler and Keiko K. Samimy (1999). In J. Sharkey & K. E. Johnson (Eds.), *The TESOL quarterly dialogues: Rethinking issues of language, culture, and power* (pp. 141–150). Alexandria, VA: TESOL.

Holland, D., Lachicotte, W., Skinner, D., & Cain, C. (1998). *Identity and agency in cultural worlds.* Cambridge, MA: Harvard University Press.

Kachru, B. B. (Ed.). (1992). *The other tongue.* Chicago: University of Illinois Press.

Lippi-Green, R. (1997). *English with an accent: Language, ideology, and discrimination in the United States.* New York: Routledge.

Montañez, L. (1993). *El racismo oculto en una sociedad no racista.* [The hidden racism in a nonracist society.] Caracas, Venezuela: Fondo Editorial Tropykos.

Pennycook, A. (1994). *The cultural politics of English as an international language.* New York: Longman.

Phillipson, R. (1992). *Linguistic imperialism.* New York: Oxford University Press.

Rockhill, K., & Tomic, P. (1995). Situating ESL between speech and silence. In J. Gaskell & J. Willinsky (Eds.), *Gender in/forms curriculum: From enrichment to transformation* (pp. 209–229). New York: Teachers College Press.

Styles, C., & Horwood, J. (Eds.). (1998). *The Oxford Spanish dictionary* (2nd ed.). Oxford, UK: Oxford University Press.

Tang, C. (1997). The identity of the nonnative ESL teacher: On the power and status of nonnative ESL teachers. *TESOL Quarterly, 31,* 577–580.

Vygotsky, L. (1978). *Mind and society: The development of higher psychological processes.* Cambridge, MA: Harvard University Press.

Weedon, C. (1997). *Feminist practice and poststructuralist theory.* Oxford, UK: Blackwell.

Chapter 6

From Learning English in a Colony to Working as a Female TESOL Professional of Color: A Personal Odyssey

Angel M. Y. Lin
The Chinese University of Hong Kong

LEARNING ENGLISH IN A BRITISH COLONY

I do not belong to the small number of people in Hong Kong born into families and communities that provide them with the ample English linguistic and cultural capital (Bourdieu, 1982/1991; Delpit, 1988) needed to succeed in school in a British colony, where English is the key to academic success and socioeconomic advancement. My parents do not speak any English. People we know all speak Cantonese, which is our daily language. I grew up in a home and community where few had the linguistic resources to use English at all, and even if anyone had, he or she would have found it socially inappropriate (e.g., sounding pompous, putting on airs) to speak English.

My chances for learning and using English hinged entirely on the school. However, I lived in a poor, government-subsidized apartment building complex (called "public housing estate") in the rural area (the New Territories) in Hong Kong, where schools were mostly newly put up in the 1960s and they had neither adequate English resources (e.g., a staff well versed in spoken English) nor a well-established English speaking and English teaching and learning tradition or school culture.

My parents were poor manual workers. They put all their hopes and expectations in their children: Illiterate in English as they were, they did not fail to be keenly aware of the fact that their children's future depended on doing well in school. In the Hong Kong schooling system, doing well in school depends on mastering the English language. My parents have passed on their work ethic to their children. We were urged day and night to "study hard," and especially to study English hard (although they themselves did not have the slightest idea as to how one could learn English well!). I remember that when I was in Grade 3, I was very frustrated by my English "story book," which was full of difficult English words that I did not understand. My teacher typically would read the story once and I could not remember how to pronounce those words afterward. The whole page was opaque and frustrating to me! I was very frightened then, because small as I was, I did not fail to realize that I was not going to do well in English.

After leaving the primary school, I achieved good results in the secondary school entrance examination and was admitted to an English medium secondary school. However, unlike when I was in Primary 3, I didn't despair. I would spend hours and hours looking up all the new words in the dictionary and writing down their pronunciations (in phonetic symbols), meanings, and examples in a vocabulary notebook, and would read them whenever I had time. My history textbook had become a rich source of vocabulary learning and soon I could catch up with the history lessons and assignments.

A Community of English Letter Writers

In my circle of girlfriends, having pen pals had become a topic and practice of common interest, and we would talk about our pen pals and discuss our excitement about trading letters, postcards, photos, and small gifts with them. We'd also show one another pictures of our pen pals. We'd share things, like different kinds of beautiful letter pads and envelopes, and talk about what to write to our pen pals. Although there wasn't a pen pal club, we had, in a way, formed our own informal pen pal interest group (without having such a name and formal structure, of course). It was a spontaneous "community of practice" (Lave & Wenger, 1991) that had emerged from our own activities and interests. Through organizations such as Big Blue Marble or International Youth Service I got paired with pen friends from England, Austria, Canada, and the United States, and we communicated regularly in English by air mail letters. Sending letters to our overseas pen friends and waiting eagerly for their replies had became everyday hobbies for my friends and me.

6. A PERSONAL ODYSSEY

Expressing Alternative and Expanded Selves in English

At about that same time, I also started to write my own private diary in English every day. I started this habit when a pen pal sent me a diary book for my birthday present and suggested keeping a diary as a worthwhile activity for me. I chose to write my diary in English because someone (a teacher? I don't remember now) had told me that finding a chance to use the language daily would improve one's English. I believed that I could write my feelings more freely when I wrote in English—I felt less inhibition and reservation. I seemed to have found a tool that gave me more freedom to express my innermost fears, worries, anger, conflicts or excitement, hopes, expectations, likes and dislikes, or my alternative selves, without constraint or inhibition. It was as if this foreign language had opened up a new, personal space (a "third space," so to speak) for me to more freely express all those difficult emotions and experiences (typical?) of an adolescent growing up, without feeling the sanctions of the adult world. I guess I was creating an expanded self in English, and English seemed to provide me with the additional resources I needed to explore myself in a somewhat different manner, in a somewhat different value system, one that appeared to be less prohibiting than my native language in some areas (e.g., in the area of explicitly articulating one's emotions such as anger).

English, it seems, had opened up a totally new space for me to express and entrust my secrets and innermost feelings. I felt safe to confide in Gretchen, my U.S. pen pal, and in my diary. I also felt that English had provided me with a tool to broaden myself, to reach out to new friends in new lands, to invent and create for myself a somewhat different self than the one my parents knew. It gave me excitement when new and lasting friendships across cultural and geographical boundaries were formed, and it gave me satisfying feelings like those that an adventurer would have when exploring a new land and new culture. Of course, all the while, I also felt that I had developed a good, healthy hobby that would help to improve my English proficiency and my performance in school, which was equally important to me. This experience of mine has made me aware of the importance of creating opportunities for students to use the language that they are learning to expand their sociocultural experiences, to explore cross-cultural issues, and to negotiate hybridized and expanded selves and identities. If they can appropriate English and penetrate it with their own meanings, intentions, and voices and use it for their own purposes, then English will no longer be a foreign or alien language—it will become a language of their own. This notion has motivated my later research and work on how to help students to hybridize English and appropriate it to express their own meanings (see Lin & Luk, 2005; Lin, Wang, Akamatsu, & Riazi, 2002).

Anticrisis: Being Made to Feel Ashamed of My Accent

In my secondary school days, English was something I believed I had mastered and owned. I felt competent and comfortable in it. It was not until my first year as an undergraduate English major in the University of Hong Kong that I was induced to feel ashamed about my own English—or, rather, made to feel that I hadn't really mastered or owned the language. Many of my peer students at the university had mostly studied English literature in their secondary schools, whereas I had only the slightest idea of what it was! When I opened my mouth in tutorial sessions, I noticed the difference between my Cantonese-accented English and the native-like fluent English that my classmates and the tutor spoke. It was, however, too late for me to be able to pick up the native-like accent then. Besides, there were not many chances for me to learn to interact informally with people face to face in English.

My disadvantage and my lack of spoken English resources became more painfully evident when, after graduation, I started teaching English in a well-established girls' school. When my most advanced students began mocking my accent in the classroom, I knew that I had to quit and return to the university to acquire more English resources and credentials.

Fortunately, I succeeded in getting a scholarship to live in the Robert Black College at the University of Hong Kong for 2 years, during which I studied for my master's degree in applied linguistics. It is a lush residence primarily intended for visiting professors, scholars, researchers, and overseas graduate students. However, they also offered a small number of residential scholarships to local Chinese graduate students to enable them to live there (e.g., subsidizing their room and board, which would otherwise be too expensive for a local student). For the first time in my life, I lived in a community and an atmosphere where English was informally used, and where I could interact and make friends with English-speaking people in my daily life (vs. in a formal lecture).

My life and career took a positive turn after my master's degree and my residential years in the Robert Black College. I had acquired both the paper credentials and the actual linguistic and cultural resources to get and properly perform the job of an English teacher. I had not (and have not) acquired a nativelike English accent, but, relatively speaking, my spoken English was more fluent and idiomatic than it was before the Robert Black College years. I no longer felt that I was an "impostor" (Bourdieu, 1982/1991), or an "incompetent" teacher, an object of mockery by my middle-class students and colleagues. I seemed to have somehow managed to enter the elite group of English-conversant Chinese in Hong Kong.

I was about to settle down with a job as an English language instructor at the University of Hong Kong, and forget about the past. After all, I had worked hard and managed to move up the socioeconomic ladder, fulfilling the expectations of both my parents and myself. I had a better job now compared with the jobs my parents had, and they didn't have to worry about my future any more.

However, when I think of all that had happened, I realize that my own chances for socioeconomic advancement seem to have hinged largely on a certain exceptional repatterning of social and institutional arrangements. Although individual hard work is necessary, it and sacrifice alone do not count much. For all the hard work in the world, I would not have been able to develop my interest in and ability to learn English had there not been some well-trained and English-conversant teachers who were willing to teach in a rural school (and this was an exception rather than the rule), and who provided me with access to some English linguistic capital. For all of my hard work, I did not manage to attend one of those well-established, prestigious English-speaking schools in the urban area, because of the prohibitive distance constraint imposed by my rural residential location. For all the hard work in the world, I would not have had access to conversational English resources had there not been an institutional arrangement to provide some local students with scholarships to live in the English-speaking Robert Black College (and again, the number of scholarships was very small). My own personal history has led me to realize that certain social and institutional structures impose strong constraints on a child's opportunities for bettering his or her life quite independent of his or her efforts and industry. For someone coming from a sociocultural and socioeconomic background like mine, the chances for socioeconomic advancement are slim, even with lots of individual hard work and enterprise. These social and institutional arrangements constrain the child's opportunities for socioeconomic advancement by denying or limiting his or her access to English linguistic and cultural resources.

It would not be too much of an exaggeration to say that success in learning and mastering English (and thus also other subjects, which were tested in English in most secondary schools) can be almost a life-and-death matter for schoolchildren in Hong Kong; their academic success, social mobility, social status, higher education and job opportunities, and very often and very immediately, in the students' as well as their important others' (e.g., their parents') minds, the students' own self-worth directly or indirectly depends on it. We may be justified to call it the "language of self-worth." Notwithstanding its being the mother tongue of only a minority in Hong Kong, English is both the language of power and the language of educational and socioeconomic advancement. It constitutes the dominant symbolic resource in the symbolic market (Bourdieu, 1982/1991) in Hong Kong.

The symbolic market is embodied and enacted in the many key situations (e.g., educational settings, job settings) in which symbolic resources (e.g., certain types of linguistic skills, cultural knowledge, specialized knowledge and skills, etc.) are demanded of social actors if they want to gain access to valuable social, educational, and eventually material resources (Bourdieu, 1982/1991). For instance, Hong Kong students must have adequate English resources, in addition to subject matter knowledge and skills, in order to enter and succeed in the English-medium professional training programs of medicine, architecture, legal studies, and so forth, if they wish to earn the English-accredited credentials to enter these high-income professions. The symbolic market is therefore not a metaphor, but rather one with transactions that have material and social consequences for individuals.

I therefore pursued doctoral studies and conducted a critical study on the sociocultural contexts of English language lessons in Hong Kong schools (Lin, 1996). However, earning a doctoral degree and entering into the TESOL academia proved to be just the beginning of another difficult journey. Looking back on my past years of experiences in the university is painful; it's like looking at one's scars and all that one has sacrificed in order to gain respect and dignity in one's job. I turn to this story in the next section.

WORKING AS A WOMAN TESOL PROFESSIONAL OF COLOR IN HONG KONG

Ever since the very moment of being hired in my former university, I have been considered as "a local classroom person" and designated to do the labor-intensive work of student practicum supervision and school placement coordination. I learnt later that, at the time they hired me, the school had two positions open. One position was to replace a local (i.e., non-white, Cantonese-speaking) faculty member who was leaving academia to return to a secondary school to become the principal there. The local colleague had contributed the lion's share of the work setting up the undergraduate programme's internship curriculum. She had been doing both the heavy administrative work of soliciting from schools every year the placement positions for the programmes, as well as developing the internship manual, assessment, portfolio, and journal protocols for the course. The other position was for someone to teach second language acquisition (SLA) and TESOL research methods.

Although I had extensive training in research methodology, including both qualitative, ethnographic methods and sophisticated statistics and measurement theories and techniques (e.g., path analysis and LISREL [linear structural relations], factor analysis, and other types of inferential statistical analyses), my employer seemed to ignore all my research training (which was stated on my CV) and just focused on me as a "local classroom

6. A PERSONAL ODYSSEY

person" because my thesis research was a sociocultural and discourse-analytic study of local classrooms. I later learnt from my Caucasian American colleague, who filled the other position, that when he was hired, he was told that they needed a local person for teaching the classroom modules and doing the work of student practicum placement coordination and thus wanted him for teaching the SLA and research methods modules.

So, from the very beginning of my existence as a faculty member there, I was both labeled and pigeonholed as a "local classroom person," which has all the consequences of giving my superiors the rationale for assigning me to the labor-intensive, administrative-heavy work that the senior Caucasian members choose not to perform. Another very useful rationale is found in the argument that they need someone who speaks the local language (and preferably a woman—isn't a woman traditionally most suitable for a public relations job?) to liaise with the schools in soliciting practicum places for our students. Whenever we counterargued that the local school personnel do speak English, the superiors would assert that it would be better to have a local person who is "more familiar" with the local schooling system to liaise with school personnel. This argument assumes that the senior faculty members from overseas (all Caucasian, native English speakers), (a) do not need to learn at least some local language of the students and teachers, and (b) do not need to better acquaint themselves with the local educational issues and schooling system. One wonders in what ways they can fully benefit our preservice and in-service student teachers if they take it for granted that it is acceptable for them to remain not very familiar with both the local educational issues and the local linguistic and cultural milieu of our student teachers and their future students. And of course, we argued the points in the way that we liked, and they assigned us the jobs in the way that they liked.

Another instance also speaks to the school's pigeonholing me as a classroom person. Some years ago, I was Deputy Programme Leader of our undergraduate TESOL programme. However, one day I was told by my Chinese male colleague who was Programme Leader that they would like to have my British colleague become the Deputy Programme Leader to boost the public profile of our TESOL programme in the local communities. A British colleague of mine, and a Caucasian British and native English speaker, did not have a doctorate but was a playwright doing some English radio educational programmes part time. The Programme Leader's exact words were: "It'd be better to have a native English speaker as our Deputy Programme Leader—it will increase the prestige of the programme, as local students and parents look up to foreign, native English speaking experts." I was asked to give up the Deputy Programme Leadership to take up the heavy administrative, coordinator work of the practicum module AGAIN (work that I had previously done for years). I protested via an e-mail to my Chinese male colleague, saying that what he proposed would only reproduce the society's denigration of local English staff. He replied that he wouldn't want to enter into such a nonfruitful argument with me, and said all he cared about was the good of the programme.

I held nothing personal against my British colleague nor my Chinese male colleague. Both of them had been and are still on friendly terms with me. I fully understand that this is what my Chinese male colleague truly believes: Putting a British name and a Caucasian face on our undergraduate programme will boost our public image. However, what I felt agonized about is that all these years of solid training and researching intensively the local educational issues had only earned me a "second-class" status in the TESOL profession. I still think that my male Chinese colleague was well intentioned (i.e., "for the good of the programme"), but he had let the ideology of native-speakerism rule him (Gee, 1996) and he was totally unaware (or refused to be aware?) of the kind of injustice he did me by reproducing this ideology that privileges White people in his actions as he exercised his power unjustly.

Every workplace is vulnerable to internal politics, and there are struggles that are related not only to race/ethnic/linguistic background or gender. Thus, marginalization *can* happen to anyone, including White male and female faculty. It is important to note that gender and racial categories should be seen as relational and not categorical, and do not invariably prescribe a particular type of social experiences for members of those categories (and membership can sometimes be negotiated). Hence, we should refrain from taking an essentializing approach to our experiences. And yet, my lived experiences of marginalization point to certain systematic ideological and institutional structures underlying them. It is to a theoretical analysis of these structures that I turn next.

GENDERED AND RACIALIZED TASK/LABOR SEGREGATION IN TESOL

My lived experiences point to a common pattern of gendered and racialized task and labor segregation; that is, women faculty of color are often assigned to labor-intensive administrative and teaching duties (e.g., I was consistently asked to do the heavy administrative work of liaising with schools for students' teaching practicum). Decades ago, feminist standpoint theorists had already pointed out the gendered labor segregation in modern academia. For instance, Dorothy Smith (1974, 1987) argued that "women's work" relieves men of the need to take care of the everyday, practical chores of the local places where they exist, freeing men to immerse themselves in the world of abstract concepts and theories. Moreover, the more successfully women perform their work, the more invisible it becomes to men. This is precisely what is experienced by faculty of color in Hong Kong. Without the heavy administrative work of women faculty of color like me to secure places for students' practicum every year, our department's TESOL programme cannot be viable. The largely White male faculty enjoys the benefits of their labor and can then focus on teaching "theoretical" courses and writing research papers or taking up leadership roles in the department. We therefore need to extend the model of the feminist standpoint theorists to point out that this segregation of labor is very often not only gendered, but also *racialized*.

We can draw a parallel between task segregation in modern academia and the well-documented task/labor segregation in 19th century United States: "A pattern of task segregation can also be historically demonstrated. Although the classical example is the sole use of black slaves in growing cotton, task segregation occurred with other racial minorities as well" (Liu, 2000, p. 1351). Liu (2000) went on to describe the internal colonialism in the United States in the 19th century, under which racial minorities such as Chinese and Black labors were concentrated in the low-priced, low-wage fields, primarily in agriculture and import-competing industries, while the majority of White workers were in the higher-priced, higher-wage fields and in noncompeting industries. I argue that such an invisible internal colonial model is also in operation in today's academia, especially in the TESOL discipline, in which a pecking order of tasks seems to exist. It is to an analysis of the epistemological and political consequences of this task hierarchy and task segregation that I turn in the next section.

THE GREAT THEORY–PRACTICE DIVIDE IN TESOL

TESOL as an institutionalized discipline is relatively young, compared with other "hard" sciences or even social sciences (e.g., psychology). As an academic discipline it has always aspired to "scientific status" by ever improving its theories through research done mainly in the positivist, physicalist tradition, and chiefly in the subdisciplines of second language acquisition and interlanguage studies. As an "applied" discipline, it has borrowed extensively from both the theories and research methodologies of other "pure" disciplines, such as Chomskyan linguistics, psychology, and cognitive science. Although recent years have seen the discipline's top journals becoming more receptive to research done in post-positivist, sociocultural, or critical paradigms, mainstream TESOL theoretical and research canons still follow the parent disciplines, which are modern academic disciplines established in the tradition of Enlightenment rationality and philosophy.

Modern disciplines born of the Enlightenment tradition subscribe to specific sets of ontological and epistemological assumptions. Under Enlightenment assumptions, the ideal agent of knowledge, the ideal scientist, is a transhistorical, unitary, individual, and disembodied mind, whose scientific endeavours are not supposed to be in any significant ways shaped or constituted by their historical, social, cultural, and institutional contexts and locations. The contents of their discoveries—the theories and findings—likewise can lay claim to the status of transhistorical, universal truths (for a summary of feminist standpoint critiques of Enlightenment epistemology, see Harding, 1996). In practice, mainstream TESOL research largely follows the paradigm of positivism and physicalism. The chief concern under this paradigm is to *operationalize* and *quantify* (i.e., define and measure in numerals) human and social phenomena (e.g., language learning and teaching) in terms of "variables," and to *verify* hypotheses about the relationships (e.g., causal or correlational relationships) among different variables (for a theoretical alternative to physicalism and positivism in understanding human actions, see Taylor, 1985).

It is not a trivial point to note that the Enlightenment philosophers were typically males who theorized and philosophized in a historical period when they occupied privileged social and economic positions with slaves and servants attending to their everyday practical needs, thus freeing them to conduct their theoretical work. Today, we can see the shadows of parallel structures of gendered and racialized division of labor in academic disciplines and in TESOL, which models itself on its parent disciplines. In the TESOL field, those who teach future professors and researchers are at the top; those who teach future ESL/EFL teachers come next; and those who teach ESL or EFL are at the bottom. It is typically females (and among *them*, many are women of color) who fill up the ranks at the bottom.

Feminist standpoint theorists have pointed out the unfortunate epistemological consequences of such gendered segregation of labor. They hold that movements for social liberation advance the growth of knowledge. As summarized by Harding, "[Feminist standpoint theorists] explicitly call for women of color, working-class women, and lesbians to be present among the women whose experiences generate inquiry. They all discuss the limitations of sciences emerging only from white, western, homophobic, academic feminism" (Harding, 1996, p. 311). In our lived experiences, we note that it is precisely this gendered and racialized theory–practice divide in our discipline that has contributed to the inadequate generation of theories of practical knowledge that are relevant to the work of frontline TESOL practitioners. The experiences and activities of the majority of frontline TESOL workers (typically female classroom teachers, and many are people of color) do not have a chance to enter into the ranks of prestigious mainstream theories and research, because these frontline TESOL workers are not given the institutional resources, time, and opportunities to theorize their experiences and share and publish them in the discipline's prestigious journals.

6. A PERSONAL ODYSSEY 75

Apart from the negative epistemological consequences, there are also grave political consequences of this gendered and racialized theory–practice divide. Because the knowledge generated by the experiences and activities of female researchers and teachers, of people of color, and of different social classes and sexualities does not have a chance to enter into the discipline's knowledge base and thus cannot contribute to the content of the discipline's curriculums, students coming from these dominated groups consistently are not exposed to the kinds of knowledge and theories that speak to and value their own lived experiences as minorities in society.

WHERE I AM NOW

Where do I stand now? I feel that I am not just an "Asian," a "Chinese," a "nonnative English speaker of color" (although people in general will still identify and classify me with such labels). I feel that I have been able to develop an identity that's broader than just being Hongkongese or Chinese, or a person of color, but as a human being reaching out to other human beings, forming friendships above and across cultural and ethnic lines; different, yet not an *other*. English is very much part of me now. Yes, I speak English with an accent, but I promise myself that when occasions arise in which some people might try to make me feel ashamed of my accent, to feel that I'm an *other*, I'll resist any negative impulses. I'll reply "I am like you, but I'm not really you," or "No, I'm not you, but I am like you" (Trinh, 1990). Like what Trinh Min-ha said: There's an *other* within every I. Perhaps I can also say this too: There's an English *other* within a Chinese I, or equally true, a Chinese OTHER within an English I.

Yet, today, I'm agonized, seeing that many students of English have such an unpleasant experience with English. Perhaps it's like how I felt when I was frustrated by the difficult English vocabulary in my textbook in Primary 3. Perhaps more importantly, such students need to develop a new relationship with English, and find new identities for themselves that are more than just "Hong Kong Chinese who need English for exams." English, as I have known it for years, is not and should not be seen as the language of only those people living in or coming from "English-speaking countries." English should not be exclusively owned by the English-speaking British, Americans, Australians, or Canadians. English—in its many diverse ways, in its many rich accents—should be accessible and should belong to anyone who wants it. English should also allow itself to be enriched, expanded, and hybridized by people living in different parts of the world. I see that nonnative English teachers and TESOL professionals of color can have an important contribution to make to TESOL in shifting the ownership of and authority over English (as communicative resources) to more learners and teachers of diverse ethnic/linguistic backgrounds in the world. They should not always be relegated to duties and roles placed at the bottom of the ranks, simply because of the market ideology that White faces sell (i.e., the ideology that asserts putting White faces and names in leadership positions add symbolic prestige to an institute and its programmes).

How do I help my students to turn English from an enemy to a friend; to make use of this medium to express, expand, and possibly enrich their lives; to transform or hybridize their current identities; to enter into a new world of possibilities as well as relationships with other cultures and peoples in the world? We cannot just ignore English, no matter how much we might wish we could; we have to come to terms with English, but not as a neutral tool of communication (albeit how much we would like to happily believe that). Instead, we have to be fully aware of its power and its gate-keeping functions, fully aware of how it gets its power over us, and yet reappropriate and hybridize it, with our own accents, and ultimately own it. I can never forget what a 14-year-old secondary school student told me: "English is so boring and so difficult, I can never master it, but the society wants you to learn English; without English, you can't find a good job!" His words keep coming back to haunt me. It's a dilemma, and I'm still working on a response to it. Perhaps the cyberage in this new millennium presents new spaces, new media, and new possibilities for experimenting with new forms of English, new hybridized identities, and new hybridized communities. Perhaps we can work toward helping ourselves to develop and engage in new practices whereby learning and speaking another language is not a continuation of the processes of *othering*, which we have already witnessed so much of in this world.

TOWARDS A COMMUNICATIVE ETHIC OF TOGETHERNESS-IN-DIFFERENCE: FROM TESOL TO TEACHING ENGLISH FOR DIALOGIC COMMUNICATION IN A WORLD OF DIVERSITY

The TESOL discipline needs to be revisioned and reshaped in our increasingly globalized world of diversity. Instead of taking as our disciplinary goal the finding and gaining of *certain* (as opposed to situated, uncertain) knowledge of the most effective technology (as if there exists a universally effective technology) to teach English to speakers of other languages, a more urgent task seems to be that of finding situated, dialogic, globalized ways of teaching and learning English for relatively constraint-free understanding and communication (Fricker, 2000) and achieving a sense of togetherness-in-difference (Ang, 2001) among people coming from very different locations (geographical and/or social) and with very different sociocultural experiences (see Lin & Luk, 2005; Wong, 2005). The traditional technicalized concerns of the discipline need to be expanded by equally im-

6. A PERSONAL ODYSSEY 77

portant concerns about how to value linguistic and cultural diversity and promote social justice in the (often hegemonic) spread of English in different parts of the world.

In embarking on this writing project, I am not aiming at "narrating [my] suffering," nor am I "invested in rewards" (Velez, 2000, p. 325). What gives meaning to this job and profession of ours as we continue to work as women faculty of color in TESOL? Because we have been sociohistorically constructed as "women," "person of color," and "nonnative English speakers," we are triply disadvantaged by all the labels of marginalization and exclusion. In the hierarchy of the TESOL industry, such pigeonholing identities have the effect of placing women of color at the bottom ranks of the profession, and forming an implicit caste system in which persons of color are consistently excluded or marginalized, with such marginalization made invisible and legitimate through all kinds of naturalized ideologies (e.g., the market ideology that White faces and names help to sell an ESL or EFL program).

With few faculty of color to serve as role models to schoolchildren of diversity, the invisible ideologies that privilege White faces and White names as legitimate speakers of English and authoritative figures/experts in TESOL will only continue to perpetuate, to the effect that children of color might also internalize the ideology that White persons are the "best" ESL/EFL teachers. It is my hope that our work will contribute to a world in which there is more intercultural understanding, and less marginalization and discrimination due to various ideological and institutional structures; a world in which children and students of different racial/ethnic, linguistic, social, and gender backgrounds can have their identities and experiences valued and their potential affirmed and developed in their English language education. That, however, cannot happen without a serious problematizing of the kinds of marginalization and exclusion that the TESOL industry and profession perpetuate.

QUESTIONS

1. If you are a nonnative speaker of English, how does your process of acquiring English compare to Lin's? If you are a native speaker and you have had the experience of learning a foreign language, how does that experience compare to what Lin encountered as she learned English?
2. Lin describes the importance of English for socioeconomic advancement in Hong Kong. Does access to English occupy this strategic position in any society in which you have lived? Are you aware of any other societies in which this is the case? Have you seen any relationship between race and access to English in any society in which you have lived?
3. Lin explains how she was "pigeonholed" and describes the disparity in job assignments between other local "classroom person[s]" and senior

faculty from abroad. How might you have reacted in Lin's place? What are some possible consequences of this disparity, other than the ones she mentions?
4. Lin describes an instance in which she was removed from her position and replaced by a colleague who was said to lend a more prestigious public image to the program in which she taught. Lin believes that an injustice was done to her. If you agree, mount an argument in her defense. If you disagree, mount an argument in defense of Lin's Chinese male colleague.
5. Lin describes racialized task segregation in the TESOL profession. Have you ever seen evidence of this? How can this type of segregation be addressed?
6. Lin refers to the "racialized theory–practice divide" in the TESOL profession, and some of its consequences. Can you think of other consequences? What do you believe is the effect of this kind of divide on teachers, learners, and others in the TESOL field?
7. Lin states that "English should not be exclusively owned by the English-speaking British, Americans, Australians, or Canadians," but that its ownership should be shifted. How do you respond to the notion of English—or any language—being "owned?" Who owns the languages you use? What is your perception of the relationship between the countries listed here and the ownership of English?
8. Lin describes a kind of tripartite disadvantage experienced by TESOL professionals of color like herself, and a "marginalization made invisible and legitimate through all kinds of naturalized ideologies." If you agree with her, what do you think some of these ideologies are, and how do you think they should be addressed? If you disagree, give your understanding of the situation Lin describes.

REFERENCES

Ang, I. (2001). *On not speaking Chinese: Living between Asia and the West.* London: Routledge.
Bourdieu, P. (1982/1991). *Language and symbolic power.* Cambridge, MA: Harvard University Press. (original work published 1982)
Delpit, L. D. (1988). The silenced dialogue: Power and pedagogy in educating other people's children. *Harvard Educational Review, 58*(3), 280–298.
Fricker, M. (2000). Feminism in epistemology: Pluralism without postmodernism. In M. Fricker & J. Hornsby (Eds.), *The Cambridge companion to feminism in philosophy* (pp. 146–165). Cambridge, UK: Cambridge University Press.
Gee, J. P. (1996). *Social linguistics and literacies: Ideology in discourses* (2nd ed.). London: Taylor & Francis.
Harding, S. (1996). Feminism, science, and the anti-Englightenment critiques. In A. Gary & M. Pearsall (Eds.), *Women, knowledge, and reality: Explorations in feminist philosophy* (pp. 298–320). New York: Routledge.

Lave, J., & Wenger, E. (1991). *Situated learning: Legitimate peripheral participation.* Cambridge, UK: Cambridge University Press.

Lin, A. (1996). *Doing-English-lessons in secondary schools in Hong Kong: A sociocultural and discourse analytic study.* Unpublished doctoral dissertation, University of Toronto, Canada.

Lin, A., & Luk, J. (2005). Local creativity in the face of global domination: Insights of Bakhtin for teaching English for dialogic communication. In J. K. Hall, G. Vitanova, & L. Marchenkova. (Eds.), *Dialogue with Bakhtin on second and foreign language learning: New perspectives* (pp. 77–98). Mahwah, NJ: Lawrence Erlbaum Associates.

Lin, A., Wang, W., Akamatsu, A., & Riazi, M. (2002). Appropriating English, expanding identities, and re-visioning the field: From TESOL to teaching English for glocalized communication. *Journal of Language, Identity and Education, 1*(4), 295–316.

Liu, J. (2000). Towards an understanding of the internal colonial model. In D. Brydon (Ed.), *Postcolonialism: Critical concepts in literary and cultural studies* (Vol. IV, pp. 1347–1364). London: Routledge.

Smith, D. (1974). Women's perspective as a radical critique of sociology. *Sociological Inquiry, 44,* 7–13.

Smith, D. (1987). *The everyday world as problematic: A feminist sociology.* Boston: Northeastern.

Taylor, C. (1985). *Human agency and language.* Cambridge, UK: Cambridge University Press.

Trinh, T. M.-H. (1990). Not you/like you: Post-colonial women and the interlocking questions of identity and difference. In G. Anzaldua (Ed.) *Making face, making soul* (pp. 371–375). San Francisco: Aunt Lute Foundation.

Velez, D. L. (2000). Anger, resentment, and the place of mind in academia. In *Is academic feminism dead? Theory in practice* (pp. 311–326). New York: New York University Press.

Wong, S. (2005). *Dialogic approaches to TESOL: Where the gingko tree grows.* Mahwah, NJ: Lawrence Erlbaum Associates.

Chapter 7

Perpetual Foreigners: Can an American Be an American?

Shelley Wong
George Mason University

EARLY PERSONAL FAMILY HISTORY: IMMIGRATION AND THE SEARCH FOR INCLUSION

I am a fifth generation Chinese American. As a TESOL professional of color looking back on all five generations, I see recurring issues that have emerged in both my family background and my experience in TESOL. My life in TESOL has reflected some of the same themes that emerged from my family's 150 year history in the United States.

The earliest members of my family to come to the United States from China were on my mother's side. The first generation, my great-great-grandfather Lee Bo-wen and great-great-grandmother Wong Ah-Ching came from China in the 1850s during the California Gold Rush days. My great-great-grandmother Wong Ah-Ching was one of the few women to come from China in those days. Much younger than her husband she lived well into the 20th century and became the family matriarch. My mother's grandfather, James Bowen, born in San Francisco, was the second generation. There are no "Bowens" in China. All the Bowens in California are related to me and are really "Lees." "Bo-wen" was his father's given name. His Chinese surname was "Lee." However, because immigration authorities didn't know that Chinese always stated their family names or surnames first, all the descendants of my great-great-grandfather, Lee Bo-wen became "Bowens."

Although born in the United States, at the end of the 19th century and the beginning of the 20th century the second- and third-generation Chinese Americans did not have the same rights as White citizens. As Takaki (1989) noted, "'Color' in America operated in an economic context" (p. 13). The dual wage system of payment to White and Asian workers in the plantations, in the food packing houses or canneries, in construction of the railroads, and in the mines pitted White workers against Asians, causing racial antagonism and driving down wages for both. The Chinese Exclusion Act of 1882, which prohibited Chinese from entering the United States, "singled out the Chinese on a racial basis" (Takaki, 1989, p. 14). Chinese could not testify in court, nor buy land, nor marry White people. There were anti-Chinese riots and it wasn't safe to be in many areas if you were Chinese—you could be attacked or even killed.

My Yen Yen (Toishan dialect term for paternal grandmother) grandmother, Alice Mar, was born in 1901 in Weaverville, a gold-mining town in northern California. Her father would carry supplies from San Francisco to Weaverville by horseback, to sell to the miners. Chinese American children were often not allowed to attend school—sometimes by law, sometimes by local custom. In my grandmother's case, she didn't go to school because she and her sisters only had Chinese clothes which they made themselves, and her older brother didn't want them to go to school because he thought that other children would make fun of them.

It was not easy to be Chinese in those days. Some of the White miners became jealous of the Chinese staking claims in the mines, and set fire to a row of Chinese houses. All the houses but one were burned to the ground. My grandmother's house, which was the last house in the row, was spared due to a change in the wind. Although their house was spared, my grandmother's family decided to move to where there were more Chinese residents.

They chose Sacramento, where my grandmother started school in a Baptist church. She was 12 years old . My grandmother worked hard in school and graduated from the eighth grade by the time she was 17 years old. After my great-grandfather died, my great-grandmother moved with her five children (including my grandmother) to Fresno. My great-grandmother supported her family by growing and selling vegetables. As a young boy my father spent summers peddling her product to other Chinese families and businesses

When my grandmother said "Americans," she meant White people. Among her generation, Black Americans, Mexican Americans, and Chinese Americans were never referred to as "American" people. That was because they weren't treated the same and didn't have the same rights. For example, my paternal grandfather was born in China. He came to California at the age of 15 and worked as a houseboy. After he met and married my grandmother, they tried to buy some property under her name. To their surprise, they learned that they were not allowed to buy the land even though my grandmother was an American citizen born in the United States.

7. PERPETUAL FOREIGNERS

She had forfeited her citizenship by marrying an "alien!" It wasn't until after World War II when the law was changed that my grandmother was able to regain her citizenship after engaging a lawyer a lawyer and taking citizenship classes.

My grandmother and grandfather had a grocery store in Bakersfield, California, where my father and his brother were reared. The two boys helped in the family business as soon as they were capable. My dad attended the University of California at Berkeley, majoring in accounting, with the expectation of taking over the family business after graduation.

LEGAL SEGREGATION: WARTIME, PEACETIME, ALL THE TIME

The Pearl Harbor attack occurred in 1941, launching our country into World War II. My dad and his brother both immediately joined the Army Air Force. My dad had just graduated from UC Berkeley. Because of his background in math, he was accepted as a navigator. Before being accepted into the Army Air Corps, my father was turned down by the Navy. At that time, African Americans served in completely segregated units in the Air Corps, whereas Asians and Latinos served with Whites. Of 360 flying officers, Delbert Wong was the only Asian American. Casualty rates for the bomber crews were high. Only 3 out of the 18 navigators who were in training with my father completed their required 30 missions. The other 15 were shot down, with several taken as prisoners of war. Stationed in England, my father flew 30 missions in a B17 aircraft over Germany. Uncle Ervin, who graduated from Bakersfield High School and who enlisted in the Army Air Corps at the same time as my father, was killed in a training accident. He was 19 years old. My grandmother was beside herself with grief at the loss of her son. She joined the Gold Star Mothers and continued to be active in the Bakersfield Chapter for years, marching as a color guard. But despite being born and reared in the United States and losing her son in WWII, she was always treated as a foreigner, and never regarded as a full American citizen.

During WWII and in all wars, including the present one in Iraq, Asian, Native American, Black, and Latino soldiers have faced a disproportionate number of casualties. They are given different jobs: the dirtiest, and the most dangerous. For Asian American soldiers and for Arab Americans today, the issue of their racial appearance becomes especially problematic, because they are seen as foreigners, and sometimes suspected of being spies or "fifth column" agents. During World War II, the United States was at war with Japan, Italy, and Germany, but Italian Americans and German Americans were not confined in relocation camps. Only Japanese Americans—suspected of being disloyal to the United States—were interned.

After completing his 30 missions in Europe, my father entered Stanford Law School under the GI Bill. This GI Bill provided many veterans with opportunities for higher education that they otherwise would never have attained. My father was the only Chinese American in his class; moreover, there were no Blacks or Latinos, and only two or three women. All of the faculty members at Stanford were White males. In 1948, my father became the first Asian American to graduate from Stanford Law School. After graduating and passing the bar examination, as a non-White the options open to him for employment were limited.

After WWII, veterans who had fought to keep America free from Hitler's Aryan racial supremacy came home to face discrimination in employment and housing. Discrimination and racial segregation were legal in the United States until the 1964 Civil Rights Act. In addition, laws to keep "racial purity" were present in many states, not only the southern states that had a history of slavery. California still had miscegenation laws that prevented Asians and other non-Whites from marrying Whites.

Because mainstream private law firms wouldn't hire a Chinese American, my father went into government service, working for the Office of the Legislative Counsel, first in Sacramento and later in Los Angeles. Subsequently he became a deputy attorney general under California attorney general Edmund G. "Pat" Brown. When Pat Brown was elected governor of California, he appointed my father to the bench in 1957. Dad was the first Chinese American to become a judge in the continental United States.

My mother, Dolores Wing, was born in 1921 in Vallejo, California, a U.S. Navy town near San Francisco. My mother was the oldest child and the first person in four generations in her family to attend college. Like most of the Chinese Americans in the San Francisco Bay Area, my parents attended the University of California at Berkeley. In the 1930s, my mother picketed at U.C. Berkeley's Sather Gate to protest the Japanese invasion of China and also to stop the United States from sending to Japan scrap metal that could be used to make military weapons. In the 1940s, she became a member of the National Association for the Advancement of Colored People. She never understood how anyone who had experienced discrimination against their race or ethnicity could then turn around and discriminate against another group. After graduating from U.C. Berkeley, she went to Smith College for a master's degree in social work. She then became a psychiatric social worker in a child guidance clinic in New Orleans. Later, after marrying my father, like many of the women of the 1950s, she stayed home to rear four children. She continued as a volunteer social and community worker. She spent her whole life as an advocate for the Chinese American community and a voice of conscience within it. She also chartered the first Chinese Democratic Club in Los Angeles.

In 1951, when my parents moved from Sacramento to Los Angeles, they were unable to buy into the newly built apartments in the Park La Brea area,

7. PERPETUAL FOREIGNERS

and had to settle for an apartment in the more racially mixed, working-class neighborhood of Echo Park. Later, when they found a lot on which to build a house, the real estate company would not sell to non-Whites. My father looked up the owner in the Hall of Records and approached him directly. The owner was happy to sell but didn't want to divide up his three lots, so Dad bought the land and, in turn, sold to a Jewish family on one side and another Chinese American family on the other side. The other neighbors circulated a petition protesting the sale, but we moved in anyway. Because I was 5 years old at the time, I was not aware of the petition, nor of the neighbors' initial hostility. It was not until the early 1960s—when my brother and I went with our mother door to door, canvassing against Proposition 13 (the first Proposition 13—to repeal the Rumford Fair Housing Act)—that we learned about this initial racism.

GROWING UP MULTICULTURAL: LOSS PREVENTION

My brothers and I grew up in the 1950s and 1960s as members of the Hollywood Los Feliz Jewish Community Center. We were one of only two Asian American families there. My mother had enrolled us as members because she liked the progressive cooperative nursery school. We celebrated Purim, baked Challah bread, and made gefilte fish and matzoh ball soup. I also participated in Jewish service projects, such as singing Hebrew songs and folk dancing to entertain the elderly, and assisting with physical therapy for a developmentally delayed child. I was a member of a girls' club—Yalim, "Daughters of Peace"—and later, in college, we marched against the war in Vietnam. My mother promoted bilingualism by speaking Cantonese at home with me and my brother Pudgy (although, being American-born herself, English was her strongest language). She set up Saturday Chinese heritage language classes at our church, which was mainly White in membership. Heritage language classes, and positive interracial and interfaith experiences, planted seeds for what I would come to value as a TESOL professional.

My family history—the patterns of exclusion that my great-grandparents, grandparents, and parents faced—have presented themselves to me repeatedly in my adult life in different contexts since I've been a TESOL professional. They have also served to heighten my awareness of what Dr. W. E. B. Dubois (1961) called "double consciousness," to look at oneself through the eyes of another. The concept of double consciousness is significant for us in TESOL, because it enables English language learners to understand where they came from, and to appreciate those who went before them. This is especially important in the United States where English dominates to the exclusion of other languages. For instance, double consciousness helps us to address the problem of language loss—a problem for indigenous students, students from former colonies, and speakers of less prestigious languages. In the United States, whether our students' home language is a world language such as Spanish, French, Arabic, or Chinese, or on the verge of extinction like Native American languages, we as teachers must teach English as an *additional* language, rather than contribute to replacing the home language with English.

Double consciousness also helps us to be aware of "false consciousness"—those taken-for-granted views of the dominant discourse that lead to self-hatred and being ashamed of parents and grandparents who speak English with an accent (Lippi-Green, 1997). Images in the media and popular culture can be extremely demeaning and derogatory for English language learners who are people of color. These images support cultural and linguistic assimilation and a subtractive rather than additive perspective to learning English. An example is the Disney movie *Aladdin*, in which Aladdin, the "good guy," has lighter skin and speaks with an American accent, whereas the "bad guys" have darker skin, fake Middle Eastern accents, and bad teeth.

FIRST TEACHING EXPERIENCES: OF PYRAMIDS AND PASS RATES

My own journey as an ESOL teacher began in Hong Kong over 30 years ago at Tak Nga Middle School, a Catholic girls' school. I had no previous training in the teaching of English. My only credentials were that I had a bachelor of arts degree in Sociology from the University of California at Santa Cruz and native English fluency. My students' nickname for me was Sauh Wohng, or "silly or bumbling Wong." I was unfamiliar with the culture of the school, which stressed obedience and respect for authority, and required prayers five times a day. In addition, not only the girls but also the teachers were required to wear uniforms. All the teachers in the school were native Chinese, with the exceptions of me and a Chinese Australian who spoke no Cantonese.

Under British colonialism, as Chinese American and Chinese Australian teachers our "English native speaker" status was mediated by our race. We fell in between the White "expatriates" and the local Chinese because of the status of English, the colonial language. The White foreigners received housing allowances and their salaries were set much higher than were those of the local Chinese. In the early 1970s in Hong Kong, although 98% of the population spoke Cantonese, English was the language of the courts and the legislature. If you appeared in court, you had to hire an English-speaking, British-trained barrister.

If you ordered a telephone in English, you would get service immediately, but if you ordered it in Chinese you could wait for up to 6 weeks.

The educational system was shaped like a pyramid, with many students at the bottom and very few at the top. Hong Kong had only two universities; hence admission, which was based on examination scores, was extremely competitive. Examinations also played a critical role in determining prospects for employment in a colonial economy. Students with better scores in English would be hired for white-collar jobs as clerks, as opposed to factory jobs in electronics. Each year students were dismissed from the school, until only the best students would remain and take the final Hong Kong School Leaving Certificate Examination. By beginning with five classes of Form 1 students and ending with two classes of Form 5 students, the school received a higher "pass rate" on the examinations. One Form 2 student who received poor marks on the examinations committed suicide.

When you enter another culture, it is easier to see hierarchies that you might take for granted as "normal" within your own culture. The experience of living outside of the United States and beginning to teach under British colonialism shaped my view of teaching in profound ways. It heightened my awareness of inequalities in education. However, many years later I would find that the same pyramid that existed in Hong Kong also existed in the United States.

EXCLUSION AT AN EARLY AGE: ON THE PLAYGROUND

One of my first memories of "race," or racial difference, was on the playground at Ivanhoe Elementary School in Los Angeles, California, in the 1950s. A blond-haired classmate stuck her fingers in the corners of her eyes and pulled her eyes up, saying in a sing-song voice, "Chinese," then she pulled her eyes to slant down and said, "Japanese," and then pointed to her own knees and said, "American knees." She laughed and ran away.

I know that I didn't report the incident to my teacher, nor to my parents, but I remember that incident very clearly to this day. I internalized the negative perception on the part of the other child that there was something funny or different about the way I looked. Did Chinese have "slant" eyes that pulled up? Did Japanese have eyes that pulled down?

Although I didn't know the terms for race, ethnicity, or nationality, I understood very clearly that I was "Chinese," not American—that Chinese and Japanese were not the same as other Americans. This particular incident marked one of my first racializing experiences. I was not really "American," just as my grandmother—despite being born in the United States—had not been treated as an American; had not gone to school until she was 12, after being driven out of Weaverville by White miners; had not been able to buy property; had lost her citizenship by marrying an alien; and had been a Gold Star Mother. She was never seen as a "real" American.

Ever since that moment on the playground, I believe that I sought to prove that child was wrong, that I took on the burden of having to prove that I was as fully American as she was. In junior high school, I rebelled against the "quiet Oriental" stereotype. In high school, I secretly smiled when I got an unsatisfactory report in math. When I went to U.C. Santa Cruz as a college student, I joined other Asian Americans who identified with the third-world student movements at U.C. Berkeley and San Francisco State to organize for ethnic studies, minority recruitment, and the demand that research serve the interests of communities of color.

I find that to this day, although my family has been in the United States now for six generations, it is often assumed from my appearance that I am not an American. At a TESOL colloquium in which I participated in 2001, a White female graduate student related that she had avoided taking a course I was scheduled to teach when she had seen my picture, because she had assumed that I was not a native speaker of English and that she wouldn't be able to understand me. Here was the Chinese Exclusion Act in the 21st century. This was not the first time I was taken for a nonnative speaker. I am frequently complimented on my English. On a picket line or in a demonstration or when passing out leaflets I have on more than one occasion been told to "go back to China." Sadly, even those of us who have ourselves been considered "foreigners" have internalized the dominant view of being American as being "unmarked" and "White." When we read an account of an American, we picture a White person rather than a person of color.

DANGEROUS DISCOURSES: RACIAL PROFILING

As teachers, we can become more aware of the discourses of discrimination in the schoolyard, the popular media, and children's literature, and talk to children about racial stereotypes, hatred, and other forms of bullying (Hill, 1995; Zentella, 2003). This is even more important for us in the United States since the September 11th, 2001 tragedies. Many ESOL students, their families, and immigrant communities have been identified as the enemy because of their religion and their appearance. In the aftermath of September 11th, a Sikh was murdered for wearing a turban.

It is important to state that people are victimized not only because they *are* gay or Muslim or Japanese, but also because they *appear* to be different from the American (White heterosexual) norm. In the midst of unemployment and plant closings in Detroit in the 1980s, a Chinese American, Vincent Chin, was beaten to death by an unemployed autoworker because the Japanese "took away their jobs." After the September 11th attacks on the Pentagon and the World Trade Center, the Los Angeles County Commission on Human Relations reported "an 11%

increase [in hate crimes] over the previous year, and the largest number [of victims] ever reported in Los Angeles County" (Zia, 2003, p. 3). Included in the 188 victims in Los Angeles County of anti-Middle Eastern/Muslim hate crimes were South Asians, Latinos, and Armenians who were attacked because they "looked like the enemy." What is particularly alarming in the current U.S. context is that racial profiling of Arab and Muslim Americans has been justified in the name of national security, adding religious bigotry to the racial dimension.

U.S. MINORITIES IN THE TESOL PROFESSION: NOT THE RIGHT MATERIAL

The patterns of exclusion that I've observed through my family history are also present in the field of TESOL. Why is it that so few U.S. people of color work in this field? When I entered the graduate program in TESOL at UCLA in 1974, there were only six U.S. minority students (two Asian Americans, two Latinos, and two African Americans) out of a TESOL certificate class of 90 students. Each year, approximately 90 students would be admitted to the 1-year graduate certificate program and, out of that class, only half (or 45 students) would be selected to continue the second year to complete the master's degree program, which involved writing a thesis.

At the end of that first year there were only two of us who made it through the three-quarter certificate program—an African American woman and me. The other four minority students left the program to pursue other opportunities because they didn't feel they belonged.

The African American student, Helen (pseudonym), who had grown up in south central Los Angeles and had majored in French, completed the certificate program. Both of us applied for the master's program but only I was accepted. Incensed, the two of us went knocking on doors to ask faculty members, "What's your commitment to affirmative action? Why wasn't Helen admitted to the program?" We were told that although Helen had good grades, not everyone could be admitted to the very competitive master's program, and Helen was not "master's material." She had not distinguished herself by speaking up in class. Here was the pyramid I had observed in Hong Kong being replicated in the United States, in my master's program.

"Master's material" or "doctoral material" is part of the meritocracy discourse that emerges from the discourse of discrimination at the university. In high school it is "college material." Sociologists of education (Bourdieu & Passeron, 1977) have pointed out that who is considered "college material" has a lot to do with the social class of the students. Working-class students, students from rural areas, and racial minority students have difficulty getting admitted into university and graduate programs. Once admitted, because they "don't fit in"—they don't necessarily look or sound like the others—they lack the mainstream "cultural capital" (Bourdieu, 1991).

Now I am a teacher educator, and I find that our field has changed very little in the last 30 years with respect to the number of U.S. minorities we are recruiting to the colleges of education and to TESOL programs in the country. Although students of color are becoming the majority in school districts across the nation, the populations of our colleges of education are overwhelmingly monolingual, monocultural and White. We desperately need to recruit racial, linguistic, and cultural minorities to all levels of education. We need teachers, counselors, social workers, educational researchers, administrators, and educational specialists of all content areas—not only TESOL/bilingual education, but also math, science, social studies, English, special education, reading, early childhood, and elementary education.

We need to recruit broadly so that the composition of our classes in the colleges of education reflects the diverse makeup of our classes in the public schools, from kindergarten to Grade 12. When there are only one or two visible minorities (whether in an elementary, or high school class, or in a graduate program of TESOL), those students may feel uncomfortable if they are asked to represent the race or native country. It is easier to be silenced with respect to questioning racist or sexist practices if yours is the only voice asking those questions, and if the responsibility for identifying or examining "the problem" rests on you rather than the institution.

It is also important to transform our perceptions of "master's" or "college" material—away from the White, monolingual, monocultural standard. Instead, we need to incorporate diverse epistemologies, perspectives, and cultures into both the curriculum and the academic standards. Looking critically at the biases involved in meritocracy is not "lowering" standards but rather providing pluralistic models of academic excellence.

CONCLUSION: STILL SEARCHING FOR INCLUSION

We need to move away from the melting pot and Americanization models of "becoming American" that prevailed a hundred years ago, and move toward models that incorporate the rich traditions and funds of knowledge (Moll, Amanti, Neff, & González, 1992) from the many different home languages and cultures of our students. Becoming American should not mean leaving one's home language and identity at the schoolyard gate. Instead, our ESL and bilingual students need to become *America*—a multiracial, more compassionate society; a chorus of multivoiced, multitextured polyphony, enriched by multiethnic artistic and spiritual sensibilities as well as intellectual traditions from all over the world. TESOL/bilingual professionals of color have a role to play in the creation of this new society.

Many years after I had moved from UCLA to teach on the east coast in the New York City area, my mother sent me a picture, from the cover of the *LA Times* weekly magazine, of an attractive young African American philanthropist. It was Helen. I read in the article that she had gotten her master's degree in bilingual education from the University of Southern California and, after becoming highly successful in educational technology, contributed to supporting the arts, particularly minority artists and projects with a social conscience.

QUESTIONS

1. What have been the experiences of immigrants to your country (if your country has received many immigrants)? If there has been a history of immigration or emigration in your family, how does it compare to the experiences of Wong's family? How does Wong's information about Chinese immigrants in the United States compare to what you have been taught about immigration in this country?
2. In your background, what do you think "planted the seeds" for what you value as a TESOL professional? How were these seeds planted, and at what stage of your life did that occur? What do you think might be some of the effects of a bilingual heritage on a TESOL professional who comes from such a heritage?
3. How do you interpret "double consciousness" as it relates to TESOL? Do you agree with Wong that English should not be learned at the expense of the student's native language? If so, why? How would you or how do you incorporate "double consciousness" in your teaching? If you do not agree, why not?
4. Have you had the opportunity to compare educational hierarchies between different countries or within your own country? Describe the hierarchies and on what they were based. What are the effects of these hierarchies on second language education in your context?
5. If you had been Wong's teacher and she had reported the incident to you, how would you have addressed it?
6. Wong poses the question of why there are so few U.S. people of color in the TESOL profession. If you have observed this phenomenon, what do you think could be some of the reasons for it? Do you think it needs to be addressed? If so, how would you address it?
7. In discussing the impact of the presence of ESL and bilingual students in the United States, Wong states that these students "need to become *America*." Do you feel that something is gained or that something is lost when ESL and bilingual students "become" the country in which they are learning English? If you are aware of the impact of immigration on countries other than the United States, how would Wong's vision of America apply to any one of those countries?

REFERENCES

Bourdieu, P. (1991). *Language and symbolic power* (G. Raymond & M. Adamson, Trans.). Cambridge, MA: Harvard University Press.
Bourdieu, P., & Passeron, J. S. (1977). *Reproduction in education, society, and culture*. Beverly Hills, CA: Sage.
DuBois, W. E. B. (1961). *The souls of black folk*. Greenwich, CT: Fawcett. (Original work published 1903)
Hill, J. (1995). Mock Spanish, covert racism and the (leaky) boundary between public and private spheres. *Pragmatics, 5*(2), 197–212.
Lippi-Green, R. (1997). *English with an accent: Language, ideology, and discrimination in the United States*. London: Routledge.
Moll, L. C., Amanti, C., Neff, D., & González, N. (1992). Funds of knowledge for teaching: A qualitative approach to developing strategic connections between homes and classrooms. *Theory into Practice, 31*(2), 132–141.
Takaki, R. (1989). *Strangers from a different shore: A history of Asian Americans*. Boston: Little, Brown.
Zentella, A. (2003). José, can you see? Latin@ responses to racist discourse. In D. Sommer (Ed.), *Bilingual aesthetics* (pp. 51–66). New York: Palgrave.
Zia, H. (2000). *Asian American dreams: The emergence of an American people*. New York: Farrar Straus and Giroux.

Chapter 8

Becoming an English Native: An English TESOL Professional of Color's Experience

Carlos Islam
The United Nations

> *My mother was half English and I'm half English too*
> *I'm a great big bundle of culture tied up in the red white and blue*
> *I'm a fine example of your Essex man*
> *And I'm well familiar with the Hindustan*
> *Cos my neighbours are half English and I'm half English too*
>
> (song lyric by Billy Bragg, 2002, "England, Half English," reprinted with permission)

I'm sitting down in a midtown Manhattan Starbucks with my laptop, in an attempt to "articulate my experiences as a TESOL professional of color" 3 days before leaving for the TESOL 2005 conference in San Antonio. I mention this because it was during an unplanned encounter at the previous year's TESOL conference that Andy Curtis first brought up this book proposal and asked whether I'd be interested in contributing a chapter. Even though I have only recently received the guidelines on writing this chapter and the parameters in which to set it, over the year I have intermittently thought about its possible content and direction. Reflecting on incidents and events that I've experienced as a result of my color started to become overwhelming, and it became difficult to decide which experiences have directly affected me as a TESOL professional. Looking back, however, I realize that because of my color I have made different life choices than have my friends from home, who are almost all White (the few who aren't White are not easily recognizable as being of color). Thus, I've decided to describe three events that I believe have taken me to where I am today in terms of geographical location (my present job in English language teaching and my place of residence—not sitting in Starbucks) and understanding of who I am (or *what* I am—I'm not sure there is a difference). The *who* I am is very much tied up in being a TESOL professional—not purely a *person* involved in the teaching of English but more significantly to me, a *person from England* involved in the teaching of English.

I'm grateful to Andy Curtis for offering the opportunity to articulate my experiences as a TESOL professional of color and reflect on some of the "critical" incidents in my life. I have come to realize that although some of the experiences have been negative, to say the least, they have contributed to steering me into a profession that I enjoy and a country that I could make my home.

MY ENGLAND: THERE AIN'T NO BLACK IN THE UNION JACK

The England of the mid-1970s and early 1980s, the decade of my teenage years, was a racially tense and economically depressed place—at least that's how I remember it. It was an era of national strikes (culminating in the miners' strike in the mid 1980s and Margaret Thatcher's infamous destruction of the unions), and the collapse of the left-wing Labour government followed by years of austere, unfriendly, uncaring, and nationalistic Thatcherite politics. It was also a time in which the National Front, an extreme right-wing political group whose major policy was the repatriation of immigrants, was garnering 10% of the vote in some parts of the country. Their repatriation policy was commonly understood to apply to people in the Black and Asian communities (whether they had been born in the United Kingdom or not) and not immigrants from Ireland, Italy, or any other White European countries. Violence and racism were also the most pungent ingredients on the terraces of most football matches I attended or watched on TV.

My world of teenage culture was dominated by scary-looking punk rockers, aggressive and even scarier skinheads, and mods,[1] the smartly dressed,

---

[1] Punk rockers, skinheads, and mods were three separate groups that made up part of the British youth subculture in the late 1970s and early 1980s. Each group followed its own dress codes and musical taste, and there was often a violent rivalry between the groups. The skinhead ethos was particularly worrying for me, because they were aligned with neo-Nazis groups and supported extreme right-wing ideas, thus making me a target for both being a mod and of color.

8. BECOMING AN ENGLISH NATIVE 95

scooter-riding, Motown-listening group to which I belonged. Hard stares and the general threat of violence were not uncommon at school or walking through the mall with friends.

At the same time, I was being exposed to iconic American culture, with the introduction to England of McDonalds, shopping malls, U.S. TV programs (*Starsky and Hutch, Dallas, The Six Million Dollar Man, Hill Street Blues, Charlie's Angels*, etc.), Cold War political posturing, and the timing of the American bicentennial along with the unforgettable TV film *Roots*, which all seemed much more glamorous and interesting than what was happening in the my own backyard. In 1977, for example, we had the Queen's Silver Jubilee, which was celebrated on my road with tea, cake, and bunting, contrast this with the epic celebrations and pageantry of the American bicentennial celebration in 1976.

In American films and TV shows of the time, the ethnic diversity (although often stereotypical) of the characters portrayed was highly salient to me. I only remember seeing the odd Black actor on U.K. television when I was growing up, and often in horribly racist shows such as *Love Thy Neighbour*, in which the father of the central family clearly didn't love his Black neighbors. Another such program was *Mind Your Language*, in which ironically, most of the cast were foreign ESL students, but they were one-dimensional stereotypical representations of their nationalities, and the comical storylines (this is not a criticism—*Mind Your Language* was a sitcom, after all) were always centered on the White middle-class hapless English teacher. The presentation of U.S. society and culture I was receiving from TV, movies, and pop music were images full of exciting multi-ethnic cities, grit, glamour, and strong forceful personalities of all colors (e.g., Kojak, Shaft, Mohammad Ali, Diana Ross, and even Benson). Having now lived in the United States for several years, it is easy to see how these fictional characters were created and how the real people of color were so successful. Especially, now that I'm living in New York, the popular culture idea of America I grew up with is somewhat corroborated. Growing up, I was also aware of the Civil Rights struggle in the United States because it was portrayed on TV, in songs and in movies, and the protagonists were charismatic and flamboyant (JFK, MLK, Malcolm X, Mohammad Ali, Jesse Jackson, and the Reverend Al Sharpton all spring to mind). I have never heard of any similar movement in the United Kingdom and growing up I was not aware of any leader of any color who spoke out against racism.

It's my understanding that, in the United States, terms used to identify different groups such as African American, Native American (or American Indian), and Irish American have existed since before the 1960s, whereas in England terms such as British Asian are much more recent. These labels can exist either to indicate the inclusive nature of the society (e.g., African

Americans are Americans) or to differentiate a group of people from the mainstream of society (e.g., "They are of African descent and happen to be American, unlike us [Anglo-Whites] who are just American" [or "who are *real* American"]). In England, the term British Asian now exists; it indicates (to me at least) that these people have British passports and citizenship but they are not English. Black people in the United Kingdom used to be (and still are to my knowledge) referred to as Afro-Caribbean or West Indian. There is no inclusion of Britishness, let alone Englishness, in the labels describing the Black population in England, and no Englishness in the labels given to any other population of color.

The descendants of Italian, Irish, and French immigrants, for example, are in the same boat as Black and Asian populations in England, in that there is no label identifying them as English. The terms Italian English, Irish English, or French English don't exist. The difference, however, between these groups and British Asians and Afro-Caribbeans is that there hasn't been a need to coin new terms such as British Italian, British Irish, or British French to distinguish them from the mainstream Anglo-Saxon English population. I don't think it is even common for a child of an Italian immigrant to self-identify as Italian, at least not at the expense of their Englishness. My experience of growing up in England suggests that children of Italian immigrants would confidently call themselves English and perhaps say that their parents were Italian.

Norman Tebbitt, who served as the Home Secretary in one of Thatcher's cabinets, famously promoted the idea of an informal test of Englishness by posing the question of cricket loyalty. It was his contention (not even a suggestion) that if you cheered for Pakistan, India, or the West Indies when they played cricket against England, you could not be English. It was as if a sporting empathy for the country of your parents' or grandparents' birth somehow made you unpatriotic and responsible for the United Kingdom's economic woes. The twisted logic came apart in my mind when I noticed that the other cricketing powerhouses, Australia and New Zealand, were not part of the test, and that there was no mention of a similar football test of patriotism for the many Irish and Italian (there weren't and still aren't any Asians—of the Indian subcontinent variety—playing in the English football league) descendants living in the United Kingdom. I'm a passionate football fan, and even though I am the staunchest of England football supporters, the sentiment expressed by Tebbitt's test often made me feel as though I didn't have the right to claim my Englishness and support my team.

Within this setting, I grew up acutely aware of my color and how it confused my sense of national identity. The growing feeling of being unwelcome in my own home (England) because of my color could be epitomized in the racist chant I heard many times in the clubs I attended as a teenager

8. BECOMING AN ENGLISH NATIVE

to listen to American 1960s Motown and soul music (which a lot of skinheads were also into, ironically): "There ain't no black in the Union Jack, so why don't we send those bastards back?" In this particular bastard's case, I didn't know where *back* would be. Would I be sent back to Spain, my mother's birthplace, or Bangladesh, my father's birthplace? Neither place was particularly appealing at the time, because I didn't know the language of either, and nor did I have any friends in either country. I thought that these were fairly important criteria for a teenager to be happy in a country. The point I'm trying to make here is that, in my view, unlike the United States, England, English society, and English institutions can exclude people of non-White origins from feeling English.

MY ENGLAND: MY EXPERIENCES

I started this chapter with a Billy Bragg lyric from his song "England, Half English," because growing up I always felt less than half-English. Both my parents emigrated to England as the 1960s began, my father from Bangladesh and my mother from Spain. I was born in London and spent most of my school years in Luton (less than 30 miles north of London). The Luton I grew up in was a hard-edged place with almost no character. It definitely was not a place people visited without a good reason.

Going into my teens, I had a fear of the word *Paki*. *Paki* is the British-English equivalent of *nigger* in the United States. It is aimed at people from Pakistan (*Paki* is derived from *Pakistani*), India, and Bangladesh, or anyone whose pigmentation is one of the varying shades of brown common to the Indian subcontinent. Although the word is short for *Pakistani*, it conveys a deep-seated and malicious hatred. *Paki* connotes unhygienic, dirty, and primitive; English spoken with an accent that's easy to ridicule; submissiveness and physical weakness. A *Paki* is very unattractive and unappealing. The word is not diminutive of *Pakistani*. It is completely missing the point to protest, "I'm not a Paki, I'm Indian." Just writing it on my laptop and saying the word in my head makes me squirm with discomfort and embarrassment.

I have been referred to as a Paki a few times in my life, and two occasions have taken permanent residence in my memory. The first of these incidents was quite early on in my high school life in Luton. I was about 12 years old, and suffering from a spell of bullying. I had never been bullied before, but I had been involved in one or two typical schoolboy fights. From what I remember, I had not started the fights; and although I came out on top, I found fighting in public intensely embarrassing and humiliating. Having said that, I had always enjoyed school life; I had lots of friends, I played for the school soccer and cricket teams, and, because my high school was about a 30-minute walk from my home, it gave me a small sense of independence and escape from the ties of my parents.

I can't remember how the bullying started or how many times it happened, but I remember it was always the same kid and his accomplice. At that time, some of the school's classes were held in temporary buildings (a bit like small mobile homes in the States) set up in one of the playgrounds and on the edge of the sports field. There were over a thousand kids at my high school at the time, and we must have been running out of classroom space. Somehow, these two kids, who were in the year above me, would get me between the mobile classrooms during morning, lunch, or afternoon break. The main bully would ask for my right hand, and I would give it to him, fearing a beating if I didn't. He then squeezed my hand, first crushing the bones together and then rubbing the bone of the little finger back and forth. This was incredibly painful and I pleaded for him to stop, which he would do only when he decided he needed another victim and was bored with me.

I wasn't consumed with fear, or too worried about the bullying, because it was always brief and I knew I wasn't being singled out (why this was of comfort, I don't know). However, I had no idea why I was being picked on. Then, one weekend day, while I was out playing near my house (almost 2 miles and a world away from school), the bully appeared alone—without his assistant bully. I was full of dread (much more than at school) as he demanded my right hand; it would be humiliating if my parents saw me being bullied or if they became involved in a confrontation with this boy. This time I decided not to give him my hand but instead to try reasoning with him. After all, his partner in crime was absent and he might be willing to think about what he was doing. So, I asked why he was doing this. "Because I hate Pakis," was his devastating response. This caught me totally by surprise. It was the first time I had to consciously deal with being lumped in with this derided group (I lived in a completely White neighborhood except for one West Indian family, and the school population was overwhelmingly White), and the kid who was dealing out the punishment for my being a "Paki" was Black. "But, I'm not a Paki," I blurted back. "My mother is Spanish." I don't know why I thought this would make a difference, why I believed he wouldn't wonder why my family name is Islam, or why he wouldn't ask where my father was from. I was just trying to save my skin (no pun intended) and that's what came out. Amazingly, it worked. The bully said something along the lines of "Why didn't you say before?" and went on his way.

Later in life, I've reflected on this experience and it's left me with a sense of shame, because I had denied part of my ethnic heritage and identity, and at the same time reinforced my own racism. I went through school, college, and university avoiding social relationships with anyone who would be classified as a *Paki* in order to avoid being a *Paki* by association.

8. BECOMING AN ENGLISH NATIVE

The second of these indelible incidents involving the term *Paki* happened a year or two after I'd left high school[2] and I was dating my first *serious* girlfriend. By this time, I was 17 and working weekends at a national supermarket chain near the town center. I was dating a typically *English* girl. She was fair skinned, blonde haired, and blue eyed. In the United States she'd be called a WASP (for White Anglo-Saxon Protestant).

She had met me for my lunch break, and we were walking arm in arm to a nearby sandwich shop when, from nowhere, I hear a loud callous shout: "Paki-lover." My initial reaction was to ignore the abuse and pretend it wasn't happening, even though my gut was churning. My girlfriend's immediate response was to shout back with as much force, "F%*$ off!" I felt uncomfortably proud of her for standing up against what was clearly wrong, and, again, ashamed of myself for not doing anything myself nor defending my girlfriend, who was obviously the "Paki-lover." It transpired that she was not so much incensed about racial abuse in general, but more annoyed that the abuser would think I was a Paki. In her mind, she was not, therefore, a Paki-lover. "But you're not a Paki," she would later say to me.

Before I started dating this girl, I had also been told by some of the mods and scooter boys[3] I used to hang out with that they didn't like Pakis but I was different. I have also been told by a few people over time that they don't think about or see my color when they look at me. The intentions of these two statements may seem to be in opposition. In the first the first type, the speaker is saying "I'm obviously racist, and I don't generally like people of your heritage and color but I like you, so you should feel privileged." The second type of statement is meant to say, "I'm not racist at all, and in fact skin color is so unimportant to me I haven't even noticed yours. You're just like everyone else to me." This second type of statement is obviously easier to hear than the first, and is encouraging in some way. My only problem is that I just don't buy it. I don't know how anyone can ignore your skin color. I'm very aware of people's color whether I've just met them or not. I notice not only their color, but also any other distinguishing features, including height, dress sense, accent, and so on. I can't help thinking that the underlying motivation for saying comments like "I don't notice your color" is that in White cultures it is accepted that being of color carries negative connotations and stereotypes (including being a Paki), and what the speaker means is "I don't want to accept those connotations when it concerns you." This may not be an accurate conclusion to draw, but I believe it to be true, and it shapes how I feel about myself in England, a predominantly White culture.

---

[2] In England, we leave high school at 16 and, if one is interested in going to university, go either to a sixth-form college for 2 years to take A-level exams, or to a technical college to study for equivalent qualifications.

[3] Mods and scooter boys used to form gangs based on their shared interests in riding Vespa and Lambretta scooters.

LEAVING MY ENGLAND

The first opportunity I had for living abroad was in Northern Ireland in 1991. I was now in my mid-20s. I had completed an undergraduate degree in political economy and a master's degree in international studies, and was taking an NCTJ[4] journalism training course in Belfast. This was a time before any cease-fire agreement and when the loyalist and unionist factions were hard at it, executing tit-for-tat attacks in each other's strongholds. As a Catholic journalist told me, "With a name like Carlos Islam and your accent, you're considered a neutral." A neutral! He was telling me that, in this context, I was in a socially and professionally privileged position. In theory, I potentially had easier access to interview local leaders and protagonists because I was English and not from Ireland, and because I couldn't be easily identified as Catholic or Protestant. For the first time I was unfairly advantaged, and I had no problem with that at all.

The summer immediately before starting my journalism training in Belfast, I had met a girl while on vacation in Spain, visiting family. I had told her that if I could get a job, I would move to Spain and give our relationship a chance. She found me a job teaching English as a foreign language (EFL) in an independent language school in the Spanish Basque country in the town where my family lived. The opportunity was perfect for me to learn Spanish, spend time with my family, and see if there was a future for this relationship.

Three years later, I had decided that English language teaching (ELT) would be my profession and I would return to England to get an master's degree in the field. In that time I had also become much more English, or I perceived myself more as English. In Spain, I was automatically considered English (not British but English) by everyone. My family and girlfriend told everyone I was introduced to, *"Es inglés"*—"He's English." All my students assumed I was English, and I was the expert on English pop culture, history, and the English language, of course. Most importantly, all the ex-patriots, who were mostly teachers, also considered me as English. I played in English teams in the soccer (or football, as we like to say) leagues, and people who didn't know my name (and some who did) referred to me as *El inglés*. In discussions with colleagues about cultural work patterns, for example, my behavior was considered "very English." Never once did I hear the word *Paki*, or did anyone say or hint at anything disparaging connected to my color. On the contrary, I would get comments such as, "I think the color of Asian and European mix is beautiful." It was my experience that Spaniards are much more vocal with their opinions about people's appearance and

---

[4]NCTJ stands for the National Council for the Training of Journalists.

8. BECOMING AN ENGLISH NATIVE

whether they think someone is attractive than are the English. When Spaniards saw my skin color, it wasn't ignored and I didn't feel judged in a negative way.

After 3 years of teaching English as a second language (EFL) in Spain, it was time to get serious about this profession and study for an master's. It turned out that the only place I could study for an master's in second language materials development (the program I was most interested in) was at the new Luton University in my hometown. The classroom environment was great. I was one of only two native speakers, and my connection with our professor, Brian Tomlinson, was very English; for one, we both support the same soccer team. Being in a minority of native speakers, I also felt English and continued to be accorded the status of the "English" cultural and language expert by the nonnative-English-speaking students. In this environment my Englishness was never questioned. These weren't the main reasons for my enjoyment of the program, and they weren't even in my consciousness at the time. The class sessions were always stimulating and thought provoking, and the assignments were very practical. I already decided this was "my" profession and I was very motivated to study and do well. On reflection, however, I also felt that being a native English speaker and being English entitled me to some authority over the nonnative-English-speaking students, I'm ashamed to say. Interestingly, I found myself antagonized by the other native speaker. This was probably due to a personality conflict, but I also think there was an element of competition over who had the authority in teaching English. In my mind, I was in constant disagreement with her, and it sometime spilled out into the class discussion. With hindsight the program not only furnished me with confidence and a qualification to get ahead in our field, but also reinforced the idea in me that the field fortified my English identity.

This feeling was sharply contrasted outside the classroom. Luton has a large Bangladeshi and Pakinstani community concentrated in a small area close to the center of town, which was on the way home from the university. This area is full of Indian grocery stores, clothes shops, and businesses. My father would like to stop there to buy halal meat, mango, and Indian desserts. Going with him brought back my teenage anxiety about being seen as a Paki and I would try to avoid going with him. But when it was unavoidable, it was horribly painful thinking that someone (someone White who would recognize me) would see me and think I was just another Paki. In my late 20s and married (to the Spanish girl who got me the job in ESL), I felt ridiculous, infantile, deeply ashamed, and racist.

Before I had even completed my coursework for the master's degree, I was on a plane headed for Japan to teach junior high and high school. Once again living in a country other than England put me in an advantaged position, especially in the professional context, but also socially, because the

Japanese I encountered were interested to meet foreigners and find out about other cultures. I was also seen as a teacher from England and as English (e.g., not just a native speaker and not American). Teaching in the Japanese school system with Japanese teenagers was an endearing experience. My overpowering memory is of hundreds of smiling teenagers saying hello, calling my name, and wanting to spend time with me on a daily basis, which gave me very different self-image to the one I had during my own schooldays.

COMING TO AMERICA

I had wanted to come to the United States to work since I graduated from university in 1989. I spent a summer after graduation working in an Atlantic City restaurant and really enjoyed the attention I received from the other staff and customers on account of my English accent. Apparently, my accent was cute, the way I talked and acted was cute, and I was cute. To them I was the cute English boy.

Getting a teaching position at the University of Maine after spending my whole teaching career in non-English-speaking countries was exciting. Maine is a big state for the northeast coast of America, but it has a small population of only around 1 million. There is little ethnic diversity and it is known to be the "Whitest" state in the United States. Maine is also the most rural place I've ever lived in, and I thought the local people were quite conservative and parochial in their view of the world. I also lived through September 11 in Maine, a place where I was the only "Islam" in the telephone directory. Despite (or because of) these elements, I felt at home living there. Both the local and campus population had a healthy interest in my ethnic background, and their notions of England, Bangladesh, and Spain all carried positive associations. I've lost count of the number of times at social events, at TESOL conferences, and during workshops I've had to respond to the question, "So, where are you from?" I always reply, "From England, but my mother is from Spain and my father from Bangladesh." I can't remember a single follow-up question about my Spanish or Bangladeshi heritage. Most responses were enthusiastic comments about England or English accents.

An English accent (from England) is undoubtedly a high-status (possibly the highest) accent in the United States. There are advantages socially and professionally, especially in ELT, in being English and having the accent. When giving conference presentations and workshops in the United States, I find it easier to get audiences on my side and to make them laugh, and their comments and questions tend to be supportive and accepting. I sense that I get the benefit of the doubt the second I open my mouth. I believe the American stereotype of the English includes being well educated, articu-

8. BECOMING AN ENGLISH NATIVE

late, and knowledgeable. It's is also my impression that universities and academics are more used to dealing with educators of color from around the world and from America. At university in England (and I've attended four and worked for one), I only ever had one person of color (a Japanese professor of ELT) teach a class. During my time as a faculty member at the University of Maine, I encountered professors from the Middle East, the Indian subcontinent, and China, as well as African American and Native American faculty. There was also an active international society and a Black and Latino society for students, which never existed in England (at least when I was a student). And Maine is the least ethnically diverse state in the country! I spent a year working at Leeds Metropolitan University in 2002, teaching graduate applied linguistics courses, and although Leeds and the university have very large British Asian populations, I don't remember coming across one Asian faculty member other than the same Japanese professor with whom I had studied at Luton University. Being the only other faculty member of color (and the only descendent from the Indian subcontinent) in the department and the only other faculty member of color on campus as far as I could tell actually helped me feel more comfortable, because I didn't want to feel like another *Paki* faculty member or as though I was being grouped with people with whom I didn't identify.

During my time working for Leeds Metropolitan University, I was fortunate enough to be sent to Durban, South Africa, to run a 3-week workshop at Durban Institute of Technology (DIT). Historically, Durban has been the center for Indian immigrants to South Africa. I was impressed to see that around half of the professors at DIT were of Indian descent, and I could see their surprise that "the professor from England" was also of Indian descent. One elderly Black professor approached me during a break to say he had been expecting a tall, pipe-smoking, white-haired professor but was pleased with what he got. He didn't say he'd imagined the professor to be White, but we both knew that's what he meant. I was told toward the end of my stay that this was the consensus among the workshop participants.

What I'm trying to present here is the feeling of being more at ease living and working outside of England. My Englishness is prominent and unquestioned, and it works in my favor. In England, I always felt that my color was an impediment, but in the United States, for instance, I feel it may have even been taken in consideration by the hiring committee at the University of Maine because of their equal opportunity hiring practices.

Having lived in the United States for 7 years now, I also feel that it's the least racist country I know. I realize that the United States has terrible racial problems, and in parts of the country the racism takes extreme proportions, but none of that had been on display in my everyday life in Maine nor the major cities I've visited. Instead, I've been greeted with pleasant conversation and a smile everywhere I've been. As an outsider, it is easy to avoid the places in the United States where you might come across racist sentiment, whereas growing up in England I found it inescapable. I know that other people of color in the United States, and I suspect African Americans and Latinos in particular have to contend with racial discrimination on a regular basis. However, my experience living in the United States has only been positive in this respect. It may in part be because of the positive attitudes a lot of Americans have toward English people and the special relationship between the two countries. It probably also has a lot to do with living in an academic environment and working in the TESOL field, which is by nature probably more open, accepting, tolerant, and diverse compared to, for example, corporate law. Whatever the reasons, this is my experience and it can't help but heavily influence my view of where I live.

I started this chapter by indicating that I have found a place I could make my home. I'm now living in New York and running the in-house English Language Programme for the diplomats and staff at the United Nations. I don't need to tell you that this is like no other city. An array of nationalities are represented in the businesses and neighborhoods (Chinatown, Little Italy, etc.). Blending national and ethnic identities is commonplace, yet everyone is American. A mixed ancestry is the norm here and you can see it in people's skin color. At the United Nations, the Whites are the minority and the current the Secretary General is Black. For some reason this makes a difference to how I feel about myself in relation to the organization. I think, simply because I am of color and the head of the organization is of color, that I don't feel marginalized or like an outsider but instead am part of the mainstream and part of the team.

A NATIVE ENGLANDER

I'm not sure how my experiences as a person of color affect me as a TESOL professional. I suppose I am more empathetic to and identify more with students of color (the majority of ESL students around the world) than I could have if I'd not been of color. I also feel that students perhaps open up more easily with someone else of color when discussing political and personal issues in class and when sharing experiences connected to their color. But, for me, the more significant connection linking the TESOL profession and my color is how the profession has allowed me to live outside of England, and how living overseas and teaching English allows me to feel about my English identity.

I no longer feel half English or a third English. I'm totally English and what else could I be? My boss sees me as English and the teachers whom I supervise see the same. Students in our program recognize that I'm English (and not American or Indian). I go to bars to watch English soccer, and when I've been to restaurants in Little India the proprietors know I have an

Indian connection but don't mistake me for Indian, Bangladeshi, or Pakistani. I don't deny my Bangladeshi heritage, although I feel closer to my Spanish side in personality. Having an immigrant background, with parents from different parts of the world, doesn't make me less than wholly English. I feel that if I went back to England and became involved in a different profession as a person of color, my sense of Englishness could possibly be eroded again.

I'm going back to England tonight for my best friend's wedding. The wedding will take place in the English countryside, and the reception will be under a marquee. I'm his best man and it's going to be a thoroughly English affair.

QUESTIONS

1. In his introduction, Islam makes a parenthetical remark about the distinction between who he is and what he is. He concludes, "I am not sure there is a difference." As a TESOL professional, does this difference exist for you? If so, what's the difference? If not, how are the two the same
2. In describing some of his early, formative experiences growing up in England, Islam gives many examples of the impact of popular American culture and media on him and his peers. If you grew up in a country impacted by American culture and media, how did these influences shape your views of American culture?
3. How would you assess former British Home Secretary Norman Tebbitt's "informal test of Englishness" based on sporting allegiances? Do such sporting allegiances exist within your context? If so, how do they manifest themselves?
4. In describing the incident of school bullying, Islam is confronted with great force by the difference between how he views himself and how another viewed him. Have you ever experienced this difference? If so, what impact did this experience have on you as a TESOL professional?
5. Islam states his belief that, as a person of color, he doesn't "know how anyone can ignore your skin color." Do you think it is possible to ignore someone's color? If so, how? If not, why not? What are the effects of ignoring or not ignoring such a feature?
6. Islam describes how he felt he benefited from the apparently positive American stereotypes of British people. Are positive stereotypes any better or worse than negative ones? If so, in what ways are they better or worse?
7. Islam makes a statement that might surprise some people living in America today, when he writes that, "Having lived in the United States

for 7 years now, I also feel that it's the least racist country I know." This is clearly true for Islam, but based on what you know about the United Sates, either directly or indirectly, how would you respond to such a statement?

REFERENCES

Bragg. B. (2002). England, Half English. On *England, Half English* [CD]. England: Cooking Vinyl CD222.

Chapter **9**

Musings of a Black ESL Instructor

Marinus Stephan
Educational Testing Service

Prior to 1997, I had never given any thought to what it meant to be a Black ESL professional. In fact, before that time, I never had to ponder what it meant to be Black. Born, raised, and educated in Suriname—a small, independent nation located on the northeast coast of South America—I rarely had any reason to think about this. Although Suriname is a racially diverse society, race is an issue largely played out in the political arena. True, there is an undercurrent of racial tension throughout the society; however, if I were to be stopped in the street by a police officer of a different race and then claimed that I was the victim of racial profiling, few people, Blacks included, would believe me. The concept of racial profiling is totally alien to Surinamese society.

Not surprisingly, therefore, I was appalled when, after 2 decades of teaching ESL, I became aware that some ESL students perceive an association between the racial identity of the ESL instructor and his or her professional knowledge, skills, and abilities. It is this recently developed awareness that has led me to question my position as a Black person in the field of ESL. In accordance with the suggestions of the editors of this volume, I first provide a brief personal and professional history of myself. I then go on to define the term *ESL professional of color*, after which I focus on some experiences that gave me pause to think about the perception that ESL students have of non-White ESL instructors like myself.

107

PERSONAL AND PROFESSIONAL HISTORY

The year 1973 is a proper moment in time to start the tale of my personal and professional history. In middle school, Spanish had become my first love, with English and history a close second and third, respectively. By 1973, my ardent desire was to become an interpreter specializing in Spanish. Because such training wasn't available in Suriname at that time (in fact, nearly 30 years on, it still is not available), I needed a government-sponsored scholarship to study abroad. However, the government's policy was—and, presumably, still is—that study-abroad scholarships were only granted to those wanting to pursue a career in a field deemed of immediate relevance to Suriname's development. Unfortunately, languages and language-related fields were not perceived as such.

Not surprisingly, therefore, the counselor at the Ministry of Education's Bureau of Student Affairs, having listened to the goal I wanted to pursue, suggested an alternative route (for the sake of ease, names of institutions located in Suriname referred to here are translated into English). First, I was to enroll in a teacher education program that provided training in the curriculum of the elementary school and, to some extent, of the middle school. After completion of this program, I could enroll at the Institute for Advanced Teacher Training (IATT), majoring in Spanish. I could then use the knowledge I gained as a springboard toward achieving my ultimate goal.

Although this alternative route would take me at least 6 years to complete, I, undauntedly, embarked on the journey that I assumed would end with me becoming an interpreter. In 1974, I enrolled in at the Christian Pedagogical Institute (CPI); 8 years and numerous visits to the Bureau of Student Affairs later, I realized that at my first visit I had clearly been misinformed, to put it mildly. Not only had my original goal essentially gone up in smoke, but I also realized that I had reached a point of no return as I had gotten deeper and deeper into the field of teaching. To begin with, by 1981, I had completed programs at both CPI and IATT. At the latter institute, I had majored in English language and literature rather than Spanish due to a change in the government's educational policy, which accorded Spanish lesser importance within the educational system than it had had previously. Moreover, by that time I had been teaching for 4 years and, consequently, had gotten used to earning an income that I could spend either wisely or wildly. So, it was by accident that I entered both the teaching profession and the field of ESL.

I started my teaching career in 1977 at I. P. J. Berkenveldschool, a Roman Catholic middle school in Paramaribo, where, over the course of the years, I taught Spanish, English, Dutch, history, and biology to seventh and eighth graders. In 1981, I joined the teaching staff of the Institute for Natural and Technical Sciences, where I taught EFL for 5 years. Now fully immersed in the teaching of EFL, I wanted to earn a university degree in English as a second language. Because this was not possible in Suriname, I decided to pursue my goal abroad, specifically in the United States. I applied to a number of colleges, and in 1986 was accepted in the master's program in applied linguistics at Indiana University, Bloomington (IUB) and Southern Illinois University at Carbondale. I opted for the former, simply because their letter of acceptance was the first to arrive. With a scholarship awarded by the Organization of American States, I commenced my studies at IUB in the winter of 1987. After I graduated in the spring of 1988, I returned to Suriname and was hired at the Institute for Language Research and Development (ILR&D).

The ILR&D was a new and improved version of the Language Institute, which, since its inception in 1968, had offered conversational courses to adults in various national and international languages. By 1986, the institute had both a new name and a new director, and by the time of my appointment, plans were well under way for a new approach regarding the teaching of conversation courses. In the end, the communicative language teaching approach—a methodology that previously had been unknown in Suriname—was adopted. The application of this methodology proved to be so successful that the institute began promoting it at the middle school level. In fact, the objective was to completely overhaul foreign language teaching at the aforementioned educational level.

To this end, numerous training programs and workshops for in-service teachers were organized; one significant change brought about by the efforts of the institute within the English language curriculum of many middle schools was the introduction of the dyad role play as a means to measure the speaking skills of the students at their exit exams. The work of the institute also resulted in the establishment of the Surinamese Association for Foreign Language Teaching, which in the first half of the 1990s organized three highly successful conferences on language teaching. I consider working at ILR&D the high point of my professional career thus far, not only because of the various successes that I am honored to have been part of, but also because of the enthusiasm and the energy of all of the people affiliated with the institute.

It stands to reason, therefore, that having to leave the institute in September 1994 to pursue my doctorate in foreign and second language education at Ohio State University (OSU) in Columbus, Ohio, was quite a bittersweet moment. Courtesy of the department of linguistics at OSU, and specifically Dr. Donald Winford, I was granted a graduate research scholarship to begin work on earning the ultimate academic degree. A respected Creolist, Dr. Winford is, among other things, greatly interested in the structure of Sranan. My involvement in his research on Sranan included transcribing and translating audio-recorded data, specifically interviews conducted in Sranan. Between 1995 and 1998, I worked as a graduate teaching associate in the ESL composition program at OSU. From 1999 to 2001, I was employed as a writing tutor at OSU's University College. In that same period, I was employed as an adjunct faculty member in the ESL programs at Columbus State Community College and Franklin University. Moreover, I worked as a writing tutor at Franklin University. Since August 2002, I work for Educational Testing Service in Princeton, New Jersey. In my capacity as an assessment developer, I create test material for the Test of English as a Foreign Language (TOEFL) and the Test of English for International Communication (TOEIC).

ESL PROFESSIONALS OF COLOR: A DEFINITION

At first glance, defining the concept of *ESL professional of color* seems simple and straightforward enough. To some extent, it can be seen as an offshoot of the term *person of color*, which "In the United States, ... refers to [a person] whose ostensible ancestry is at least in part African, Asian, Indigenous, and/or combinations of these groups and/or White or European ancestry" (Helms, 1995, p.189). As such, this term is juxtaposed with the term *White people*, which, in the United States, refers to "those Americans who self-identify or are commonly identified as belonging exclusively to the White racial group regardless of the continental source (e.g., Europe, Asia) of that racial ancestry" (Helms & Piper, 1994, p. 126). These definitions suggest that, ordinarily, people perceive an association between someone's phenotypical features (e.g., skin color and facial features) and the racial class to which that person is assumed to belong. Hence, when one speaks of skin color, one indirectly speaks of racial classification. Presumably, then, the most obvious definition of this concept might be "a person of color who has had a certain degree of academic training in the teaching of English as a second language (ESL) and is actively involved in the field through teaching, research, or both."

However, this commonsense definition, based on the combined elements of race/ethnicity and formal knowledge, harbors certain dangers that may be detrimental to adequately dealing with the concerns of people of color. More specifically, the racial element of the definition by default excludes White people; at the same time, it not only automatically presumes the inclusion of all people of color but it also seems to oblige them to adopt certain attitudes that they, for whatever reason, may be reluctant to adhere to (or reject altogether). I arrive at these conclusions at least in part by my inquiry into race as a feature of the pedagogical and social dimensions of the ESL classroom (see Stephan, 2001). In this context, the pedagogical dimension refers to the extent to which goals, beliefs, and values that ESL instructors hold regarding their day-to-day teaching are inspired by issues of race. The social dimension, on the other hand, refers to the impact that

9. MUSINGS OF A BLACK ESL INSTRUCTOR

issues of race may have on the social interaction between student and teacher.

What are the problems associated with interpreting the concept of ESL professional of color as referring solely to people of color? For the reader to make sense of my answer to this question, I first need to make a statement: I perceive an inextricable link between the concept of the ESL professional of color and the "cartoon American syndrome." I credit Jack, a White male ESL instructor, for bringing the term *cartoon American* to my attention. This term, I argue, has two dimensions to it. The first is that many people, particularly foreigners, have a characteristic image of North Americans in general and U.S. residents in particular as people who have blond hair and blue eyes—thus, as Caucasians. The second dimension is that in the minds of these people, the typical North—that is, White—American has a sophisticated command of English, whereas those who are not White do not. (For a detailed discussion on this issue, the interested reader is referred to Lippi-Green, 1997; and Matsuda, 1991). Thus, they perceive an association among race and linguistic knowledge, skills, and abilities.

Obviously, these perceptions carry over to the ESL classroom. As Fels (1994) observed, "When students from abroad arrive at our United States institutions of higher education, they will unpack more than their suitcases. They will also unpack the social, intellectual, and cultural baggage that has been packed for or by them" (p. 2). Presumably, then, in the mind of certain ESL students, the more an ESL instructor deviates from the cartoon American image, the less she or he is perceived as being capable of adequately meeting their linguistic needs. Thus, skin color, one of the observable characteristics used to distinguish various racial groups (Helms, 1995), can be an asset or liability, particularly when it is associated with the instructor's credibility.

My argument that the concept of the ESL professional of color is inextricably linked to the cartoon American syndrome is bolstered by the writings of various scholars. Thus, for instance, Amin (1997, 1999, 2000), Nero (1998), and Tobash (1996) have established that some employers and ESL students perceive non-White ESL instructors as being less reliable and trustworthy in meeting the linguistic needs of ESL students than are their Caucasian counterparts. In this respect, it seems appropriate, moreover, to refer to Romney (1998), who pointed out that one of the specific objectives of the International Black Professionals and Friends in TESOL is to "counteract stereotypes and negative images of African Americans and other US minorities abroad that affect beliefs held by EFL students about professionals of color" (p. 10). Furthermore, in speaking of "the concerns of Black professionals," Romney presumably had in mind their worries, uneasiness, and anxiety about the way in which their phenotypical features affect how they are professionally perceived.

Dealing adequately with the anxieties of non-White ESL instructors requires not just the dedication of these instructors but also the devotion of White ESL professionals. Consequently, if the concept of the ESL professional of color is limited to those instructors who are not or do not perceive themselves as Caucasian, this may suggest to White ESL instructors that they are excluded from contemplating how skin color and, more generally, racial categorization exert influence over people and events in the ESL classroom. Specifically, their exclusion exempts them from having to question and challenge the privileges associated with being White. This is evident from my colleague Jack's mode of thought. He declared:

> If it is the case that I conform to [my students'] idea of the stereotypical American [i.e., one who has blue eyes and blond hair], then I don't have to think about how my being White affects the way I approach and deal with students in the classroom. That is one of the luxuries of being the dominant White, Anglo-Saxon Protestant: You don't have to think about [being White]. It's not fair, but that's life. (p. 157)

Thus, if the concept of the ESL professional of color simply refers to people who are not of European descent, then it offers a legitimate escape hatch for ESL professionals of Caucasian origin who prefer not to question the effect of skin color in particular and racial categorization in general on the pedagogical and social dimensions of the ESL classroom. This, then, is the first problem I detect when the concept of ESL professional of color solely applies to people of color.

The second problem is that the exemption of White ESL instructors to question White privilege places the onus of determining and understanding how issues of race may impact the pedagogical and social dimensions of the ESL classroom solely on non-White ESL scholars, a fact that may cause the latter to feel quite vulnerable. With that vulnerability may come a certain degree of reluctance to consider the aforementioned impact. The sentiments expressed by Mukembe, a Black ESL instructor I interviewed during the course of my dissertation research, made me acutely aware of this sense of vulnerability and reluctance. Once, when he had given his students a text on the topic of interracial marriage, some of his students informed him afterward that the topic had caused some embarrassment among other students. Mukembe went on to note:

> From that time on, I said, "Hey, watch out, it is not good to bring up issues like this because it would embarrass other people." And who knows, maybe some students may be so offended that they may complain to a hierarch and when it gets to that point you never know what may happen. So I just try to be cautious about issues like these. My intention can be a good one, that is, I want to show the students the significance of racial issues. But the students, given their sensitivity and the cultural differences between them and myself,

may interpret it otherwise. So in order to avoid these kinds of things, my attitude has been to avoid [issues of race] altogether. (Stephan, 2001, p. 171)

Thus, Mukembe's worst fear seems to have been that negative reactions on the part of his students regarding discussion of a controversial topic such as race might ultimately have repercussions for his job. He, obviously, is not alone in this assumption. According to Totten (1992), fear of jeopardizing their job is one of the reasons why teachers, irrespective of the subject they teach, refrain from addressing social issues in the classroom.

The final problem is that the inadvertent exclusion of White ESL instructors may result in trivializing or even negating the important contribution that White ESL instructors can make with respect to enhancing awareness and acceptance of others among their students, particularly with respect to race. As Alderfer (1994), discussing his involvement in research on issues of race, argued, "What I [as a White person] have to contribute to the joint undertaking of improving race relations is knowledge about [W]hite people and our ways of dealing with race" (p. 214). Thus, Stephan (2001), for instance, quoted Lindsey, a White female ESL instructor, who claimed:

> Most of my students come to the United States with a media perspective of this country, and the media is pretty one-sided and usually very positive [toward] American culture. As a result, many students enter the ESL classroom with a very skewed viewpoint on what, say, an Indian is. … [A]t … schools where I've been employed, I brought in what I thought was a survey of American society: members of the Native American, Hispanic, Black, and Gay and Lesbian organizations on campus, as well as personnel from the disability student center. Moreover, whenever possible I try to talk about such issues as homelessness, bias, prejudice, and racism. I try to bring these matters up because I am concerned that the students won't have an arena outside of the classroom to ask questions about that. They might encounter it, but they won't be able to feel comfortable, or have someone who they could ask questions of. I want to give them a chance to see some of the things that they might not have experienced in a media-safe environment. And so I do believe that issues such as these should be brought up in the ESL classroom whenever possible. (p. 164)

The fact that Lindsey makes it a point to expose her students to, among other things, issues of race, indicates that she is, in essence, working toward greater acceptance of people of color in general and in the ESL profession in particular. If an ESL professional of color is strictly perceived as being a person of non-Caucasian origin, then Lindsey's efforts may largely go unrecognized.

So how, then, do I define the concept of ESL professional of color? I would suggest that the phrase *of color* might here be interpreted as "devoted to color" or "concentrating on color," rather than interpreting it as an identity marker. Based on this interpretation, then, an ESL professional of color is anyone within the ESL profession who is devoted to or concentrates on inquiry into how issues of race—for instance, racial classification, racial identity, racial prejudice, racial preference, and racial experiences—impinge on the pedagogical and social dimensions of the ESL classroom.

ON BEING A PERSON OF COLOR IN THE ESL PROFESSION

Although I have been an ESL professional since 1977, it was not until 2 decades later that I first perceived an association between my racial and my professional identity. At one point in 1997, when I was an ESL instructor in a writing program at a university, my students—who were primarily of Asian origin—expressed dissatisfaction with my performance in their end-of-term evaluations. Their reports prompted a request from the director of the program for some soul searching. One issue that came up during this process was whether I believed the students were racially biased against me. Because of my previous experiences, primarily gained in Suriname, I readily dismissed that idea. There, language instructors (English teachers included) have always been men and women of African, Chinese, East Indian, European, and Indonesian descent. These instructors represented the racial composition of Suriname, and if I, or any of my peers for that matter, had at any time questioned their teaching skills and abilities, it was never on account of their racial background.

Consequently, while working as an EFL instructor in Suriname, I had no reason to believe that my students were racially biased against me. Moreover, I assumed—perhaps naively—that my teaching in the United States would not alter this belief. What I also failed to realize was that not all students of color may necessarily perceive themselves as such, or place much importance on being people of color; consequently, they may not necessarily develop an affinity with a teacher who is of color and perceives himself or herself as such. My view of interracial relationships between teacher and students in the ESL classroom was forever changed, however, as a result of a brief newspaper article brought to my attention by one of the ESL program coordinators. The article read:

> Hollywood insiders say Jackie Chan has backed out of doing "Confucius Brown" with Wesley Snipes for racial reasons. Chan had second thoughts about doing it after deciding that his fans in Asia would have trouble handling the movie's interracial relationship. (Levins, 1997, p. 2A)

Assuming the report was accurate, I interpreted it to mean that an interracial working relationship between a Chinese and a Black actor is likely to be perceived as inappropriate by Asian audiences; hence, Mr. Chan's decision to withdraw from the project. It is perhaps somewhat ironic that about the same time that this article was published, Norment (1997) reported that Mr. Snipes, who is African American, was romantically involved with an Asian model. Moreover, in all fairness to Mr. Chan, it should be added that in 1998 he made a hit movie that featured the Black actor Chris Tucker in a leading role. Nevertheless, the article from which this was taken created a greater sense of awareness on my part regarding the issue of race in the ESL classroom than any scholarly article on the topic might have done. If it is true that Asians have difficulty in accepting a Black man projected on a screen, what, I wondered, did my Asian students make of the physical presence of a Black person in the classroom who is also assumed to be the authority within this particular setting?

This question prompted me to conduct an inquiry into race as a feature of the pedagogical and social dimensions of the ESL classroom; more specifically, it became the focus of my dissertation and most certainly a critical event in my professional life. The interested reader is referred to Stephan (2001) for details on the findings; here, I briefly address one question the study sought to answer—namely, the extent to which the participating ESL students exhibited a disposition toward a particular category of ESL instructor. Among the 174 participating students were 138 Asians, 14 Europeans, 9 Africans, 8 Middle Easterners, and 5 South Americans. To get a clear picture of the preference of the participants, they were given two scenarios. The first asked them to rank order four ESL instructors (an Asian American, a Black American, a Hispanic American, and a White American) according to their preference. The second scenario requested them to rank order groups of ESL professionals based on the geographic origin and the linguistic background of these instructors (i.e., respectively, whether they came from Asia, Europe, or Africa, and whether they were native or nonnative speakers of English). The participants were told to assume that all ESL instructors were similar in terms of qualifications, teaching skills, and abilities, as well as experience.

With regard to the first scenario, for 134 (77%) of the participants, the White ESL instructor was the preferred instructor. Among the Asian and European student participants, the African American instructor was perceived as the last resort (i.e., the ESL instructor they would turn to in the absence of instructors for whom they had a greater preference), whereas the Asian American instructor was perceived as the last resort by the African, Middle Eastern, and South American student participants. As for the second scenario, nearly 74% of the 174 student participants preferred native-English-speaking ESL instructors from Europe to ESL instructors from Africa and Asia, irrespective of whether the latter were native or nonnative speakers of English. Moreover, nearly 45% of 174 student participants rated nonnative-English-speaking ESL professionals from Africa as "the last resort." It should be pointed out that the study assumed that the students associated the terms *African, Asian,* and *European* with the traditional classification of humanity, in this case, Black, Mongoloid, and White, respectively.

My first reaction to these figures was one of surprise. Having read of the reports by Amin, (1997, 1999, 2000), Nero (1998), and Tobash (1996), it had become apparent to me that ESL students preferred White ESL instructors to those who are non-White, so that in and of itself did not come as a shock to me. What I had not been prepared for, however, was the sheer magnitude of the students' preference. To put these figures in some perspective, if these statistics were the outcome of a political election, political analysts would most likely speak of a landslide victory. True, nearly 80% of the student who participated in the study were Asians, and that could have had its bearings on the outcome. However, the reports mentioned here suggest that there is very little, if any, correlation between the race of the students and their preference for White ESL instructors.

At the defense of my dissertation, one of the committee members raised the question how this and other knowledge I had gained through the study might affect my perception of and relationship with my students. I responded that I would make every effort not to let it interfere with the way I deal with the students, but I had to admit that as a Black, South American, nonnative-English-speaking ESL instructor, being perceived as "the last resort" could never be far from my mind. Since 1999, I have become very sensitive to students' attitudes toward me, and find myself asking the question that, prior to then, had never occurred to me: Is the student's attitude toward me based on my being Black, being a nonnative speaker of English, or both? It is a question similar to the one people of color in countries such as the United States, Canada, and England constantly have to ask themselves: Am I being treated in this particular fashion because of the color of my skin? Moreover, had I been a woman, I most certainly would have had to add the issue of gender to the equation.

Two instances may serve to highlight the tension I have only recently begun to experience resulting from my professional and personal identity. I preface these experiences by acknowledging how difficult, if not impossible, it is to unequivocally state that racial bias was at the heart of these experiences. As an acquaintance of mine once asserted, whenever one interprets a particular situation or experience with racial bias in mind, one runs the risk of reading far more into that particular situation or experience than there actually is to it. The reader is, therefore, requested to keep this assertion in mind as I recount my experiences.

In the spring of 1999, I was teaching a class consisting largely of immigrant students originating primarily from the Middle East and Eastern Europe. I knew none of the students prior to the start of the quarter and, as far as I could tell, none of them knew me. Moreover, I don't think they could have heard anything negative about me that would have caused them to perceive me as incompetent or unsympathetic. To begin with, I had joined the program in the winter quarter of 1999, and thus was about to embark on only my second quarter with that particular program. Moreover, to the best of my knowledge, there had been a good working relationship between the students and myself during my first quarter. That is, the instructor evaluations the students had completed at the end of the winter quarter did not reveal any negative information with regard to my competence or my relationship with the students. Consequently, the developments that occurred in the spring quarter of 1999 left me thunderstruck.

Already, in the first week of that quarter, I could sense that some of the students were questioning my authority and credibility. As the quarter progressed, the tension only mounted. Some students were openly challenging my explanations of linguistic items, in spite of the fact that the explanations provided by the textbook were at the heart of mine. From the third week onward, I dreaded every class session; however, once each session started, my anxiety largely disappeared. I provided the students with at least two opportunities to air their grievances, and learned, among other things, that they wanted me to speak slower, give them fewer assignments or more time on assignments, and other issues related to the day-to-day running of the sessions. I tried to comply with their requests wherever and whenever possible, but although the tension on their part subsided somewhat it never completely disappeared. Therefore, I could not rid myself of the impression that were other grievances that, for whatever reasons, the students did not wish to reveal. I could only guess what those might have been until late in the quarter one possibility presented itself—a possibility that I had and still have difficulty accepting.

Toward the end of the quarter, one student confided in me that a number of students wanted to petition the chair of the department to have me replaced; however, so I was told, the plan was abandoned when the champions of the petition failed to garner unanimous support for it. What shocked me most in hearing these revelations was the fact that idea of the petition had been launched in the second week of the quarter. As hard as I thought, I could not imagine anything I might have said, let alone done, within the first 7 to 14 days of the quarter that could have upset some of the students to such an extent that they would go so far as to file a request to have me replaced. Consequently, the only reason I could think of was that, in the eyes of these students, I did not fit the image of the cartoon American, and therefore must not have been thought capable enough to meet their linguistic needs. Whatever I might have said or done—or, perhaps, did not say or do—had confirmed their suspicion and had, subsequently, led to a call for action.

The second experience I wish to discuss here occurred in my capacity as a writing tutor. At one school where I worked in this capacity, I was, in addition to being the only male, also the only person of color and the only nonnative speaker of English. The structure of the tutoring program was such that, on any given day of tutoring, two tutors were on duty during the same period of time. I have on numerous occasions observed that my colleague's schedule—whoever that colleague happened to be—was filled; what is more, on a few occasions that colleague even had a wait list. At the same time, all the time slots listed under my name were open. Concerned as to how this phenomenon might strike the director of the tutoring program, I brought this matter to her attention on at least three different occasions. She was always very understanding and told me that I did not need to worry. Her explanation for the phenomenon was that some students take a liking to a particular tutor and, consequently, tend to schedule their tutorials with that person simply on account of that liking.

For all its plausibility, the director's argument raised more questions than that it provided answers. To begin with, why did the students seem to not like me? One might argue that that was the result of a negative experience they might have had with me, and that they not only stopped coming, but moreover, informed others about the negative experience they had had with me, which prompted other prospective clients not to seek my counsel. I reject such an argument, however, because each time that I conveyed my concerns to the director, she assured me that she had not heard a single note of discord from anyone relative to my tutoring duties or otherwise. The fact that I was invited term after term to join the tutoring program was testimony of her sincerity. Hence, when a negative attitude on my part toward the students is taken out of the equation, I can think of only two other reasons why so few clients sought my counsel: either because I was a nonnative speaker of English, or because I did not fit the image of the cartoon American—perhaps both.

On various occasions, tutees raised the question of whether I was a native speaker of English; one even asked the question twice, as if to be certain that she had heard me right the first time. Much as I regret having to deny my identity, I have decided that whenever this is raised to give an affirmative answer if it helps to foster a healthy student–teacher/tutee–tutor relationship. Because of my investigation, discussed earlier, I cannot rid myself of the nagging suspicion that the color of my skin is a barrier for some students. Or, in the absence of any hard evidence in this specific case, it is perhaps best to argue that I did not strike the tutees as the "typical" American, at least as they perceive of this concept. Even framed in this way, however, the issue of racial bias can neither be excluded nor ignored.

CONCLUSION

Judging from the goals of the International Black Professionals and Friends in TESOL, the overall objective of this TESOL caucus might be described as enhancing the visibility of people of color within the profession.

9. MUSINGS OF A BLACK ESL INSTRUCTOR

As the various scholars mentioned here have indicated, the presumed current lack of visibility of this particular group of ESL professionals cannot be viewed independently from the misconception among some ESL students and employers that ESL teachers of color are less capable in meeting the students' linguistic needs than are their White counterparts. Although ESL teachers of color are presumed to be primarily responsible for establishing a higher degree of visibility within the profession, the responsibility can never be solely theirs. Just as it takes a village to raise a child, so, too, I argue, does it take every single individual within the ESL profession to create awareness among ESL students and employers that people of color can be just as capable in teaching ESL as can Whites. Consequently, everyone who works toward creating this kind of understanding is an ESL professional of color, irrespective of his or her racial or ethnic background.

QUESTIONS

1. Having read a summary of Stephan's personal and professional history, what would you identify as some of the key influences that have shaped/molded him as a TESOL professional of color?
2. Stephan identifies "the impact that issues of race may have on the social interaction between student and teacher." What are some ways in which this impact may manifest itself in such student–teacher interactions?
3. Stephan refers to Fels' (1994) use of the "suitcase" metaphor in describing what international students bring to American classrooms. What social, intellectual, and cultural baggage might your students bring to your classroom? What baggage might you bring to your classroom?
4. Stephan refers to teachers deciding whether or not to address social issues in the classroom. Have you had to make such decisions? If so, what issues did you choose to raise, which did you choose not to raise, and how did you decide?
5. What are your beliefs about where the onus of dealing with issues of race lies or should lie? Do White TESOL professionals have the same responsibility as TESOL professionals of color where race is concerned?
6. Stephan gives an interesting—and perhaps somewhat controversial—definition of TESOL professional of color. Do you accept his definition as it is given? If so, why? If not, how would you change it?
7. Has your authority or your credibility as an instructor ever been challenged in the way Stephan describes in this chapter?
8. Stephan presents the results of a study that revealed that ESL students prefer White teachers and native-English-speaking teachers. Have you ever seen evidence of these preferences among your students? How would you react to such preferences if you became aware of them?

REFERENCES

Alderfer, C. P. (1994). A white man's perspective on the unconscious processes within black–white relations in the United States. In J. Edison, R. Trickett, J. Watts, & D. Birman (Eds.), *Human diversity* (pp. 201–229). San Francisco: Jossey-Bass.
Amin, N. (1997). Race and the identity of the nonnative ESL teacher. *TESOL Quarterly, 31*(3), 580–583.
Amin, N. (1999). Minority women teachers of ESL: Negotiating white English. In G. Braine (Ed.), *Non-native educators in English language teaching* (pp. 93–104). Mahwah, NJ: Lawrence Erlbaum Associates.
Amin, N. (2000). *Negotiating Nativism: Minority immigrant women ESL teachers and the native speaker construct.* Unpublished doctoral dissertation, University of Toronto.
Fels, D. (1994, November). *Imagining America: A study of assumptions and expectations among English as a Second Language students from Japan.* Paper presented at the Annual Meeting of the Speech Communication Association, New Orleans. (ERIC Document Reproduction Service No. ED389026)
Helms, J. E. (1995). An update of Helms's white and people of color racial identity models. In J. G. Ponterotto, J. M. Casas, L. A. Suzuki, & C. M. Alexander (Eds.), *Handbook of multicultural counseling* (pp. 181–198). Thousand Oaks, CA: Sage.
Helms, J. E., & Piper, R. E. (1994). Implications of racial identity theory for vocational psychology. *Journal of Vocational Behavior, 44,* 124–136.
Levins, H. (1997, August 6). People. *St. Louis Post-Dispatch,* p. 2A
Lippi-Green, R. (1997). *English with an accent: Language, ideology, and discrimination in the United States.* New York: Routledge.
Matsuda, M. J. (1991). Voices of America: Accent, antidiscrimination law, and a jurisprudence for the last reconstruction. *The Yale Law Journal, 100*(5), 1329–1407.
Nero, S. J. (1998). Parallel perceptions of world Englishes and Ebonics. *TESOL Matters, 8*(5), 15.
Norment, L. (1997). Wesley Snipes on his hot career, black women, interracial relationships, and his multimillion dollar hide away. *Ebony Magazine, 53*(1), 188–190, 192, 215, 216.
Romney, M. (1998). Caucus status approved for International black professionals and friends in TESOL. *TESOL Matters, 8*(2), 10.
Tobash, L. (1996). Sociopolitical concerns addressed at TESOL '96. *TESOL Matters 6*(4), 22.
Totten, G. O., III, & Schockman, H. E. (1994). Introduction. In Totten, G. O., III, & Schockman, H. E. (Eds.), *Community in crisis: The Korean community after the civil unrest of April 1992.* Los Angeles: Center for Multiethnic and Transnational Studies, University of Southern California.
Stephan, M. H. (2001). *Lifting the veil of silence: An inquiry into race as a feature of the social and pedagogical dimensions of the English as a second language classroom.* Unpublished doctoral dissertation, Ohio State University, Columbus.

Chapter **10**

The World Away From Home[1]

Gertrude Tinker Sachs
Georgia State University

Shortly after my arrival in Hong Kong in 1991, I went into a local supermarket to buy some supplies. I was dumbstruck when I rounded a corridor to encounter a shelf with a prominent display of "Darkie" toothpaste. The Darkie toothpaste tube had a picture of a very Black-faced man starkly contrasted against his huge, wide, red grinning lips to show his very white teeth. I stood for a few minutes staring at the display.[2] People came and went but no one appeared to be bothered by this. I felt that I was the only person who was upset and I wondered to what kind of country I had come. I was to find out in very intimate ways over the next 12 years.

My first experience of living in a foreign culture was in the 1980s, during my years of graduate studies in Toronto, Canada, but my experiences there were relatively sheltered ones because my life was regimented and restricted to the rigorous timetable of meeting assignment and dissertation deadlines. When I did go out, it was usually to school, the library, church, or

---

[1] I am grateful to Wanjira Kinuthia, Rachel Grant, and Shelly Wong for constructive feedback on this chapter.

[2] The stark Black face and the contrasting very large white teeth made me think of the 19th century minstrel shows in the United States, during which Blacks and former slaves were caricaturized by Whites. See the following for more insights: Bean, A., Hatch, J. V., McNamara, B., & Hatch, J. V. (Eds.) (1996). *Inside the minstrel mask: Readings in nineteenth-century blackface minstrelsy.* Hanover, NH: Wesleyan University Press; Cockrell, D. (1997). *Demons of disorder: Early blackface minstrels and their world.* New York: Cambridge University Press; Grubar, S. (1997). *Racechanges: White skin, black face in American culture.* New York: Oxford University Press.

121

my part-time music lessons. When I took a break on a sunny weekend to walk along Bloor Street or Yonge Street, the narrow sidewalks were crowded with hordes of people of many ethnicities and sexual orientations, which truly reflected the strong diverse multicultural lifestyle of Toronto.[3] My academic life, however, was restricted mostly to interaction with my all-White professors and a few international students. However, two contrasting experiences in Toronto brought me face to face with some of the realities of life as a person of color in multicultural Canada. The first is an experience that I will never forget and the second shows the need for educating ourselves and all those who teach about nonstereotyped "others."

TEACHING A MASTER'S LEVEL COURSE AT THE UNIVERSITY OF TORONTO

My coursemate had asked me to teach her master's-level course on reading for one night because she was unavailable. I felt more than competent. I had conducted numerous teacher education workshops in the Bahamas and had always been well received. In addition, I was working on a doctorate in that field at the same university. The classroom was small and held about 15 part-time students, all of whom were full-time teachers. They were all female and White. I had done adequate planning and felt ready for the class. I introduced myself and explained why I was there. There were a few sniggers from the women directly in the front of me. I continued, but the three women in the front kept laughing and talking in whispers for quite some time. It was becoming impossible for me to ignore the situation because the room was small, everyone could hear and see them, they were disturbing the flow of my thoughts, and above all they were totally disrespecting me. I had already given them a look that signaled my unhappiness with their continued chatter, but soon I realized that I had to exert my "authority" as lecturer or be totally disrespected. I was scared, because I had never had to exert authority over White people before—they had always been the authority figures in my life as teachers, nuns, or priests. Dare I do it now?

My self-integrity was on the line and I would not be further humiliated. So, I took a bold step and told those disrespectful White women that they were disturbing the class and me, and that I would appreciate it if they would stop their chattering and laughter. The class grew very quiet and I continued the lesson. At the end of the class, one of the other students came to me and apologized for her classmates. I felt utterly small and so shattered for days, weeks, and months afterward. It was my first encounter teaching

---

[3]See http://www.city.toronto.on.ca/about_toronto/index.htm for detailed information on the City of Toronto's multicultural composition. Of the 2.48 million who live in the city, 43% reported being part of a visible minority (e.g., Chinese, 10%, South Asian, 10.3%, Black, 8.3%, and Filipino, 3.5%). There are 79 ethnic periodicals in the city. Accessed Nov. 16, 2005.

White people and I wondered if this was how it would be if I had to do it again. I had never been disrespected in a teaching situation before. What was wrong? Was something amiss with my language or my different accent? Was my content incorrect? What could it be? Was it because I was a Black woman and they could not see pass my Blackness to understand or appreciate what I was saying? I agonized over this experience for years and became very aware of my interactions with White people and how they responded to me or me to them.[4]

A second pivotal experience in Canada taught me some valuable lessons. Earlier, I had felt the sting of being disrespected; now I saw the power and possibilities of education in a place that embraced learning about "others."

TALKING ABOUT THE "ISLANDS" TO TEACHERS FROM TORONTO

This second experience in Toronto confirmed a lot of things for me. One of my coursemates asked me to give a talk to teachers from one of the boards of education in Ontario. The teacher felt that many Toronto teachers were classifying all students from the Caribbean countries in a similar fashion, because they lacked knowledge about the students' backgrounds. Many of their students lived in the Jane-Finch corridor,[5] a melting pot of working-class immigrants from many countries. Students from the Caribbean were being assigned to ESL classes because teachers could not understand their English.[6] The teachers also assumed that the Caribbean students' schooling had been inferior to what they were receiving in Toronto. I accepted the challenge as an opportunity to learn more about both what was happening in the Toronto schools and about the Caribbean. Even though I am from the Bahamas and we share much in common with the island nations from the Caribbean region, actually, at that time, Bahamians in general were not very familiar with the workings of other countries from the region. My own colonial education had been sadly lacking, and I had studied only my own country's history and geography at Teachers' College, so I grasped this opportunity.[7]

At the talk, I wanted to dispel myths about the "islands," as they were commonly referred to by teachers. I knew that Canadians hated being mistaken for

---

[4]Houston, M. (1997). When black women talk with white women: Why dialogues are difficult. In A. Gonzáles, M. Houston, & V. Chen (Eds.), *Our voices: Essays in culture, ethnicity and communication* (pp. 187–194). Los Angeles: Roxbury.

[5]See McLaren, P. (1980). *Cries from the corridor: The new suburban ghettos.* Toronto: Methuen. See also McLaren, P. (2003). *Life in schools: An introduction to critical pedagogy in the foundations of education* (4th ed.). Saddle River, NJ: Pearson Education.

[6]See Nero, S. (2001). *Englishes in contact: Anglophone Caribbean students in an urban college.* Cresskill, NJ: Hampton.

[7]This situation has long been rectified. Also, through Caricom and other Caribbean regional bodies, organizations, and events, the Bahamas is much more integrated with our southern neighbors.

Americans and saw their country as distinct from the United States, and so I used this analogy to show that, similarly, people from the Caribbean hated been lumped together without distinction because each country was different. I also wanted teachers to know that each island had schools of a range of backgrounds similar to those in Toronto. Thus, accordingly, there were schools with high- and low-income students, excellent resources and teachers, and high standards and expectations. I talked about standards for admission to the University of the West Indies and the College of the Bahamas and the types of examinations that students were expected to pass at different levels under the old British system. I then spoke about language and the varieties of languages that exist in the Caribbean, particularly the varieties of English. Because I had just completed my master's thesis in the area, I had lots of examples, albeit more Bahamian ones.[8] I also addressed accents, which, for some teachers, were the main reason for misplacing students in ESL classes. I talked about the beauty and variety of West Indian accents, because audience members were unfamiliar with them and could not understand them. Additionally, I discussed what people on the "islands" do for a living, because there was a common misperception that many of us lolled about on the beaches all day.[9] In general, this lack of cultural knowledge about others and the assumed superiority of another culture was an eye-opener for me, especially because of the high-stakes consequences for the students.

I am aware that I made many people uncomfortable by what I said, because I challenged their perceptions with solid information supported by current research findings on the issues. However, discomfort is sometimes necessary to sensitize others and awaken in oneself the negative repercussions of different ways of thinking.[10] Although there was a degree of discomfort manifested in the body movements and facial expressions of some of the teachers, everyone appeared to be receptive to what I was saying and they all listened carefully and interacted nicely. This fully White audience gave me a very different reception than what I had experienced in my last encounter. I was satisfied after this experience, although I remained hounded by the first for many years.

My somewhat sheltered Canadian experiences provided me with some resources to confront life in a vastly different cultural context, such as Hong Kong. The Canadian experiences, coupled with my own cultural and spiri-

---

[8]See Tinker Sachs, G. (1984). *Dialect and reading: The question of interference*. Unpublished master's thesis, University of Toronto, Canada.

[9]See Winer, L. (1993). Teaching speakers of Caribbean English Creoles in Northern American classrooms. In A. W. Glowka & D. M. Lance (Eds.), *Language variation in North American English: Research and teaching* (pp. 191–198). New York: Modern Language Association of America.

[10]See Lin, A., Grant, R., Kubota, R., Motha, S., Tinker Sachs, G., Vandrick, S., & Wong, S. (2004). Women faculty of color in TESOL: Theorizing our lived experiences. *TESOL Quarterly, 38*(3), 487–504, for examples of the need for creating discomfort when discussing sensitive and difficult topics in academic environments.

tual resources that I possessed from my Bahamian heritage, enabled me to face the challenges.

GROWING UP ON THE "ISLANDS"

I grew up in the Commonwealth of the Bahamas, where skin color is an issue both within and outside of the predominantly Black population. The remnants of our colonial legacy and "slave mentality" remain entrenched within the peoples of African descent; even today, there is still a preoccupation with skin hues and color. Across racial lines are class lines associated with race or ethnic group. The original peoples of the Bahamas were the Lucayan Arawaks whose presence was eradicated by the arrival of Christopher Columbus and his men.[11] Historically, Whites in the Bahamas have been the landed class before, during, and after the days of the importation of slaves, 1656–1804.[12] During the time I was growing up, they remained the power brokers and government leaders. Even though their numbers were considerably smaller than those of the Blacks, and they lived in different communities, their economic presence was felt. As children, we were aware of them because of the way our parents spoke about them. I was often told by my mother that "Sir Harry Oakes is not your father,"[13] which meant that she was not wealthy and could not afford the many different things my two brothers and I wanted. We knew there were differences and discriminatory practices because our parents told us about not being able to go the Savoy Theatre or into certain stores on Bay Street,[14] but these differences and practices did not have much impact on us because our world was filled with very strong significant others, mainly Black people along with some of the nuns and priests in our school and church who were mainly White Americans.

It was not until universal suffrage in 1962 that the Black majority of both genders had a true voice. In 1967, the first Black majority government was elected. Later, on July 10, 1973, we discarded our British colonial shackles and became an independent nation. At the time of independence, I had recently graduated from high school. The independence celebrations, of which I was a part, played an instrumental role in affirming my sense of

---

[11] For an excellent critical view of the arrival of Columbus and what his coming did to the indigenous population of the Bahamas and surrounding territories, see chapter 1 of Zinn, H. (1999). *A people's history of the United States 1492–present.* New York: HarperCollins.

[12] See Murray, A. G. (1999). *Bahamian history highlights.* Nassau, Bahamas: Media Publishing.

[13] Sir Harry Oakes was a wealthy Canadian gold miner who resided in the Bahamas. For more details, see the annual publication *Bahamas handbook* (2004). Nassau, Bahamas: Etienne Dupuch Jr. Publications Ltd.

[14] For more details on the impact of slavery and discrimination in the Bahamas, see Saunders, G. (1995). *Slavery in the Bahamas 1648–1838.* Nassau, Bahamas: The Nassau Guardian. See also McCartney, D. M. (2004). *Bahamian culture and factors which impact upon it: A compilation of two essays.* Pittsburgh, PA: Dorrance.

pride and self-esteem in who I was as a young Black Bahamian person. I can recall at this very moment the thrill I felt as the Union Jack was lowered and the British national anthem was sung for the last time, followed by the raising of the Bahamas flag and the singing of our own national anthem, "March on Bahamaland," for the first time.

Several years later, armed with a Commonwealth scholarship, I had the opportunity to leave the security of my homeland to study in Toronto, Canada. Leaving home to live in another country is a traumatic experience for anyone, and I was no different. Even though I had traveled abroad, I had never lived alone for a prolonged period in another country, far from family and friends. I had read and studied enough about racism for it to be a concern, but what was uppermost in my mind at that time was assimilating into the university culture and doing well in my program. A few years later, I found myself in Hong Kong, wondering what my life was going to be like in a place where a Black-faced man with a big, wide Aunt Jemima[15] grin was looking at me from the mounds of toothpaste stacked high on the prominently placed display counter.

LIFE IN HONG KONG

As I got to know Hong Kong and its people, I discovered that most people did not want to talk with me about the related issues of Darkie toothpaste ("Darkie" toothpaste has now become "Darlie" toothpaste).[16] Those who did speak with me waved it off dismissively by saying that people were racist or that people were still backward in their thinking, but that was as far as they would go. There are many taboo topics in Chinese culture and in Hong Kong. Racism and discriminatory practices remain taboo in the classroom, but in the later 1990s these issues were given more attention by the press. What I experienced in Hong Kong as a TESOL professional of color speaks to the need for positive representation in all forms in our work, regardless of one's ethnicity or cultural heritage.[17]

---

[15]Aunt Jemima is a cultural trademark created by industrialists to advertise pancake mixes and syrups. In 1893, the Black woman wore and apron and a bandana headband reminiscent of the apparel worn by slaves. Today, she appears without the apron and kerchief on products sold by the Quaker Oats Company.

[16]Darkie toothpaste was sold by Hawley and Hazel, a Hong Kong-based company. It was later acquired by Colgate. After an uproar by Americans about the marketing of Darkie toothpaste, Colgate changed the name to the more sanitized "Darlie" toothpaste. Instead of being a totally Black-faced man, the face became half Black and half White, and remains so today (at the time of the preparation of this chapter). However, the local Cantonese name has not been changed. It is still called *Haak Yahn Nga Gou* or "Black Man's Toothpaste." One can purchase the original Darkie toothpaste on ebay; prices range from 99 cents to $17.75. I also saw it advertised on the Internet for $25.00. "Darlie" toothpaste is also marketed in other Asian countries. In Japan it is known as "Mouth Jazz Toothpaste."

[17]Yes, we are all called to be cultural workers. Freire, P. (1998). *Teachers as cultural workers: Letters to those who dare to teach*. Boulder, CO: Westview; Shor, I., & Freire, P. (1987). *A pedagogy for liberation: Dialogues on transforming education*. New York: Bergin & Garvey.

10. THE WORLD AWAY FROM HOME

Hong Kong is known as one of the "Tigers" of Southeast Asia, because of its booming economy. It is in strong competition with Singapore and Japan and now, since its return to Mainland rule in 1997, it pits itself against Shanghai in terms of sustaining its status as a leading place for international business and commerce in Asia. It is a very modern city, with an excellent infrastructure and transportation system. In January 2005, the *Hong Kong Monthly Digest of Statistics* reported that Hong Kong's population was 6,841,900. In the last census (March 2001), 5.1% (343,950) of the population was determined to be "ethnic minorities," or people who were of non-Chinese ethnicity such as Asian, European, American/Canadian, or Australian/New Zealander. Of this 5.1% of the population, the largest non-Chinese group was Filipino (41.4%), followed by Indonesian (14.7%), mixed race (5.7%), British European (5.5%), Indian (5.4%), Thai (4.2%), Japanese (4.1%), Nepalese (3.7%), Pakistani (3.2%), other European (2.9%), American/Canadian (2.7%), Australian/New Zealander (2.0%), and Korean (1.5%). The smallest ethnic minority group, called "Others," represented 0.8% of the total non-Chinese groups (i.e., less than 0.05% of the total population of Hong Kong). This group was comprised of Black people and any other ethnic groups. Only Whites were reported for the American/Canadian, Australian/New Zealander, and European groups.[18] The population demographics of Hong Kong's "ethnic minorities" is an indication of the very low number of people of African descent in Hong Kong. However, many of the Asian ethnic minorities have skin of a much darker hue than that of their Chinese compatriots, and this too impacts how they and other "dark-skinned" people are perceived and received in Hong Kong and in international contexts.[19]

In Hong Kong, I was employed first as a lecturer and then as an assistant professor in two institutions, both in the capacity of TESOL teacher educator. My work mainly involved conducting research and teaching pre- and in-service teachers of English as a second/foreign language at the graduate and undergraduate levels. The nature of my teaching and research work took me into primary and secondary school classrooms all over Hong Kong. I visited

---

[18]*Population census: Thematic report—ethnic minorities.* Hong Kong: Census & Statistics Department, Hong Kong Government. Retrieved February 8, 2005, from http://www.info.gov.hk/censtatd/. It is also interesting to note that 73.4% of the elementary occupations (e.g., domestic helpers, cleaners, messengers, hand packers, etc.) were non-Chinese Asians, whereas over 90% of the Europeans, Americans/Canadians, and Australian/NewZealanders were in the "professional" category (e.g., managers, administrators, etc.).

[19]Local Hong Kongers generally do not like dark-skinned people, regardless of their country of origin. Filipino maids are often rejected by employers because they are too dark. See, for example, Torda Lowe, C. (2000). *The outsider's voice: Discourse and identity among Filipino domestic workers (FDWs) in Hong Kong.* Unpublished doctoral dissertation, Department of English and Communication, City University of Hong Kong. See also Tinker Sachs, G., & Li, D. C. S. (forthcoming). Cantonese as an additional language in Hong Kong: Problems and prospects. *Multilingual: Journal of Cross-Cultural and Interlanguage Communication.*

my undergraduate preservice students on their practice teaching, and I worked with other graduate in-service teachers who participated in several different projects that I conducted over the 12 years I spent in Hong Kong. My work also afforded me numerous opportunities to participate in international conferences locally, around the region, and in other parts of the world.

In visiting primary and secondary schools in Hong Kong, I was always given a welcome of some form. My welcome to the school ranged from whoops and loud laughter to stunned silence. I often experienced the ripple effect as I walked along the corridor to arrive at the class that I was observing. The instantaneous reaction of the students upon seeing a person of my skin color inhabiting their world was so powerful that many students jumped out of their seats and shouted and pointed while laughing loudly—this happened in every class until I arrived at my destination, and sometimes here too the response was shocked silence or screams and shouts. What was always interesting to me was the reaction of my own student teachers to the response of their students. In most cases, none said a word to me about it, and neither did I bring it up. I conspired to the unwritten code of secrecy about the taboo subject. I realized that this was an uncomfortable experience for most of my student teachers and I did not want to add to their embarrassment or discomfort. Some of their students often broke the ice by shouting out, "Michael Jordan," "Whoppi Goldberg," or any other Black person they knew from the media. I have also been called "jyù gulik"[20] (Cantonese for "chocolate") by a Form 1 student. These ice-breakers prompted me to laugh and made the situation easier for my student teachers.

After numerous visits to most schools, students were no longer surprised to see me. In fact, after the observation, many students in the class would speak to me, say goodbye, or give me a sweet or a love note. During the class activities, I walked around and supported my student teacher's work. This gave me a chance to assess the impact of his or her teaching input, clarity of instruction, or the effectiveness of the task. This also provided me with an excellent opportunity to be a cultural broker. I taught the students. I held on their desks, I touched them on their shoulders or their heads. I looked into their eyes to check for understanding, I smiled, I marked their work, I complimented, and I explained what to do. I was often called "lóuhsì" or the more formal "sinsàang" ("teacher"), by the students. Many goodbyes echoed in my ears as I left the classroom. Sometimes, after the lesson, halting conversations in English were initiated by those same students during the recesses.

All the research projects that I conducted in Hong Kong took me into secondary or primary schools where I worked in close contact with the teachers and their students. This often meant assisting with the teaching of

---

[20]Yale romanization is used for all Cantonese in this chapter.

the classes, sometimes teaching together with the teacher or sometimes teaching alone in front of the teacher. I cannot recall ever being openly disrespected by the students of my student teachers. In fact, I was very much loved and welcomed with open arms by most of them, especially the primary students on those projects that ran for several years in the same school. However, there were occasions when my research assistants and I encountered negative comments about my presence. Following is an excerpt from one of my letters home that describes an incident that occurred in one of the schools:

> Well, I was at one of our project primary schools, as usual when some of the kids see me there is a huge reaction. Apparently, one of them had made some racist remarks and my research assistant (and former student), May (pseudonym), told me later what they had said. The boy had said something like—he smelled something awful when I passed. May was so upset. We had just been talking about racism at lunch and then this happened. I was quite pleased that she felt comfortable enough with me to tell me what the student had said. I asked Wendy (pseudonym), our research officer, to contact the English department head at the school to report the incident. (April 1998)

In my university courses, I invariably began the first lecture by introducing myself and my country. Most students that I met had never heard of the Bahamas, and the vast majority of them had never encountered a black-skinned person before or had ever had close contact with one. To get to know my students better and to develop a more than superficial appreciation of their culture, I enrolled in Cantonese classes: first at the local YMCA; then in an exchange program with my own students; and finally for a more rigorous, intensive course at the Chinese and Yale Center at the Chinese University of Hong Kong, where I studied part time for two full semesters. My learning of Cantonese greatly facilitated my acculturation into the Chinese community.[21] I could go to the local "gaaisíh," or market, buy my fresh fish, vegetables, and fruits, and negotiate the price. I could talk with the people in the local restaurants and order a simple meal, and I could ask for directions to the numerous schools that I had to visit. Most of all, my student teachers were proud that I could speak some functional Chinese and even bragged to their own students about it. When I interacted with my students' students, they often tried to speak to me in Cantonese, and when I said "néih góng Yingmàhn seehar la!" (try to speak English), they accepted it.

The courses I taught had very heavily packed content, so there was limited room to address cultural diversity issues or critical issues in English language teaching and learning, although I squeezed these themes in when I could. On

---

[21]See Tinker Sachs, G. (2002). Learning Cantonese: Reflections of an EFL teacher educator. In D. C. S. Li (Ed.), *Discourses in search of members: In honor of Ron Scollon* (pp. 509–540). New York: University Press of America.

my master's-level course, which I cotaught with a colleague and later on in another postgraduate course, I began to incorporate more critical pedagogical issues of power, race, gender, and representation in my work. For the most part, time was inadequate for the attention that needed to be devoted to these important areas of our work in TESOL. One project that I was engaged in with other colleagues made it very clear that there was a need to bring critical issues to mainstream educators' attention. Our project was commissioned by the Hong Kong government's Equal Opportunities Commission, and we did a large-scale survey on various forms of representation and stereotyping in Hong Kong's students' textbooks and educational materials. In interviews for one aspect of the project, teachers were asked to respond to the representation of Black people in their schools' textbooks. Those teachers who said that there was discrimination or stereotyping in their school textbooks qualified their claims with comments such as:

> Chinese appear most in textbooks, except situations like introducing classical dress of various racial groups or mentioning about the structure of the population in Hong Kong.
>
> Textbooks rarely mention people from racial groups other than Chinese.
>
> To emphasize the difference in culture, Africans are illustrated as primitive, [with] bare feet, necklaces made of bones and *they are always starving*. (teacher's emphasis).
>
> Shows the traditional image of Africa, for it is poor and starvation happens frequently.
>
> Black and White people were coming from two extremes. Black people are associated with: war, poor, minority, not educated, needing help, and can make no achievements. White people are wealthier.
>
> Textbooks rarely mention poor people in China, since many related materials are not available.[22]

These teachers recognized the limitations of their textbooks, but all of us, as educators, need to challenge government officials and textbook writers about the dangers of accepting what is presented in the educational resources that we use.

A CULTURAL AMBASSADOR

As the sole representative of my cultural group in the educational circles in which I moved in Hong Kong, I could say that my work brought me pro-

---

[22]Candlin, C. N., Li, S. S., Lin, A. M. Y., Tinker Sachs, G., & Keobke, K. (2001). *Research on the content analysis of textbooks and teaching materials in respect of stereotypes*. Hong Kong: Centre for English Language Education and Communication Research, Department of English and Communication, City University of Hong Kong.

10. THE WORLD AWAY FROM HOME

found pleasure and a great deal of satisfaction. I engaged with primary, secondary, and university students, teachers, and educational professionals from varied sectors across Hong Kong, and I found myself accepted for the most part on account of my contributions. However, in the type of work that I do, I would occasionally get glimpses of what lies beneath the proverbial, Western-perceived "inscrutable Chinese mask."[23] The following excerpts from my letters to family and friends reveal some glimpses of what I saw. For example:

> One afternoon as I was sitting with a group of my student teachers having tea, one student said to me with some wonderment, "Chinese people believe that you can't give a Black person chocolate because they would not be able to see it." She looked at the palm of my hand before continuing, "I guess that is not true." (Summer 2003)

One of my primary teachers made a surprise comment one evening during class recess. I had been sharing writing samples of my 10-year-old friend, whom I sometimes informally "tutored" with the class. The friend was the son of my beautician of whom I had become very close to over the years, so much so that we had had several meals together at each other's homes. Here is the excerpt from the letter home reporting on this incident:

> My teachers were generally impressed by the development of Tony's writing but they could not understand why I was doing it (I was not being paid to "teach" him). I told them, his Mom had wanted me to tutor him but I refused as I simply do not have time to tutor anyone. ... [B]ecause I always go there for facials, I told his Mom to let him talk with me which is what most kids in HK need as they have no one with whom they can practice English, so I thought this was a nice way to help out. Then one teacher asked me during the break if Tony was afraid of me. I was flabbergasted. Now, exactly why should Tony be afraid of me? When I told Tony's Mom what the teacher had asked she exclaimed, "Tony likes you!" She was amazed by the teacher's comment herself. (summer 2000)

The *South China Morning Post* (SCMP), the local English newspaper in Hong Kong, tracks the race issues in Hong Kong. It was interesting to read about Bratz dolls, the People's Choice Toy of the Year in 2002. After the SCMP had reported how the world's top-selling dolls had gone on sale in Hong Kong without the Black doll, because "market research has shown that Black dolls are not popular here and we couldn't market the doll here," (p. 3), Hasbro, the manufacturer, quickly found supplies for the Hong

---

[23]See Bond, M. (1991). *Beyond the Chinese face: Insights from psychology.* New York: Oxford University Press; Bond, M. (1996). *The handbook of Chinese psychology.* New York: Oxford University Press.

Kong market to complete the display of the Chinese, South American, and Caucasian dolls.[24]

One of my students had invited me to give a workshop for her Form 3 secondary students in English summer camp and to judge their dramatizations, which were done in English. Here's what I wrote about this experience at the time:

> When I got to the school, the students were ready. There were three presentations (about 30 students in all)—the acting was okay and the English was generally weak as these students have very little chances to speak in English outside of their English classrooms. What was interesting though were the topics they chose for their plays—Little Red Riding Hood, Snow Black (not Snow White) and Cinderella. The Snow Black one was interesting because the way they depicted "black" said so much to me—black—was the ugliest person—was the person who had to do all the menial tasks—was the one no one would marry—the one they wanted to kill—but at the end she was the one who married the prince—why did he marry her—because "she was so black and ugly."

Another incident reflected the ways of thinking that need to be challenged:

> Yesterday, I marked some of my students' assignments. One student wrote for one of his answers—"to invite expatriates i.e. white people into the classroom so that the students could hear native speakers use English." I wrote back to him, "not all expatriates and native speakers of English are white!"

All educators must be seriously concerned about the origins and perpetuation of negative and limited ways of thinking about other cultural in-groups and out-groups. We must problematize and explicitly address issues of race in our primary, secondary, and university classrooms. Instruction should be multidimensional in form to address the different mediums that support and promote the negative stereotyping of any group. Giroux (1997) noted that the electronic media—television, movies, music, and news—"have become a powerful pedagogical force, veritable teaching machines in shaping the social imaginary of students in how they view themselves, others and the larger society" (p. 295).[25] I would supplement Giroux's words by adding "and how they view others in the world." However, the entire blame cannot rest on the shoulders of the media. It is also important for us to understand how some of these attitudes developed his-

---

[24]Parry, H. (2003, January 19). Bratz are reunited as Sasha arrives. *South China Morning Post*, 3.
[25]Giroux, H. A. (1997). Racial politics and the pedagogy of whiteness. In M. Hill (Ed.), *Whiteness: A critical reader* (pp. 294–315). New York: New York University Press.

10. THE WORLD AWAY FROM HOME   **133**

torically and therefore became ingrained in people's ways of viewing themselves and others in the world.[26]

THE STATE OF THINGS

After the terrible, devastating impact of severe acute respiratory syndrome (SARS) on the Hong Kong economy in 2003, the Hong Kong government launched several advertisements to lure Western tourists back. One part of this campaign was to offer local Hongkongers postcards of Hong Kong to send to our friends overseas, to encourage them to come and visit us. I was very excited to receive my postcards. I had shared Hong Kong's pain and ostracism during the SARS outbreak and I wanted to do my part to show that we were up and running and had recovered. When I got to the post office and received my cards, I felt a sinking feeling as I looked at the faces of Hong Kong displayed on the beautiful card, with Hong Kong's spectacular Victoria Harbour in the background. Not one face looked like mine or shared my skin tones: There were eight snapshots one was of two Caucasian young women and the other was a Eurasian girl. All the others were of Hong Kong Chinese. What happened to me?[27] I showed the card to several people. They admired it, but I said to them, "I don't see me there." Most people did not know what I was talking about. In the meantime, on March 21, 2003 (Wu, 2003), the SCMP reported that race discrimination complaints have increased fivefold in 4 years (the Equal Opportunities Commission believes that this is probably due to greater public awareness). Finally after years of posturing, the Hong Kong authorities have agreed to strengthen existing anti-racism legislation (Shamdasani & Lee, June 9, 2003). However, in the meantime, pregnant Hong Kong women will not ingest tea, Coke, coffee, soy sauce, chocolate, or black sesame seed to reduce their chances of having a dark-skinned baby. Instead, they consume milk or soy bean milk, water, and fish soup to encourage paleness, and sales of skin-whitening products (to those who can afford them) are booming!

Indians have been in Hong Kong for more than 160 years and have been instrumental in the development of commerce. In a talk given by the then Financial Secretary, Mr. Donald Tsang, to the Hong Kong Indian Associations and the Indian Chamber of Commerce, February 9, 2000, Mr. Tsang noted that:

---

[26]In support of the work I do in this area, I have not been successful in finding any references that could shed significant light on how the Chinese in general have viewed Blackness and in particular how Hong Kong Chinese view Black people. This is clearly an area in need of research.

[27]Despite the relatively small numbers of dark-skinned people in Hong Kong, I had been hoping for an Indian whom I would categorize as dark-skinned or nearer to me in skin pigmentation.

Some of our abiding institutions have the indelible hand of Indian merchants on them. I imagine that many people are not aware that a Mr. Dorabji Naorojee, who arrived in Hong Kong in 1852, started what is now the famous Star Ferry company—developing it from a single steam launch into a major cross-harbour ferry service. Another merchant, Mr. N. Mody, later to become Sir H. N., was the driving force behind the establishment of the University of Hong Kong. A leading Indian firm of the day, Mody and Paul Chater, was Hong Kong's first and largest firm to deal in stock exchange and share brokerage. And last but certainly not the least, members of the Indian community have made valuable contributions to the Hong Kong civil service. That is quite a legacy and it continues even today. ...

This chapter was about the place I lived and worked for the past twelve years. What I have described here was the context within which I worked, lived, and played. I see my work in Hong Kong as the work of an educator, any educator, in any corner of this globe, to unravel, challenge, and transform the negative attitudes and beliefs that permeate our lives about people who are different from us. Negative attitudes, unfortunately, are often passed on from one generation to the next and will continue to be unless we, as educators, take action in our curriculum and on all fronts to change them. Most of all, people of other cultures and ethnic groups need to be represented in all corners and pockets of the world to counter stereotypic views and bring their experiences and histories to others in a personal way.

QUESTIONS

1. How do you think you would react to the caricature described by Tinker Sachs in the first paragraph? Would you find it shocking? Why do you think she was "dumbstruck"? If you are a person of color, have you ever seen caricatures of your racial group?
2. Do you feel you have ever been disrespected by students because of your race? Do you feel you have ever been disrespected by students for any other reason?
3. Have you ever found that colleagues or students held misconceptions about your country? Your culture? Your language background? Your race? If so, what were the misconceptions and what were they based on? How did you address the misconceptions?
4. In the census information cited by Tinker Sachs, she states that "Only Whites are reported for the American/Canadian, Australian/New Zealander and European groups." What is your response to this?
5. Tinker Sachs describes some representations in students' textbooks and educational materials in terms of "limitations." How do you feel about these representations? Have you ever seen materials with the kinds of limited representations she refers to? How would you address

the limitations of these textbooks and other materials? Do you see the same "dangers" that Tinker Sachs sees?
6. Do you agree with Tinker Sachs that "All educators must be seriously concerned about the origins and perpetuation of negative and limited ways of thinking about other cultural in and out groups?" If you agree, why and how would you address these "ways of thinking" with your students?
7. Tinker Sachs warns against the assumption that "what we teach in English is apolitical." Do you agree? Why? If so, in what ways is the teaching of English political?
8. Tinker Sachs describes how she believes "stereotypic views" should be challenged. Do you agree? What other ways would you add? What do you believe is the role of TESOL in challenging "stereotypic views?"

REFERENCES

Hong Kong Government Press Release. (n.d.). *Donald Tsang's speech*. Retrieved June 10, 2005, from http://www.info.gov.hk/gia/general/200002/09/0209117.htm

The Hong Kong Monthly Digest of Statistics. (2005, January). Wan Chai, Hong Kong: Hong Kong Government.

Shamdasani, R., & Lee, E. (2003, June 9). HK moves back to outlaw racism. *South China Morning Post*, 1.

Wu, E. (2003, March 21). Race discrimination complaints increase five-fold in four years. *South China Morning Post*, 2.

Chapter **11**

English Teaching and Ethnic Origin

Anam K. Govardhan
Western Connecticut State University

Never in my wildest dreams did I imagine that being an Indian and a "person of color" would be a disadvantage in the world outside India. In spite of limited opportunities and stiff competition in India, I had no problem in acquitting myself creditably as a student, researcher, and teacher. However, the moment I left India, I realized that I was in a world where I was judged based on the color of my skin and how I spoke English, and not on what I have to offer. After teaching English to both native and non-native speakers of English in the United States, Nigeria, and India for nearly 30, years and writing and presenting nearly 100 lessons on how to improve written and spoken English on television in India and Malaysia, I feel immense satisfaction that I had the will and perseverance not only to overcome many obstacles, humiliating experiences, and loss of self-confidence, but also to seize every opportunity that came my way to prove and excel in my chosen field. I am sure that my experiences are not isolated ones, but I hope they will stir a debate leading to the full and complete acceptance of the significant role of professionals of color in the ever-growing field of teaching English as a second language around the world.

Growing up in independent India, which was a result of Gandhi's relentless fight against colonialism, oppression, and discrimination, I believed that hard work, self-confidence, and good ethics would be sufficient in order for me to realize my dreams. The only dream I ever had was to be—an English teacher. In pursuit of my dreams, I attended Madras University, one of the most prestigious universities in India, for my bachelor's, master's, and doctoral degrees in English. In order to fine tune my teaching skills, especially teaching English, I also attended the Central Institute of English and Foreign Languages at Hyderabad, India, from where I received the postgraduate diploma in teaching English. Armed with the best education and training to teach English, I had no problem securing teaching positions whenever and wherever I wanted in India. However, the situation was completely different when I decided to teach English outside India. Through very painful experiences outside India, I realized that although English is my best-known language and I have advanced degrees in English literature and English language teaching, I am a "nonnative speaker of English" to non-Indians, and therefore I am not considered as good as one from the so-called "English-speaking countries."

In order for the reader to understand my dilemma as an Indian teacher of English, it may be necessary for me to explain briefly the history and role of the English language in India, and why Indians are not nonnative speakers of English in the sense it is widely used in the United States and other countries. The British came to India well before they came to the United States or any of the other so-called English-speaking countries. By 1600, they had established a trading post in India through the charter of the East India Company granted by Queen Elizabeth I and, thus, laid the foundation for the British Empire. The British played a very significant role in the history of India as traders, missionaries, bankers, administrators, educationists, rulers, and so on. for nearly 350 years. India gained independence from the British only in 1947, but retained the English language and made it as its own. In the next few decades, English went from being the language of the "colonial masters" to the most preferred and widely used language in India.

Today, although only 5% (approximately 50 million) of India's population of more than one billion people claim English as their mother tongue (*English Language Gazette*, 1996), nearly 350 million Indians are bilingual. In fact, there are more people in India who use English in their day-to-day activities than in all the so-called English-speaking countries put together. In India, English is the preferred language of business, banking, commerce, media, higher education, and science and technology. Due to the important role that the English language plays in India, every child who attends school—at any level—learns it and uses it. English has provided both integrative and instrumental motivation for Indians in an otherwise multilingual, multiethnic, and multireligious society. It has brought Indians together, exposed them to the Western style of education, helped democracy to take deep roots in the country, and opened up a world of employment opportunities for Indians outside India.

Like any Indian, I was exposed to English all of my life. I was hardly 5 years old when I started learning English. It was one of the subjects studied right from Day 1 at school; however, English was and is taught by Indians. When I was young, both inside and outside of school young people were constantly reminded that English was the passport for lucrative employment or university education. Naturally, everyone at school spent great amount of time learning and practicing English. At home in my extended family, I had six of my cousins, who were college educated, and they constantly spoke in English among themselves, because speaking in English was a status symbol too. One of my cousins traveled to the United States on an exchange visit in the early 1950s and, at about the same time, our family played host to two visiting American youths for brief periods ranging from 4 to 6 months. Hearing my cousins and the Americans speak in English, I longed to be able to speak English like them one day. With that motivation, I was able to pursue my interest in English through school, college, university, and beyond.

In spite of English being the dominant language in India, English spoken in India has a local color. Even among Indians, accent varies depending on where one goes to school and how much exposure one has to the English language; therefore, a visitor to India is likely to hear different varieties of English. Nevertheless, English spoken in India is intelligible and serves the important function of communication between Indians and foreigners, and among Indians themselves. In spite of reluctance in some quarters to recognize the English language that Indians speak as a legitimate variety, Indians use it effectively and proudly claim it as their own. Today, the largest circulated English daily newspaper in the world is *The Times of India* (www.timesofindia.com); Indians are among the most sought-after professionals around the world, not only due to their expertise in various fields but also because of their strong communication skills in English.

Like most Indians, I realized that English was the only way I could get out of my little town, go to college, get a job, and make a decent living. Because I was interested in literature in general and English literature in particular, I set my goal as becoming an English teacher. Thus, English has become the motivation and inspiration for me, and the encouragement I received from my English teachers throughout my schooldays helped to foster the same. After finishing my high school in my little town, I moved to Madras, a teeming metropolis, and had greater exposure to English at both school and workplaces. Personally, I had the most productive period of my life in Madras, because I honed my English language skills working under Anglo Indian supervisors, and studied under eminent Indian professors of English language and literature.

After receiving my master's degree in English language and literature, I decided to attend the Central Institute of English and Foreign Languages (CIEFL) in Hyderabad, which in the 1970s was the only institute of its kind in India that provided training to teach English. A year later, I received my post graduate diploma in teaching of English at CIEFL, returned home, and began my career as an English language teacher. Simultaneously, I also worked on my doctorate in English (a comparative study of Oliver Goldsmith and Gurajada Appa Rao, an Indian writer), which I successfully completed in 1981. With a permanent teaching position in a college and growing recognition in the field, I, like most of my countrymen, should have been content looking forward to monthly paychecks and annual pay raises while preparing students for university examinations. However, lack of opportunities to travel, lure of financial gains, and a spirit of adventure prompted me to accept a teaching position in Borno State of Nigeria, a West African country, in 1981. The assignment also turned out to be the first among a series of challenges, because I had to prove again and again that I was a qualified and competent professional who could teach English effectively. The greatest challenge I had to face related to overcoming the stereotypes that Nigerians and other foreigners had of Indian teachers of English.

Like India, Nigeria is a former British colony and therefore a member of the British Commonwealth. When I arrived there, Nigerian administrative structure, educational system, law and order, and so on resembled that of India. Thanks to a newfound wealth in oil, Nigeria embarked on universal education, and therefore needed teachers to staff the numerous schools and colleges that the government started all over the country. Foreign-born and foreign-trained teachers in all disciplines were actively recruited because Nigeria could not find sufficient numbers of qualified and willing Nigerians to teach, especially in the northern part of the country.

Although outwardly Nigeria appeared to be treating all foreigners alike in terms of service conditions and compensation, the reality was that the civil service commission ranked professionals based on their national origin, and Indians were placed generally at the bottom in terms of both postings and compensation. When I was offered a particular grade level and step in the pay scale, I accepted it gladly because it afforded me an opportunity to see some other part of the world, which I would not have been able to do otherwise. However, when I started working in the Nigerian school system, I realized that in spite of my advanced degrees and several years of teaching experience, the state public service commission had placed me lower than native English speakers who had only bachelor's degrees and in some cases no experience at all. For example, White Canadians with bachelor's degrees were placed at a higher grade level than I was, although I had the highest qualifications among all of the teachers in the school. What was more disturbing was that one of my colleagues did not even possess a college degree, and yet the authorities thought that, by virtue of being a native speaker of English, this individual was qualified to teach English. To add insult to injury, that particular individual was also given maximum flexibility

11. ENGLISH TEACHING AND ETHNIC ORIGIN 141

in terms of working conditions. I learned later that the Filipinos, Pakistanis, Bangladeshis, Sri Lankans, Ghanaians, and so on were also facing dilemmas similar to mine.

Growing up in democratic India and having participated in movements to eliminate discrimination of any kind at workplaces and educational institutions, I was aghast to see for myself firsthand how Nigerian government officials meted out different treatment to people based on their national origins. When I raised this issue, the head of the institution explained to me that the recruiting agency (the state public service commission) had always acted in this way, to the chagrin of the natives, too. Although I was very upset at the way I was treated by the state civil service commission, I had the greatest satisfaction of my life when I realized that my students liked my teaching methods and knowledge of the subject. They recognized my commitment to my profession and felt very comfortable approaching me for help with their problems both in and out of school. Because it was a teacher's college, the student teachers looked up to me as their role model. Ultimately, it was my students who helped me to keep issues related to compensation and service conditions out of my mind, so that I could instead focus on teaching. To this day, my Nigerian experience has fostered in me a desire to give my best wherever I am without being bothered by other considerations.

My Nigerian experience also convinced me that I should never give up my fight for justice and equality. Nigerian colleagues and the principal of the college showed their solidarity with me when the disparity in compensation was brought to their attention. It was not long before the principal of the college took me personally to the office of the secretary in the ministry of education, who gave me a patient hearing and promised to rectify the mistake. Although my compensation package was not revised at the teacher's college, I was encouraged to apply for a position at an autonomous institution under the auspices of the ministry of education. After a series of interviews and presentations, I was offered a position as the head of the English section, with a compensation packet, which was almost twice of that I had received at the previous institution. Further recognition came when I was invited to teach at a nearby university as an adjunct professor. Even now, I cannot find a rational explanation of why even educated colored people in Nigeria resorted to the same sort of discrimination that they fought against the British.

During my stay in Nigeria from 1981 to 1985, I had several opportunities to visit Western Europe. My experience in Europe further prepared me not to be shocked by blatant discrimination outside the workplace. For example, on my very first trip outside India in December 1981, when I approached a police officer at the Rome airport to ask for directions to the transit lounge, he whisked my colleague and me to the airport police station for a body search, and made us shiver for well over 15 minutes on a wintry morning before letting us to continue our journey. A year later, in that same famous city, I was humiliated in a hotel lobby by a bellboy, who refused to help to put my luggage in an airport shuttle although he did so obligingly for all of the other, White guests. Similar treatment awaited my family (including a 3-year-old girl and a 5-month-old baby boy) and me when we landed in London's Heathrow airport on January 1, 1985. Although as Indian passport holders we were not required to obtain visas to visit Britain, the immigration officer decided to keep us at the counter for almost an hour, and finally let us go only after he had verified my savings with a leading bank in London. These incidents confirmed my worst fears that the world had not moved past the days of Mohandas Gandhi in South Africa and Martin Luther King in the United States.

At the beginning of 1985, due to deteriorating economic conditions in Nigeria, I joined the exodus of expatriate professionals looking for employment opportunities in other countries. Although I found that teaching English was an attractive profession in the Middle East, Southeast Asia, Far East, and Polynesia, I also noticed that the employers from these regions required an applicant to be a native speaker or possess a degree from any of the so-called English-speaking countries—namely, Australia, Canada, New Zealand, the United Kingdom, and the United States. With advanced degrees in English from India and more than 10 years of teaching experience in India and Nigeria, I could not even get an interview from any of the employers because I could not meet at least one of their requirements (i.e., I was not a native speaker of English, and my degrees were not from an English-speaking country). I therefore decided to go to the United States and work toward a degree in TESL. However, the United States proved to be even more challenging than I had imagined it to be for Indians. For example, in spite of a string of degrees in English language and literature, I was asked to prove my proficiency in English by taking the Test of English as a Foreign Language (TOEFL) and Test of Spoken English (TSE). The irony was that although the departments of English in U.S. universities accepted my proficiency in English language and competency to teach, the bureaucrats in the admissions offices of universities insisted that I take the English language proficiency exams along with students that I was supposed to teach.

Both as a graduate student and teacher, I had to face the stigma of being a nonnative speaker of English and the presumption of incompetence and lack of proficiency in English; therefore, I had to prove that I was not only as good as the so-called native speakers but also better than them. It was obvious to me that a different yardstick was being applied to evaluate my credentials as a student, a researcher, and a teacher. Facing up to those challenges kept me and still keeps me on my toes, in spite of the fact that I have earned another doctorate in English (this time in the United States), am tenured as a full professor of English at my present university, and serve as a reader for several English language proficiency tests conducted by the Educational Testing Service and College Board. Even in the face of these numerous achievements, I am always confronted by one question: When am I going to be accepted as a native speaker of English, and are my achievements worth the emotional and physical stress that I am enduring?

The first institution I attended in 1985 was a state university in a southwestern state of the United States. Although some faculty members were tolerant toward foreign students, others had a condescending attitude—which undermined one's self-respect and self-confidence. One faculty member in particular, who was also the graduate coordinator in English, never let go an opportunity to recount his mostly negative experiences dealing with foreign students. He particularly referred to an Indian student's total ignorance of the Americans' coveted "personal space," much to the dismay of foreign students and glee of ignorant American students in the class. Many other faculty members exaggerated foreign students' anxiety about their grades as "obsession," whereas today, as a professor at a university in the United States, I find my American students exhibiting the same anxiety about grades. The international student office on the campus always included as a part of its orientation a session on bad breath, poor communication skills, lack of hygiene, and so on, and in the process perpetuated negative stereotypes of foreign students in general, and Asian students in particular.

To make matters worse, all the foreign graduate students in the English department, especially Asians, came under severe scrutiny. During the 2 years I spent at this university, a majority of foreign students had to transfer to other departments on the campus, and in some cases to other universities, for reasons I need not enumerate here. As a teaching associate in English, I had the opportunity to teach writing to ESL/foreign students as well as to American students in the regular composition program. In the regular composition program, students were initially dismayed to find a foreign-born person of color teaching English, but they were tolerant of my accent and found me a helpful instructor. In fact, they never complained of my accent interfering with their understanding of my instruction in the class. However, the situation was slightly different in the ESL class, in which a majority of ESL students appreciated what I was doing. The exceptions were some students from Saudi Arabia, who constantly challenged my grading and knowledge of the subject. They used to boast that they had been taught English by British and American teachers back home, and therefore did not want to be taught English by an Indian. The implication was that only the British and Americans, in the perspective of these Saudi Arabian students, should be teaching English.

My experience at this university as a student and an instructor made me aware that the world outside India was not ready to accept an Indian teaching English. I was convinced more than ever before that both the informed and uninformed believed that being a native speaker of English was synonymous with proficiency in the English language and expertise in teaching English. For the second time in my career, when I applied for teaching positions around the world, I realized that education and experience in the United States did not improve my chances at all, because the employers wanted only native speakers of English to teach English. The United States was an exception, because employers never openly declared their preference for a native speaker of English, whereas all of the other countries categorically mentioned in their advertisements that they preferred only native speakers from Australia, Canada, New Zealand, the United Kingdom, and United States. After having attended several job interviews in which I also had the opportunity to speak with several non-Whites from the so-called native speaking countries, I was convinced that the employers—especially those from the Far East, Southeast Asia, and the Middle-East—were looking for only those applicants with Anglo Saxon heritage under the false notion that only they spoke the Standard English. Although linguists have exposed the myth of Standard English, employers have used it to exclude non-Whites from the so-called native-speaking countries and others who are qualified to teach English. My own example might illustrate how the so-called nonnative speakers of English have been systematically weeded out of the job market.

Unable to find a teaching position in the United States, Japan, Korea, the Middle East, Papua New Guinea, and son on, I returned to my home country, India, where I worked as a student counselor with a binational center from 1987 to 1990. In my role, I was advising Indian students about opportunities and challenges that they might face in the universities and colleges in the United States. During that period, I also had the opportunity to continue my interest in teaching English by writing and presenting English grammar lessons for the public television's program on distance learning in Madras.

In 1990, my love for research and teaching brought me back to the United States for the second time. This time, I joined a state university in Illinois to complete my doctoral program in English with concentration in English as a second language. My experience at this university was totally different, because I found the faculty and students to be better informed about foreign students in general and Indian students in particular. Many students in the doctoral program in English have also had experience either teaching or living in a foreign country. The faculty, especially those in the linguistics program, had been very appreciative of each student's contribution. The department maintained faith in my ability and gave me an

11. ENGLISH TEACHING AND ETHNIC ORIGIN

opportunity to teach both native and nonnative speakers of English. In short, I had nothing but positive experiences learning and teaching at this university. As a result, I also regained my confidence as a person and an ESL teacher, which in turn facilitated the completion of my second doctoral program at this university in only 4 years.

During my stay at this university in Illinois, I had to experience another instance of shock and humiliation in the form of rejection of my application for a teaching position in English at a Korean university, based on my "Indianness." In 1993, while I was working in the ESL lab at the Illinois university, I had a visiting professor from Korea as one of my students. He told me that he was very much impressed with my performance as a tutor and my knowledge of the subject. Encouraged by him, I applied for a teaching position at his university. He took special interest in me and monitored the application process. One day, he came to share with me the happy news that the authorities at his university were very impressed with my credentials and would be sending me a contract proposal for employment soon. My expectations were very high and I was already preparing for my dream assignment in Korea. Unfortunately, 2 days later, my friend told me that he had received a fax from the authorities in his university informing him that they were not interested in me because I am an Indian and therefore not a native speaker. (Today, it is gratifying to note that the TESOL organization has come out strongly against employers requiring that only native speakers can teach English.

During the final year of my doctoral program, my odyssey in search of a job began in the fall of 1993 and ended successfully in the spring of 1994, when I accepted a position at a state university in Connecticut. Because I had never been to Connecticut, I did not know what to expect. It did not take me long to realize that there were very few non-Whites in the part of the state where the university is located, and only a handful at the university. Although I was elated to get a full-time position, I was not sure about the challenges I was to face at the university. Being the only foreign-born colored person in the English department, I was unsure about the reception I would get from my colleagues. To begin with, colleagues' attitude toward me ranged from being indifferent to grudging acceptance. The attitude of the staff with whom I had to interact on a daily basis could only be termed as total indifference or condescending. They would speak to me slowly, thinking I would not be able to follow them. For example, whenever I approached the department secretary, she would bend toward me to catch every syllable that escaped my lips. Invariably, she would also ask me to repeat whatever I have said. My experiences at other offices of the university were not very different from the English department, which forced me to prefer written communication in order to correspond with the university administration. Having been at this university for more than 10 years, I have noticed very little change in the attitude of the staff. Many of my colleagues from other departments openly expressed their surprise at finding me teaching English at both the undergraduate and graduate levels. With the creation of an affirmative action office and the state government's drive to increase the diversity on the campus, there is a greater awareness among students, faculty, and staff about different ethnic groups in their midst.

The greatest satisfaction that I have today is that I have successfully completed 10 years of teaching and research at my present institution. I have compiled a very impressive list of publications and presentations at national and international conferences, including several at the annual TESOL conventions. In addition, I have written and presented nearly 100 lessons on English grammar and communication skills (both written and spoken) for television stations in India and Malaysia. I have received several professional achievement awards from the university in recognition of my research work in my field. Based on the annual student evaluations, active participation in the academic functions of the university, and my contribution to the field of English language teaching, the university has not only given me tenure but also promoted me to the rank of professor. Irrespective of the recognition received in the form of promotion and tenure, I continue to look for innovative ways to improve my teaching and pursue my interest in discourse analysis, although research is not a priority at this institution.

When I look back at the challenges I faced both as a student and as a teacher, I feel good about myself, because I never lost faith in myself but instead faced the many challenges with fortitude. As a teacher, I realize that I have to teach not only in the classroom but also outside of the classroom, to create a better world that offers a level playing field. My experiences have also taught me to adapt to new cultures and new settings as quickly as possible. For example, in India, I was taught to be humble and not to crow about my achievements in public. In the United States, I have learned to be unapologetic about highlighting my achievements and importance to my students, colleagues, and administrators as a way to gain acceptance and command respect. Today, whenever and wherever I get an opportunity, I do not feel shy about informing my colleagues, students, and staff about me, my heritage as an Indian, the role of the British in India, and the importance of English in India and other Commonwealth countries. In other words, by engaging in educating the less informed, I hope to help the people around me to become better informed and be able to make more informed decisions about both people in general and people of color in particular.

QUESTIONS

1. Govardhan refers to "the full and complete acceptance of the significant role of professionals of color" in the field of TESL. Do you think such acceptance is possible? If so, how? If not, why not?

2. Govardhan explains why Indians might not be thought of as native speakers of English. What is your definition of a "native speakers of English?" On what is this definition based? Do you think the definition changes depending on whether the person defining the term is or is not a native speaker of English?
3. Govardhan describes the roles that English plays in India today. What roles does English play in your country today? Have those roles changed over time? If so, in what ways?
4. According to Govardhan, the English spoken in India has "a local color." Does the English spoken in your country have any local color? If so, what are the colors, where do they come from, and how are they responded to and perceived?
5. Govardhan writes about "the fight for justice and equality." Why do you think the combative metaphor occurs so often in discussions about justice and equality? If it is a fight, who are the key combatants and why are they engaged in such a fight?
6. Govardhan refers to the institutionalized perpetuation of negative stereotypes of foreign students. Are there any such stereotypes in your institution? If so, what are the effects of these stereotypes?
7. Govardhan contrasts his negative experiences with a set of very positive ones. If you have had similarly negative experiences, have you also had positive ones?
8. A recurring theme within Govardhan's narratives is self-esteem and self-confidence in relation to how we are treated by others. Have your self-esteem and self-confidence been impacted—positively and/or negatively—by colleagues reacting to you based on your appearance? If so, try to describe the experience(s).

REFERENCES

English Language Gazette. (1996, March). London: English Language Gazette Limited, p. 1.

Chapter 12

Not a Real American: Experiences of a Reluctant Ambassador

Mary Romney
Quinebaug Valley Community College

PERSONAL AND PROFESSIONAL HISTORY

I am an African American of Caribbean descent, born in New York City in the 1950s. My father was an immigrant from the Caribbean island of St. Maarten in the Netherlands Antilles, and my mother, who was born in Quincy, MA, was the daughter of immigrants from St. Maarten. Thus, I am a first generation U.S. American on my father's side, and a second generation U.S. American on my mother's side, but all four of my grandparents and all of my traceable ancestors were from St. Maarten/St. Martin. The dual spelling reflects the island's status as a dual-nationality territory, which it has been since the 17th century when the Dutch claimed half of the 37-square-mile island and named their part St. Maarten, and the French did the same on the other half, which they named St. Martin. Today it is the world's smallest territory to be shared by two governments.

I have always felt that being of Caribbean descent and interacting with many Caribbean people for most of my life has sensitized me not only to the breadth of ethnic and cultural variety among people of West African descent in the Americas, but also to the cultural diversity of the Caribbean itself. The bicultural heritage of St. Maarten is one such example. Other, perhaps more familiar, examples are Jamaica, where East Asian, South Asian, West African, Western European, and Middle Eastern heritages have created a multiethnic society, or Curacao, where Western European, West African, and Middle Eastern heritages have forged a multicultural society.

I believe that my appreciation of linguistic diversity originated as much from my family and my Caribbean heritage as it did from my education and my upbringing in multiethnic New York City, where I was exposed to many languages and cultures from the time I was born. In addition to his native English, my father learned to speak Spanish, Portuguese, Italian, Dutch, German, and Papiamento (a Portuguese-based Creole spoken in Curaçao). Hence, during my childhood, I never thought it unnatural or unusual for people to know more than one language. Somehow I always knew that I'd be at least bilingual. My family, like many (perhaps most) Caribbean families, was characterized by emigration, full of people living on different islands and in countries outside the Caribbean. In our case, members of our family lived in the United States, the Netherlands, and France, in addition to the Caribbean islands of Aruba, Curaçao, and St. Maarten.

Until I was 18, I lived with my parents in East Elmhurst, a middle-class, African American neighborhood in the borough of Queens New York City. Although I lived in Queens, I grew up in Manhattan. Without high-quality education available in the immediate area where we lived, my parents sent me to a private elementary and high school in Greenwich Village (a neighborhood in Manhattan), which I attended from kindergarten through high school. Geographically distant, it was a world away from Queens. This was perhaps my first cross-cultural migration—the first of many I would make as a student, and later as a TESOL professional. Of the children who attended the school, about 85% were Jewish, about 10% were African American, and another 5% were of various other heritages. I have always felt enormously privileged that I grew up in the Greenwich Village of the 1950s and 1960s. This was the age of the civil rights movement, the Vietnam War, the assassinations of Malcolm X, the Kennedys, and Martin Luther King, Jr. I can remember exactly where I was and what I was doing when I was wounded by the news of each of those losses. I remember my reactions and those of the adults around me. I remember the hope, pride, and enchantment I felt on the day Dr. King won the Nobel Peace Prize, because I was amazed that an African American individual could receive recognition of the highest order in the world beyond the United States. So I began to believe that perhaps we, too, as African American people, could take our place among the peoples of the world because we actually had something of value to contribute. As I went through my middle school and high school years, these impressions lay dormant in my mind.

Greenwich Village was the seedbed of so much of the creativity and activism of the times. I was directly exposed to so much of the cultural self-examination and upheaval of that era, as Black people in the United States began to discover and assert their own identity. Perhaps it was then that I began to think of myself as a citizen of the world beyond the United States. This nascent self-image might be why I was so attracted to the study of foreign languages, especially Spanish, the national language of more nations than any other language. I remember thinking of Spanish as a vehicle with which to reach out to people of African descent in other countries.

Hence, I pursued the study of Spanish in both undergraduate and graduate school. At the age of 18, I left New York to go to college. My undergraduate education was spent at Middlebury College, in Vermont, where I majored in Spanish. Immediately after graduation, I continued at Middlebury's Graduate School of Spanish in Madrid, Spain, for an master's degree in Spanish. When I finished that degree, I stayed in Spain for another 7 years, and taught English as a foreign language during my entire stay. After moving back to the United States, I returned to school, this time to Teachers College (TC) at Columbia University in New York, for an master's degree in TESOL, and then at the same institution for an master's degree instructional technology and media.

My entry into the world of TESOL began while I was studying in Madrid in 1975, through my introduction to the enormous demand for the study of English in Spain. Since then I have always held ESL or EFL positions in the United States or Spain. After completing my second degree at TC, I worked in an EFL program in Barcelona, Spain, for 3 years before I found my present position in the United States, which I have held since late 1992.

It was while I was living in Spain for the first time—from 1975 to 1982—that I began to become aware of the role of English outside the United States, and to learn about perceptions of its native speakers, as well as perceptions of the United States and its people. How these perceptions affected my professional life is what I address in this chapter. However, before I do that, I need to address how I believe English colors the linguistic landscape inhabited by many of our students and colleagues around the world.

ENGLISH, ITS SPEAKERS, AND ITS PERCEIVED SPEAKERS

I believe that the English language *is* all its speakers—that is, native, nonnative, Creole, World English, or whoever they are, the world over. This may seem obvious, but I think that it needs to be made explicit in relation to English because English is a world language—perhaps the only truly world language, with speakers in every part of the globe. Even if there are languages with many more native speakers (e.g., Chinese or Hindi) other languages do not have large bodies of nonnative speakers or large numbers of nonnatives trying to learn them, and they do not have the same role in the world as English does. I now realize that my Caribbean heritage is largely responsible for my perception of English as a world language and my belief that all its speakers should be equally recognized and valued. Being of Caribbean descent has exposed me to much of the diversity of the English language as it is used in the Americas. A variety of Englishes has always been a part of my life: Caribbean English, African American vernacular English, Standard American English, and British English. Thus, I have always been aware of the diversity of its speakers. Growing up in New York City also exposed me to a huge variety of nonnative speakers.

If English is truly a world language, then the perpetuation of a Eurocentric (and ethnocentric) view of English is unfair to its native (and nonnative) speakers worldwide. Again, this is because the language *is* all its speakers. That the language consists of all its speakers may not be the perception of many people, because the value and legitimacy of many varieties of English throughout the world is constantly challenged. Ebonics and World Englishes are among those English languages whose value and legitimacy are often challenged, sometimes to the point where some World English speakers are even placed in ESL courses. For example, see Nero (2000, 2001) for thorough discussions of the academic situation of some speakers of Caribbean Creole English.

One way in which this Eurocentric notion of English is perpetuated is through the TESOL profession, because of the low numbers of people of color in the profession in the United States and in many other contexts. Without diverse models of English speakers as their teachers in the United States, one result is that ESOL students emerge with a skewed perspective of whose language it is, whose English is acceptable, and, therefore, who should be their teachers.

These perspectives have been reinforced by the popular culture. They engender a kind of "linguistic racial profiling," as I have come to call it. The term *racial profiling* is used in the United States in criminal justice contexts, specifically to refer to situations in which police suspect certain people of criminal activity, based not on evidence but rather on the appearance of the individuals whom they target. The appearance of the suspected individuals is perceived by police to be similar to that of some actual convicted criminals.

In any case, none of this is to deny the European origins of the English language. Rather, I wish to adopt an inclusive perspective on the English language, and to affirm that it is also the language of many people of non-European descent who are willing and qualified to share their knowledge of it with students. In fact, the majority of English speakers worldwide are people of color and nonnative speakers (Crystal, 1998). The notion that the majority of English speakers are people of color, however, is not part of the general perception of the English language. It is not the perception of those outside the TESOL profession (e.g., our students), and it may not even be the perception of many non-TESOL educators in the United States and many other countries.

EFFECTS OF THE POPULAR CULTURE ON PERCEPTIONS OF PEOPLE OF COLOR IN GENERAL AND TESOL PROFESSIONALS IN PARTICULAR

From what I have observed, it is largely through the popular culture that people all over the world believe they learn about the United States. It was not until I began teaching English in Madrid that I began to understand the extent to which perceptions of African Americans abroad are influenced by what may be the United States' main export commodity, and arguably its most powerful one—the popular culture, in the form of TV, movies, and music, both live and recorded. The United States could very well be the country that people all over the rest of the world believe they know the most about, even if they have never been here. Because the United States continues to be the object of the dreams and aspirations of many people worldwide, it is the destination of immigrants and refugees from practically every country. What has largely been responsible for the dissemination of information, misinformation, and an array of impressions of the United States has been the popular culture. This was true long before CNN and the Internet.

During the first time I lived in Spain, television was centralized and broadcast nationally (i.e., the entire country saw the same thing on TV at the same time). Another significant factor was that it was faster, cheaper, and easier for the national TV networks to buy old TV programs from the United States than to produce their own shows. Many American TV series were up to 10 years old, but with no context and little background knowledge of the United States and its culture, the viewing public in Spain interpreted these shows as being contemporary, and their content as accurate reflections of life in the United States. Overwhelmingly, although not exclusively, images of African Americans on TV and in most of the rest of the popular culture were stereotypical and negative. African Americans were generally depicted as poor people, servants, sidekicks, criminals, entertainers, and athletes. Their behavior and their characters were portrayed as primitive, unsophisticated, violent, or dangerous. These characterizations appeared not only in fictional movies and TV, but also in documentaries. As if to add insult to injury, many of these imported TV shows and movies sometimes contained questionable and inaccurate translations from English into Spanish, or they contained materials for which there could be no accurate translation because of cultural and linguistic differences. Many were "B" movies, of such poor quality that they were not among major releases in the United States and had not been widely seen by U.S. audiences.

I soon learned how these images were likely to be interpreted by individuals with whom I interacted over the years, many of whom expressed very similar ideas. Witness these excerpts from memories of a few of my conversations with students, colleagues, and acquaintances in Spain:

- Typical of many casual conversations with students and other people in Madrid, between 1975 and 1982:

  "White people are not allowed to enter Harlem, are we?"

  "Of course you are. Everyone is allowed to go there. Where did you get the impression that you could not?"

  "From American TV programs I've seen."

- From a discussion with students in my EFL class in Madrid, ca. 1980, of an article in an American news magazine that reported on an event in the United States:

  "The Blacks reacted in that way because Blacks are very dangerous," said one student. "And very violent," added another.

  "Why do you say that?" I asked, trying not to show any emotion.

  "Because we always see it on TV and movies," said the student.

  "What kind of TV shows do you watch? What kind of movies do you see?"

  "American TV shows and American movies."

  "And you *believe* everything you see on TV?" I said, in horror and disbelief.

  "Yes. If it's on TV, it must be true," said the student, in a matter-of-fact way.

- Typical of many casual conversations with students and other people in Madrid, between 1975 and 1982:

  "In New York, you Blacks live in Harlem, right?"

  "No, not *all* of us. I've never lived there."

  "You haven't? So are you from a Black neighborhood or a normal one?"

  "But that's not a fair distinction. Black people in the United States live in normal areas, too."

  "No, that's not what I've seen on TV."

- From a conversation with a Spanish colleague in Barcelona, while looking at a photo of a local professional basketball team in planning a special activity for the students at the institute where I was teaching, in 1992:

  "I could invite the Americans on the team to come to and talk to our students," I said.

12. NOT A REAL AMERICAN: A RELUCTANT AMBASSADOR 155

"Yes, that would be great. Some real Americans!" he said, with wide-eyed enthusiasm.

"These three are American," I said, pointing to two Black players and a White one, "and so is this one," I added, pointing to another White member of the team.

"Yes, but I mean the *real* Americans, not the Blacks," he said, smiling politely.

As ethnocentric and insensitive as I considered these comments to be, I am sure that they were not made with any deliberate derogation, insult, or even racism intended by those who spoke them. They were only intended to reflect the perceptions of their speakers. What shocked me most was not the pervasiveness of negative stereotypes, but rather how willingly they were accepted as being true. What was equally surprising was the discovery of how easily the people seemed to abandon their beliefs in most of the stereotypes. The beliefs were widely held, but not deeply rooted. Usually, as soon as my students were presented with convincing evidence that contradicted what they had seen, they seemed willing to accept a different perspective. And after discovering that I did not fit the stereotypes to which they'd been exposed, most of my students treated me as an individual, in ways that many Blacks are not treated as individuals in the United States.

I do not believe that Spain has been alone in importing these types of popular culture, nor do I believe that it has been possible to avoid stereotypical images of Blacks and other U.S. minorities in the popular culture. I have heard reports of the same types of negative images in the popular culture of many other countries in Europe and Asia. Those in the marketplace where these images are bought are obviously not to blame for the quality of the images or for perceptions of their veracity. Of course, this issue is much more complex than what I can discuss here, but I believe that it is the creators of the content as well as the actors who accept such denigrating roles who should share the blame.

An observation of the popular culture and of many other institutions in U.S. life—from economics to education to politics—will reveal that African Americans live on the margins of society in the United States. Among my students in Spain and among people in other countries, I have found an understanding of this marginalization to be lacking. That African Americans are pushed to the margins and held there by a combination of discrimination and unequal distribution of resources is a fact that I have never felt completely successful at explaining to people outside the United States.

In any case, this marginalization is one reason why Blacks have not always been perceived as "real Americans" by those outside the United States. Fictional and real-life roles played by White Americans, although not always positive either, tend to be central rather than marginal. Of course, this is partly because Whites are in the majority in the United States, but it is also because of how U.S. minorities are perceived in the minds of many creators of the popular culture, the marketing for which is designed to appeal to, rather than challenge, stereotypes. Because non-Whites have been excluded from the mainstream and therefore from *images* of the mainstream, even in a country described as a "melting pot," the image of the people of the United States that exists in the collective mind of the international community has traditionally been a Eurocentric one that excludes people of color.

EFFECTS OF MARGINALIZATION ON AFRICAN AMERICAN TESOL PROFESSIONALS

If Standard English is the language of the mainstream in the United States, then the result of all of this for myself and other Black people in the TESOL profession is that there are many students and employers who do not perceive African Americans as being fully legitimate speakers of English. The belief is that African Americans cannot be fully legitimate teachers of Standard English if they are not fully legitimate speakers. Inextricably linked to marginalization are notions of inferiority, either conscious or subconscious. It is from these notions that the concept of a substandard variety of English spoken by Blacks in the United States originates. Caribbean and African Blacks have also been victims of these perceptions, but it is African Americans who are usually overgeneralized as speakers of "Black English," also known as Ebonics. This overgeneralization has serious consequences for Black TESOL professionals if employers subscribe to it; in my experience, many employers do.

Many employers, especially those outside the United States, have had limited if any direct interaction with African Americans, so they may not be aware that there are many African Americans who are not speakers of Ebonics and who are native speakers of Standard English. Again, these employers' perceptions are often influenced by the popular culture and their own observations of the minimal roles that African Americans have traditionally played in mainstream society in the United States and in other countries from which many employers usually seek to hire (native-speaking) English teachers (e.g., Britain or Canada). I am not defending partiality toward native-speaking English teachers here, but merely referring to it as another element among those with which many employers are led (or, I would contend, deluded) into making their hiring decisions based on a specific image of the people they wish to employ. In any case, with the expectations of their students in mind, many (if not most) employers, in the United States and abroad are likely to hire teachers who conform to the image of "real Americans" (or real Britons/Canadians) held by their students. These expectations create preferences in hiring, and these preferences lead to what I have previously referred to as "linguistic racial profiling." Whatever its label, the demand for teachers of a certain image is tantamount to discrimination. Compounded with the expectations of students and the demands of employers is the fact that discrimination is not illegal in most countries of the world, which makes this entire issue even more complex for TESOL professionals of color.

However, the essential element in racial profiling of any sort—linguistic, criminal, or social—is the extent to which individuals are perceived to fit a certain image. Thus, it is based on assumptions rather than on reality. Where TESOL is concerned, Black professionals do not generally fit the image of what a mainstream, Standard English, native speaker should *look* like, even if Black professionals *sound* exactly like mainstream, Standard English, native speakers.

I should point out here that it is not only outside of the United States where the issue of conformity (or lack thereof) to the image of the "real American" exists. Exclusion from the domain of "real Americans" is shared by other people of color inside the United States, most notably Asian Americans and Latinos. African Americans are not the only victims of racial profiling, linguistic or otherwise. Of course, the irony of the "real American" label is that it could be argued that the only people to whom it rightfully belongs are people of color. They are the descendants of the indigenous peoples who originally inhabited the North American continent—Native Americans, or Indians, as they are known today.

RECOGNIZED AND UNRECOGNIZED MINORITIES

Most Blacks in the United States probably know the feeling of being in the minority in many contexts. From my life in the United States, I was already familiar with the feeling of being one of only a few Blacks, or the only Black, or the first Black in many professional, academic, and social situations. However, living in a country where you are part of a recognized minority group is different from living in a country where there are almost none of your people. This was the case during the time I lived in Spain.

Throughout my entire career in the TESOL profession, I have been a member of the faculty of several institutions that did not have many other people of color working for them. I have almost always been either the first, or the only, or one of very few Black people on the faculty of the institutions where I have taught, both abroad and in the United States. This has often caused me to think of myself as a kind of representative of other African Americans because I believed that many of the faculty and staff—and, most important, the students—have had limited previous contact with other

Black people. This has made me feel that I have had to occupy the uncomfortable position of being a kind of ambassador—a reluctant one.

Suspicious, sometimes convinced, that many students and colleagues would treat me according to their preconceptions of Blacks rather than as an individual, I have always been aware of the tension between collective image and individual reality. I realize now how much effort I have put into making my interaction with students as positive as possible because it might be the only direct contact those students would have with an African American. Perhaps this has been a subconscious effort to counteract the negative images to which I thought they had been exposed. I believed in many cases that, for most of them, having an African American teacher might be a learning experience in and of itself.

WIDER PARTICIPATION AND OTHER CHANGES THAT ARE NEEDED IN THE TESOL PROFESSION

Although a lot has changed in Spain and the rest of the world since the mid 1970s and early 1980s, and even the early 1990s, I would say that, on the whole, my total of 11 years in Spain were overwhelmingly positive. I enjoyed life there through so many experiences that I could never have had in this country. I was fascinated by Spanish culture and captivated by the generosity and openness of most of the people, their spontaneity, their sense of community, and their respect for history. I was also grateful for the opportunity to view my home country through a lens that is only available from the outside, and to learn how it was viewed by others.

In the United States, a lot of progress has been made in terms of the movement of Blacks and other non-Whites toward the mainstream and away from the margins. Public and private institutions of education, politics, and commerce are more inclusive than they have ever been. This is also reflected in the popular culture, where there is wider and more varied representation of Blacks and other U.S. minorities. However, there is still a long way to go. Apart from the obvious need for the popular culture to change even more than it has, there is also a need for direct interaction, on the one hand, between those who are most adversely affected by how they are projected in the popular culture, and on the other hand, audiences of the pop culture. Direct interaction is the best way I am aware of to counteract harmful stereotypes.

That a lot of progress remains to be made is nowhere more evident than it is in the TESOL profession in both the United States and many other countries. If it is direct contact that demolishes barriers between groups of people and destroys stereotypes, then what is needed in the TESOL profession is more direct interaction between TESOL professionals of color and English language students all over the world. This can only be accomplished if there are more TESOL professionals of color in areas where they are underrepresented. TESOL professionals of color and nonnative English speakers need to gain more visibility not only with their presence, but also through the creation of more ESOL materials, wider participation in the TESOL association, and the encouragement of more people of color and nonnative English speakers around the world to join the profession. The profession, as it is practiced in the United States, would be more representative of the English language if more U.S. minorities not only entered the profession but also if they taught abroad. This is what will counteract stereotypes and provide such U.S. TESOL professionals of color with invaluable professional, personal, and cross-cultural experience, as well as unique perspectives on their country, which can only be acquired from living abroad. TESOL professionals of color are needed to orient people all over the world to the realities of the English language—who speaks it and who is qualified to teach it. We must work toward helping others accept perceptions of English that legitimize all Englishes and all people who speak them, so that all who inhabit the English language landscape worldwide can find acceptance in any part of it.

QUESTIONS

1. What influenced your earliest notions of foreign language, second language, and native language?
2. Have any historical events shaped your worldview as it relates to language or to race?
3. How do you respond to the position that "If English is truly a world language, then the perpetuation of a Eurocentric (and ethnocentric) view of English is unfair to its native (and nonnative) speakers worldwide ... because the language *is* all its speakers?" Do you agree or disagree with this position? Why?
4. Do you believe that stereotypes are harmful? Why or why not? If you believe they are harmful, what can be done to counteract them? Is this something that ESOL teachers should address? Have you been the object of stereotyping? If so, explain the context and describe what occurred.
5. As a TESOL professional, how would you respond if, during a class, your students demonstrated the kind of "racial reasoning" depicted in the conversations?
6. If you are a TESOL professional of color, what has been your experience trying to find employment? If you are an employer of TESOL professionals, how do you attempt to address the kinds of issues and concerns in this chapter?

7. If you have taught English outside your country, have you experienced the feeling of being a kind of "ambassador?" Do you feel that ESOL teachers represent more than just the language?

REFERENCES

Crystal, D. (1998). *English as a global language.* Cambridge, UK: Cambridge University Press.

Nero, S. (2000). The changing faces of English: A Caribbean perspective. *TESOL Quarterly, 34,* 483–510.

Nero, S. (2001). *Englishes in contact: Anglophone Caribbean students in an urban college.* Creskill, NJ: Hampton.

Chapter 13

Out of the Safety Zone

Suhanthie Motha
University of Maryland, College Park

EARLY PERSONAL AND PROFESSIONAL HISTORY

> There is no better point of entry into a critique or reflection than one's own experience. It is not the endpoint, but the beginning of an exploration of the relationship between the personal and the social and therefore the political. (Bannerji, Carty, Dehli, Heald, & McKenna, 1992, p. 67)

Taking Bannerji et al.'s sage advice, I use my personal history as a point of departure for this reflection on my positionality as a TESOL professional of color. I was born in Sri Lanka and am ethnically Tamil. My parents moved to the San Francisco Bay Area when I was still an infant and then to Canberra, Australia, when I was 4. I came in contact with very few people of color during my early years in Canberra, thanks to a racist immigration policy that restricted, with few exceptions, "non-White" immigration. During my adolescence, we spent 4 years in Nouvelle Calédonie, a small French colony in the South Pacific where French had been introduced to the Black Melanesian population by White immigrants. At the time, Nouvelle Calédonie was occupied by France despite a strong insurgent force. I moved to Canada to attend university and completed an undergraduate degree in French and English literature from the University of Toronto. Eventually I wandered serendipitously into TESOL, which soon became my professional home. I received my master's and doctoral degrees from the University of Maryland, College Park, where I currently teach.

I have come to understand race and language as being intertwined with each other in thorny, complicated ways. My interest in the relationship between race and language minority status is rooted in my life. As a child, I never learned Tamil, the language of my ancestry, nor Singhalese, the official language of Sri Lanka. As I grew up in Canberra under the shadow of the White Australia policy, complete assimilation was our family's primary mission, and in this context learning a language that was so strongly disassociated from Whiteness contradicted that end. However, my heritage language loss began much earlier than our immigration to Australia, before I was born, during the days of British colonialism in Sri Lanka. At that time, my grandparents began to speak only English with their offspring. Their choice was guided by the structure of their contexts—they used English in their everyday interactions while running businesses that catered to the British, and they knew that the language offered a cachet. English served them well. It solidified their socioeconomic status in a context that coupled social privilege with English language. As an adult looking back, I am aware of continuous messages about the supremacy of Whiteness, particularly British Whiteness, and of Whiteness being doggedly and consistently socially constructed as normative. I remember, during visits "back home" to Sri Lanka, seeing my cousins returning from elocution classes (which are wildly popular in Colombo) and practicing their Henry Higgins-style drills, repeating "How now brown cow?" over and over in clipped British accents.

I am also aware of discourses that resist those same dominant metanarratives. My mother tells of her grandfather's political activism, his committed participation in pro-independence movements and eventual election to the first senate of the newly established dominion of Sri Lanka. This grandfather exemplifies for me the struggle that I and many of my family members face: the dilemma of "being oneself" (Du Bois, 1996), of using cultural capital, including English language proficiency, to advantage without selling out. To this day, I often catch a jumble of colonial and anticolonial discourses swirling around in my head, and these complicate my understandings of what it means to be a TESOL professional of color.

"YOU SAY 'TOM-AY-TO' …"

A taut and reciprocal relationship exists between racial and language (including accent) hierarchies. I recall being specifically conscious of the coconstructed and subtle nature of this relationship shortly before I began my doctoral studies. I was teaching ESL at a small university in the San Francisco suburbs, and in the context of a lesson, I used the word *tom-ah-to*. A student asked me, "Isn't it *tom-ay-to*?" I replied, "It depends on where you come from. I say *tom-ah-to*, but most Americans say *tom-ay-to*."

13. OUT OF THE SAFETY ZONE

I suddenly sensed that I was losing credibility. Reflecting on the interaction later, I realized that my fears were related to my race. I didn't want students to think that I was teaching them a form of English associated with my race if they believed that form of English would not serve them well. Were my insecurities a reaction to students' facial expressions? Was it all in my head? I hastened to explain, defensively; "I'm from Australia, so I say *tom-ah-to*." Somewhere in my subconscious mind, aligning myself with Australia rather than Sri Lanka gave me legitimacy.

Did it give me legitimacy in students' eyes, or only my own? If I accept that Australian English is more socially legitimated than is Sri Lankan English, what am I saying about my cultural identity? I'm embarrassed to admit that I then added; "The British say *tom-ah-to*." The British affiliation was the trump card of valid pronunciation. How would students have reacted if I had said, "In Sri Lanka, it's pronounced *tom-ah-to*?" (This is, indeed, exactly how it is pronounced in Sri Lanka.) I was uneasy with what I was saying, but I wasn't specifically conscious of why. It occurred to me only after later reflection that my attempts to distance myself from my racial identity only served to reinforce inequitable language hierarchies.

CRITICAL CONDITIONS

Today, almost a decade later, I teach ESOL teacher candidates. I find myself increasingly troubled by the ways in which race is addressed (or, often, not addressed) in my classroom contexts. My discomfort tends to be personal and is sometimes related to my own racial identity. In many instances, race feels to me like an enormous elephant standing silently in the room, plainly visible to everyone present and yet somehow unmentionable. I usually audiotape my classes, and in listening to the tapes later I'm struck by both how often we are able to avoid direct discussion of race and how awkward the conversation becomes when I do specifically force myself to name race in a discussion that I had perceived to be dancing around the edges of the subject.

Much of my reflection as a TESOL professional of color has been provoked, ironically, by the critical conditions surrounding the one non-TESOL class that I teach, so it is in this context that I embed the remainder of this chapter. It is a master's level diversity class that is required for an intensive teacher certification program. Because it focuses specifically on diversity, it lends itself to open and explicit discussion of race and racism. The racial identities of class members make it particularly interesting. In every section that I've taught, almost all of the teacher candidates have been White (60 of the 64 students who have been in the class over the past 5 years), and all but one spoke English as a first language. Our university is located in a school county in which more than 90% of the student population is of color, and close to 10% are labeled LEP ("limited English proficient") by the county. Within the educational research community, recent interest has been devoted to the challenges facing White teachers teaching in classrooms of children who are racial minorities, which is an area that merits attention. However, I've been reflecting lately on a set of different but related challenges: those facing teacher educators who, like me, are racial minorities teaching in classrooms of predominantly White teacher candidates. In a world in which race and gender shape everything—the ways in which we construct our own and each others' identities, the ways in which we learn, and the ways in which we teach—what happens when a minority teacher educator guides a class of White teachers preparing to teach linguistic and ethnic minority students? What are the meanings of racialized and gendered identities constructed in the context of these classes? What role do I, as a woman of color, play in teacher candidates' shaping of their own positionalities and teaching identities?

I want to pause and reflect on these issues at this time, because right now, far from feeling that my pedagogy is benefiting from experience, I am sensing that with every passing year my classroom is increasingly becoming a site that supports and even strengthens the racialized discourses of society at large. My goals for the class are to reflect on the connections among difference (including racial difference), power, and identity, and to deconstruct our biases. However, I have recently been encountering what I interpret as a growing student resistance to antiracism. I'm surprised by the candor with which some students articulate resistance, and I am interested in the conditions that make possible openly expressed support for the racial status quo in this country.

My own race is salient in these interactions, as I become more and more aware of and even self-conscious about my racial minority status during discussions of class readings that critique racism. In conversations with other TESOL professionals of color, I hear numerous stories of overt discrimination within educational institutions, including the academy. Nussbaum (2000) advised us to delve deeper into a structural analysis of the conditions that make blatant racism possible, and in response I offer a discussion of some recurring themes that have surfaced repeatedly and disturbingly throughout my teaching life and play what I perceive to be a silencing or marginalizing function. These influence the ways in which I teach, learn, and coconstruct my own identity and those of others. The themes include an outright denial of racism, a sense that responsibility for antiracist work rests with racial minorities, the construction of women of color as less authoritative teachers, and an overwhelming concern for the comfort levels of Whites resulting in a persistent redirecting of focus from the needs of minorities to the needs of dominant groups. In this chapter, I explain how I see these assumptions becoming discursively constructed and provide examples of each. I then move on to detail the ways in which these conditions influence my positionality and teaching practice as a woman of color in academia in general, and in TESOL in particular.

Denial of Racism

During the most recent semester that I taught the diversity course, a recurring theme surfaced: a thinly veiled denial of the existence of racism (Kubota, 2002). It took various forms, such as the implications that (a) minorities make complaints that they link to race but that are actually unrelated to race, (b) that minorities spend too much energy constructing race-related negativity in their everyday lives, and (c) that minorities today are complaining about bygone injustices, among other arguments.

For example, in a film we watched in class, a Black man made reference to being spit on, and a White female student criticized him for citing the event as a significant racial incident in his life. She suggested that the true problem emanating from this incident was not that the character was spit on, but that he then constructed the spitting as being racially motivated. She and the other students who spoke up during this discussion believed that the man's reaction contributed to racial divisiveness. This argument places the blame for racial tension on minorities, implying that they imagine their negative experiences to be rooted in racism. I saw this statement as part of a larger social set of discourses that claim that racism is largely nonexistent but that it cannot be put to rest because of the fanciful minds of racial minorities.

Similarly, in response to the wariness and fear of police brutality that Black men have spoken of feeling as they drive through the streets in White dominant suburbs, a student commented, "They're talking about being fearful of different people and different places, it's like they focus on it … but if you think of it as a fearful experience all of the time, you have these negative thoughts in your head, and then you have these negative thoughts about the people that you're fearing, when you may not have any reason to fear." I replied, "So are you saying that they don't have any reason to fear? That their fears are unfounded?" The student then elaborated, "I feel like they just need to focus on not fearing different situations … focusing on it, it seems really not productive to me…. It seems like you're expending a lot of negative energy that doesn't need to be there."

These discourses, which suggest that minorities spend too much energy constructing race-related negativity in their everyday life experiences, are effective in redirecting blame for racial tension back to the racial minority. Additionally, on several occasions students suggested that minorities complain about the distant past. For instance, one student repudiated a complaint about slavery, asking, "How many years go by before you drop it?"

These charges ignore the modern-day legacy of centuries of historical White domination globally, and furthermore ignore modern-day racism, both structural and individual. The question "How many years go by before you drop it?" suggests that no racial injustice has taken place since slavery ended and that the descendants of slaves are complaining about historical events that they've only read about, which have no effect on their current-day lives. The composition of the class is important: If there had been even one African American in the class, it is possible that many of those discourses would not have been permissible. Practically speaking, it would have been impossible for anyone to ask aloud how many years have to go by before African Americans stop complaining about slavery. This observation raises a complicated issue: The creation of conditions that quash racist discourses in teacher education classes may not be the desirable end, because silencing speech does not necessarily mean changing ideology. The fact that a person is not expressing a troubling thought does not mean that he or she is not thinking and believing it.

Sense That Responsibility for Antiracism Rests With Racial Minorities

I find myself struggling against a set of discourses, those of "reaching" students who are not interested in challenging discrimination and of "not alienating" my audience. These discourses place responsibility for the dominant group's learning about antiracism on members of minority groups. The second time I taught this diversity course, I found myself struggling to connect with one student, Wayne, and sought the advice of other faculty in the program. Concern for reaching and not alienating Wayne was universally of the highest concern among the faculty to whom I turned.

In one assignment, I asked students to read Peggy McIntosh's (1997) essay "Unpacking the Knapsack of White Privilege." I tried to problematize the notion of unearned privilege by having students choose any facet of their own identities in which they believed they held privilege and then to write their own invisible knapsack. White, male, able-bodied, Christian, heterosexual Wayne turned in a paper about how he didn't have privilege because he considered himself to be poor. He embraced meritocratic ideologies that linked work ethic to race, and he implied that I had been hired on the basis of my skin color and regardless of my qualifications. I was terrified that if I showed anger or impatience, I would alienate him, and in retrospect I realize that I invested a great deal of energy in constructing myself counter to the angry minority woman identity of which he had spoken disparagingly.

Roxana Ng (1993) wrote about a critical incident in her teaching life, a time when a student repeatedly called her "a woman out of control" as he complained about her feminist teaching to an administrator. Although I hadn't read her article at the time that I met Wayne, the stereotype her student invoked is all too familiar. Lin et al. (2004) used several examples to illustrate the power of the dominant image of women of color as emotionally unstable, angry, and unreasonable, explaining that "Invoking the unsmiling 'angry woman of color' stereotype is a discursive ploy that silences and subordinates the voices of women of color" (p. 497).

Wayne and I had many conversations about the assignment and about the notion of privilege, and between these I talked to the faculty around me, feeling rather intimidated by Wayne's determination and annoyed by my own trepidation. The faculty were supportive and gave me caring and thoughtful advice. However, throughout these discussions, the responsibility for reaching Wayne continued to rest squarely on my shoulders, as though he would be doing me a favor if he deigned to consider the material I was hoping to teach. I received comments such as:

- "What's your intention? If your intention is transformation, you need to be careful that he doesn't turn you off because then he'll never hear what you have to say."
- "You have to think about what's more important to you, Wayne doing the assignment or Wayne understanding the notion of privilege."

I have become increasingly troubled by discourses that feed the fear of alienating dominant groups, and by practices (which I have participated in and contributed to) that charge minority groups with responsibility for reaching and raising the consciousness of members of dominant groups.

A further problem exists with accepting that initiating antiracist work should be the responsibility of minorities. It leads us to the related assumption that minorities are the primary or even only beneficiaries of antiracist work. In actual fact, antiracism serves all people. All humans suffer from the construct of oppression, regardless of at whom it is aimed. Oppression robs both oppressed and oppressors of their humanity (Freire, 1970). When certain voices are silenced, all humans are deprived of those perspectives.

The Construction of Women of Color As Less Authoritative Teachers

One White male professor offered to discuss the situation with Wayne, suggesting, "Sometimes, for someone like Wayne, it doesn't mean as much coming from someone like you because it looks like you're arguing for your own rights. Sometimes it carries more weight coming from someone who looks like him." I've no doubt that this analysis was accurate. However, to have him speak to Wayne on my behalf would have cemented the subordinate position of my voice and would have underscored this: As long as I remain female and Asian (both of which are likely), my voice will never command the legitimacy and authority of a White male voice, and I will always be dependent on the White males around me to serve as my mouthpieces. Developing an authoritative voice poses a serious challenge for any woman of color within academia (Moses, 1997). I struggle to claim the same authority established by my White male colleagues, but complexly intertwined with what Carty (1992) referred to as "outsider within" status is my positioning as a woman of color in the context of larger social power relations. Classrooms do not exist in vacuums, and thus the perceived legitimacy of what I say and teach within this classroom is connected to how women of color globally are positioned in relation to power and authority.

A tension exists—building a united front and developing a community of allies is an important part of any social justice project. However, there is a difference between intervening on behalf of a woman of color and joining a united battle against racism. Antiracist movements are strengthened when they include White allies. For instance, when our program coordinator, a White man, advocates against racial injustice, he helps to shape the fight against racism as a fight that should be engaged in by everyone, not only those of color.

Discourses of Safety

In discussions of diversity, discourses of "safety," "vulnerability," and "risk" privilege the interests of dominant groups over the project of social justice. The effect of this language on minority group members is to marginalize us as concern is refocused back to the welfare of those from dominant groups. For instance, at TESOL 2003, discussant Aneta Pavlenko stood up at an academic session and criticized the tendency of teachers to bend over backward in an effort to make dominant-group students feel comfortable in conversations about difference. She said, "I want them to be uncomfortable." An audience member added, "Safely uncomfortable," and assent was audible throughout the room. I wrote it down in my notes and took it home to stew about.

Safety and comfort are not synonymous and this show of concern for the "safety" of students from dominant groups makes me uneasy. I in fact challenge this construction of "unsafe." Classroom discussions about race don't make students from dominant groups unsafe. They do not increase the likelihood of their being sent to jail, shot, put to death, or denied employment or housing, which are the consequences for minority children when discrimination is not deconstructed and challenged. Using the language of safety and vulnerability in discussions of diversity—the same language that is used to challenge discrimination—minimizes the experience of discrimination, the experience of truly being unsafe. What does it mean to be "safely uncomfortable?" Adding "safely" to "uncomfortable" does more than mitigate the point—it runs dangerously close to nullifying it. I am not discounting the importance of safe discussion, because it is important if space is to be created for a struggle against systematic oppression and an examination of how racist ideologies serve to reinforce privilege. However, this concern for safety must be balanced against social justice and must not be allowed to redirect our focus from subjugated groups, who have historically been left out of the picture, back to dominant groups.

DISCUSSION

Throughout the various sections of the diversity class, I have found myself struggling on a tightrope walk between on one hand trying to support students' generation and construction of their own knowledge, including respect for their experiences and positionalities, and on the other hand heeding my burning desire to tyrannically tell them what I think they should think. My attempts to ask provocative questions were often unfruitful. And despite the support of excellent readings and resources, I was seldom successful in depicting antiracist work as everyone's charge and not the responsibility of only minorities. This entire struggle was embedded in the context of a self-consciousness that, as I advocated for minority rights, I was often advocating for myself as the only person of color in the room, and for the teacher candidates' hypothetical future students who were so far removed from their current lives that they were almost invisible throughout these conversations.

One effect of barely cloaked denials of racism is the fostering of a commonsense ideology that accepts that complaints about racism—particularly minorities' complaints—are unfounded. The acceptance of this ideology lays out a terrain in which minorities' complaints about racism (including mine) are preemptively disarmed. I see the ideology established in my classes as connected to a broader societal trend toward liberal, as opposed to critical, multiculturalism (Kubota, 2002). Liberal multicultural discourses pay lip service to multiculturalism by emphasizing the customs and values of different groups and embracing an egalitarian and even meritocratic philosophy without attention to social injustice and inequity at the structural level. Because liberal multiculturalist discourses are prevalent and normalized throughout U.S. society (Bonilla Silva, 2004), they are the dominant discourses that surface in my classroom. One way to address these issues in a classroom context is to encourage students' explicit attention to the ways in which liberal multiculturalist ideologies can lead to victim blaming, color-blindness, and an obscuring of power and privilege (Kubota, 2002) using authentic examples (e.g., from media, textbooks, and classroom interaction transcripts).

Changing the racial compositions of our classes can play a role in eroding this commonsense ideology. Our teacher education classes need to be diverse so that multiple perspectives are represented. One token minority is inadequate—being the sole minority voice is an unfairly heavy load for a single individual human being to take on. Increasing diversity in teacher education classes requires more than simply admitting more minorities. For truly equitable experiences, colleges of education need to invest in minority recruitment, minority scholarships, and mentoring and advising of minority students once they are admitted.

Colleges of education need to invest in increasing diversity of not only teacher candidates but also teacher educators through minority recruitment and careful mentorship for new hires. My experiences have brought home the importance of not just academic but also emotional support for faculty of color. As I began teaching the diversity class, I spoke to other faculty in my program but found myself still feeling discouraged and truly wondering whether one individual can pose any significant challenge to racism and sexism. Sometimes you need to go further afield to find support. Much of mine comes from beyond the walls of my institution, from both scholars of color and White scholars in other parts of the country and indeed the world. Establishing collectives, support groups, and allies is a crucial part of scholarly development for minorities, because it allows one to help oneself at the same time as supporting others.

I pause to underscore the importance of mentorship. As I began my graduate coursework in the early 1990s, I was (and continue to be) deeply affected by a relationship with a mentor who is a Chinese American female professor, Shelley Wong. Simply seeing a woman of color in academia influenced me—until this point, I don't think that I truly understood how seeing someone you identify with in a desirable position makes that position truly accessible to you on a subconscious level.

Bonny Norton (2001) wrote compellingly of the lure of an imagined identity or imagined community; that is, a fantasized affiliation with a certain group, often intangible and not immediately accessible. Norton connected our investments in imagined communities to our participation in our futures. Until I met Shelley, I was oblivious to just how tightly racial difference and identity connect to imagined identities. While I was working on my undergraduate degree, my professors were almost all White and male. I'd certainly never known any faculty who were women of color. On some level, knowing Shelley opened up academia as a career option for me but also drove home my awareness of the naïveté of many of my previously held beliefs about race and gender—for instance, my assumption that if minority role models are not available to minority children, they can simply look to members of dominant groups as exemplars. For example, in my earlier years, I saw no reason that a little Latina girl couldn't look to George Washington as a model. Beyond the iconic value of Shelley's mentorship, she opened up a world in which pedagogy and scholarship could be chaotic, brazenly political, brimming with caring and investment, and connected to my reality. These characteristics of Shelley's teaching are all departures from traditional models of teaching and are connected to ideology, which in turn is connected to identity, including racial and gendered identity. There is something special about the experience of being an outsider and a minority that adds layers of richness to the perspective with which one views the world and consequently changes the way one teaches. My experience being mentored by Shelley emphasizes for me the importance of providing minority children with classroom teachers who are also of color. The inequitable teacher–student relationship in the classroom is only exacerbated when the figure of authority—that is, the teacher—is White, and the student a racial minority.

Now, more than a dozen years after I met Shelley, as I engage in conversations with other women of color, I hear over and over about the crucial role that their relationships with mentors and like-minded scholars, both racial minorities and Whites, play in their professional and personal lives. Some of them point to sisterhood with women on the same trajectory, some describe what bell hooks (1989) termed "other-mothering." In my own life, these relationships have made the difference between remaining in pursuit of a career as a change agent and being socialized into silent compliance (or even, potentially, sliding quietly off an academic career path, as happens disproportionately to women of color; see Hornig, 2003).

QUESTIONS

1. Motha describes how English was associated with race in Australia, and with socioeconomic status in Sri Lanka. Are you aware of other countries where either of these associations is made? Have you ever observed or experienced this connection?
2. If Motha accepts that Australian English is more socially legitimated than is Sri Lankan English, what is she saying about her cultural identity? How would you have reacted if you had been a student in that class? Would her alignment with Australia have given her more credibility in your view?
3. Race is referred to by Motha as "an enormous elephant standing silently in the room, plainly visible to everyone present and yet somehow unmentionable." Have you experienced this feeling about race in your classrooms, either as a student or as a teacher? Describe your experience(s). If you have not experienced this, why do you think it might be "unmentionable?"
4. Motha refers to social discourses that "claim that racism is largely nonexistent but that it cannot be put to rest because of the fanciful minds of racial minorities." How would you respond to this argument if it came from your students or classmates?
5. What is your response to the notion that U.S. minorities and people of color should be solely responsible for initiating antiracist work, and that they are the sole beneficiaries of antiracist work?

6. The concept of safety and comfort for members of dominant groups during discussions of race and other differences is a major issue for Motha. She quotes Pavlenko, who said that she wants students from the dominant group to feel "uncomfortable." How would you respond to Pavlenko? How would you define safety and comfort? How would you respond to Motha's contention that classroom discussions about race and other differences "don't make students from dominant groups feel 'unsafe'?"
7. Motha describes the effect of a mentor on her academic and professional life. Do you agree with her about the importance of role models in the lives of students? What do you think is the value of role models and mentors? Have you had these kinds of relationships with your students? With your teachers? If so, describe them, and how you believe they have made a difference.

REFERENCES

Bannerji, H., Carty, L., Dehli, K., Heald, S., & McKenna, K. (1992). *Unsettling relations: The university as a site of feminist struggles*. Boston: South End Press.

Bonilla Silva, E. (2004). *Racism without racists: Color-blind racism and the persistence of racial inequality in the United States*. Lanham, MD: Rowman and Littlefield.

Carty, L. (1992). Black women in the academy: A statement from the periphery. In H. Bannerji, L. Carty, K. Dehli., S. Heald, & K. McKenna. (Eds.), *Unsettling relations: The university as a site of feminist struggles* (pp. 13–44). Boston: South End Press.

Du Bois, W. E. B. (1996). The Oxford W. E. B. Du Bois Reader. Oxford, UK: Oxford University Press.

Freire, P. (1970). *Pedagogy of the oppressed*. New York: Continuum Publishing Co.

hooks, b. (1989). *Talking back: Thinking feminist, thinking black*. Boston: South End Press.

Hornig, L. (2003). *Equal rites, unequal outcomes: Women in American research universities*. New York: Kluwer.

Kubota, R. (2002). Critical multiculturalism in second language education. In B. Norton & K. Toohey (Eds.), *Critical pedagogies and language learning* (pp. 30–52). Cambridge, UK: Cambridge University Press.

Lin, A., Grant, R., Kubota, R., Motha, S., Tinker Sachs, G., Vandrick, S., & Wong, S. (2004). Women faculty of color in TESOL: Theorizing our lived experiences. *TESOL Quarterly, 38*, 3.

McIntosh, P. (1997). "White privilege: Unpacking the invisible knapsack." In B. Schneider, (Ed.), *Race: An anthology in the first person* (pp. 120–126). New York: Crown Trade Paperbacks.

Moses, Y. (1997). Black women in academe: Issues and strategies. In L. Benjamin (Ed.), *Black women in the academy: Promises and perils* (pp. 23–38). Gainesville: University of Florida Press.

Ng, R. (1993). "A woman out of control": Deconstructing sexism and racism in the university. *Canadian Journal of Education, 18*(3), 189–205.

Norton, B. (2001). Non-participation, imagined communities and the language classroom. In M. Breen (Ed.), *Learner contributions to language learning: New directions in research* (pp. 159–171). Harlow, UK: Pearson Education.

Nussbaum, M. (2000). *Women and human development*. Cambridge, UK: Cambridge University Press.

Chapter **14**

Confessions of an *Enraced* TESOL Professional

Ahmar Mahboob
University of Sydney

PERSONAL HISTORY

I am a child of the diaspora—a model product of the postcolonial world. My parents were born in British India in the 1930s: my mother in Bhopal and my father in Gorakhpur, Uttar Pradesh (U.P.). Both sets of my grandparents migrated to Karachi in the late 1940s as British India was splintered into two antagonistic nation-states. Having moved to a "new" country, my grandparents struggled to make a life for themselves and their children. I am lucky in that my grandparents considered education to be of extreme importance and took all steps to make sure that their children (my parents) were educated. For my mother, this meant that she had to travel to Lahore to take her matric examination. For my father, it meant that he had to travel to and live in Peshawar to complete his bachelor of arts degree. They both earned their master's degrees from Karachi University: my mother in psychology and my father in English literature. This was in the early 1960s. My parents, like many other young, educated urbanites of the time, were actively involved in left-wing politics. However, the government was turning sharply to the right. Thus, with growing political instability and a violent crackdown on left-wing politics, my family decided to move to the United Arab Emirates (UAE) in January 1975. I was 39 months old.

My formal schooling started in UAE. I attended a school for Pakistani expatriates in Sharjah. The medium of instruction in this school was English, which meant that all subjects were taught in English. At school, we were actively discouraged to use any language other than English. At home and in other contexts, I grew up speaking a mixture of English and Urdu—depending on the domain of the conversation and the people involved. The series of migrations that started with my grandparents had yet to settle. From UAE, I moved back to Karachi for 1 year 1985–1986. Not being able to settle down in General Zia-ul-Haq's Islamicized Pakistan, my parents decided to move back to UAE. We lived there for another 2 years and then moved back to Pakistan—this time we moved to Gilgit (a small city in the mountains of northern Pakistan), where my parents taught English to children at a local school. In addition to my parents, there was a British couple who were also teaching English at this school. This couple was one of my early professional inspirations—I, like them, wanted to travel the world and support my travels through teaching English. Of course, this was rather naïve of me; I later discovered that they could do this because they were "native" speakers of the language, and they were White and in demand. I did not qualify for the jobs that came naturally to them.

My year in Gilgit was a series of unforgettable experiences. Just to give you an impression, we lived without running water or electricity—and this was in the late 1980s! I enrolled in a local intermediate college (equivalent to U.S. high school) in Gilgit. During one vacation, I went to Karachi to visit my brothers who were going to college there. On the way back, I was trapped in a landslide and was unable to return to Gilgit. With the winter approaching and the school back in session, it was decided that I would transfer to an intermediate college in Karachi. After graduating from the intermediate college, I found a job as an English teacher—my only qualification being that I was proficient in the language and had always scored high grades in the subject. For a year, I taught English to elementary and secondary school children, but I felt unqualified. In November 1990, I began attending Karachi University. I completed my bachelor's degree (Hons) in English literature in 1994, and my master's degree in linguistics in 1995. This stay in Karachi, from 1989 to 1995, marks the longest period that I continuously lived in one city—6 years!

Feeling unsatisfied with my academic qualifications and with a thirst to learn more, I arrived in the United States on June 19, 1995, to continue my higher education. This was a major move for me. Although I had lived in various places, this was my first exposure to the West. I soon learnt that I had to retool myself to survive in this society.

I lived in Bloomington, Indiana, from 1995 to 2002. However, I did not live there continuously. I was only there during the school year; in the sum-

14. CONFESSIONS OF AN *ENRACED* PROFESSIONAL   **175**

mers (for at least 3 months each year), I would either travel to another country to teach English, or visit my family in Pakistan. On these trips to Pakistan, I worked/volunteered at local educational institutions as an educator or a researcher.

My experiences and exposure at Indiana University, some of which I share in this chapter, have shaped my academic life. My interest in and focus on NNEST (nonnative English speakers in TESOL) issues, World Englishes, and teacher education developed during my stay there. In addition to my academic understanding, my work visits to various countries during the summers helped me develop localized understanding of these issues.

As a graduate student at Indiana University, I was also quite active in the local TESOL affiliate. I was elected the vice president of INTESOL in 2001, and the president of this organization in 2002. In July 2002, before I completed my doctorate, I was offered a tenure-track position at East Carolina University, NC, and left Indiana. Although I found the department and the university very supportive, I felt the political atmosphere in the United States in general, and in Greenville, NC, in specific, to be increasingly suffocating, especially for a person with my South Asian Muslim heritage. I soon started looking for jobs outside the United States and was offered a position in the department of linguistics at the University of Sydney. I arrived in Sydney on June 28, 2004. At the time of writing, I plan to live in Sydney—however, with my history, I cannot guarantee how long I will stay here or where I will go to next. Such is a story of a child of the diaspora.

THE CONCEPT OF *ENRACEMENT*

Let me start the formal part of this chapter by reflecting on the chapter's title: "Confessions of an *Enraced* TESOL Professional." *Enraced*, as you know, is not a word that you will find in your dictionaries. *Race* as defined in my student-time (Pakistani) copy of *Oxford Advanced Learner's Dictionary* (Cowie, 1989) is a noun that means: "any of several large subdivisions of mankind sharing physical characteristics, eg colour of skin, colour and type of hair, shape of eyes and nose" (p. 1030). However, to me, *race* is not only something that describes us, but is also something that is performed to and by us—it is a verb. And so, based on the analogy of *rage : enrage* ("make (sb) very angry"; *Oxford Advanced Learner's Dictionary*, p. 400), I have created the word *enrace*: to make or cause somebody to become (very) raced. The verb *enrace* represents actions/negotiations through which we acquire our awareness of race. The verb *enrace* does not only mean that we are enraced by others—that others cause us to construct our racial identity—but, also that we enrace others—that our actions, behaviors, and/or discourses lead to a (re)negotiation of other people's racial awareness. This process of enracement is a result of our negotiations and interactions with people (both of our own race and other races) and is partly grounded in how other people view, experience, and/or stereotype our race and how we view, experience, and/or stereotype them. This form of negotiation and identity building is, of course, not restricted to the issue of race, but extends to other forms of human stereotypes, beliefs, and/or orientations (e.g., gender, ethnicity, language [including accent], creed, sexual orientation, and so on). However, in this chapter, I restrict myself to reflecting on issues of race (with some discussion of language as it relates to race).

The process of enracement may or may not be a positive one. It is possible that our negotiations with individuals may result in a positive reflection of our racial identity, but it is also possible that they may result in a negative experience. It is also very possible that racial identity is not a subject of a particular negotiation at all. Similarly, our own actions and behavior may also lead to a positive or a negative evaluation of other peoples' racial identities. However, in many instances, we tend not to focus on our own actions/behaviors toward others as acts of enracement. We prefer to talk about how our racial identities are negotiated through our (unfortunate) experiences and tend to forget how our actions might impact others. In the narratives that follow, I include incidences that helped me define and evaluate my own racial identity, and episodes in which I feel that I caused others to enrace their identities. Let me start with two episodes that exemplify this.

Narrative 1: On Being Enraced

When I first came to the United States as an international student in the mid-1990s and entered my first class, I could sense that everyone turned around to look at me. I felt as if I were guilty of something and had transgressed an unmarked boundary. Although it is possible that I was being overly sensitive about other students' gazes, I felt insecure at that moment in time. I felt that they were looking at me because I was the only one in the room with dark skin color (and a sing-song South Asian accent). It wasn't that the people in this instance were rude or anything, it was just the way they looked at me. It marked me as an outsider—an other. This feeling impacted my behavior and confidence. I felt that I said the absolute wrong thing every time I opened my mouth: I wanted to say one thing, but uttered the opposite. I was also very conscious of my accent/language. Although a proficient speaker of Pakistani English, I suddenly felt that my English was not good enough. I lost all confidence. It was not until a few weeks into the semester that I regained my confidence and redeveloped a positive self-identity.

Narrative 2: On Enracing Others

During the same time as that of Narrative 1, I noticed that most of the international students in the class were from Asia—many with very marked accents and ungrammatical English. They were what many *desis* (people from South Asia) call *chaptas* or *chinkas*, and there are not many positive stereotypes about them. I therefore subconsciously maintained a distance from them and focused my energies to make friends with the Anglo Americans. I did not attempt to make friends with the Asian students and they made no attempts to befriend me. It was not until a few weeks into the semester that a casual comment from a classmate made me realize what I was doing: I was letting my own racial stereotypes influence my behavior with the others in my class. This realization helped me reflect on and change my behavior. I actively developed friendships with several of my Asian classmates, a few of which we still maintain via e-mail and phone calls. However, I often wonder and feel guilty about how I might have enraced some of them and how my behavior might have made them feel about their race and their English language proficiency.

These two contrasting but overlapping events define the scope of this chapter. The simultaneity of time and place of these two narratives shows how we can enrace and be enraced by others at the same time. Another aspect of enracement that these two brief narratives show is that racial prejudices do not only come into play between members of a majority and a minority group, but also between members of different minority groups (the Asian students and I were both members of visible minority groups in the United States). Additionally, they show that a narrative on race does not only relate critical incidences in which one describes how one's race becomes an issue for others, but also is a reflection of how one's own stereotypes and racial prejudices impact one's relationships with others. Finally, the narratives suggest a link between race and language (that is explored later in the chapter).

At this point, I would also like to admit that this sharing of my experiences about race is neither comfortable nor easy. Although it is hard to revisit events when my racial identity was given precedence over my professional abilities, it is even harder to admit my own past biases and prejudices and how they colored my behavior. It is in sharing this racial misbehavior that I use the term *confessions* in the title of this chapter. I am greatly ashamed of how I might have behaved in the past and apologize to those whom I might have offended.

ON BEING ENRACED IN TESOL

In Narrative 1, I recalled how I was the only student with a dark skin color in my initial graduate courses in the United States. Although this was of surprise to me then, it is an even greater surprise to note that in my 6 years as a graduate student and now 3 years as a university-based educator, I have come across only one graduate student who was Black and none with my own skin color (although I have met and seen a few at conferences). This observation leads me to think that there is something about race that relates to our chosen profession. However, when we take in the larger global picture, this race–TESOL relationship cannot be sustained: Most English teachers in West Africa (and other parts of Africa) are Black; most English teachers in South Asia are of my skin color. Thus, a claim that race is intrinsically tied to the TESOL profession is not really accurate. Nevertheless, the fact remains that people with these racial/cultural backgrounds are a minority in applied linguistics and TESOL programs in the United States (and, in my recent experience, in Australia as well). I believe that the reason for this low representation lies in other places: limited access to economic resources to pursue education in the West, low status of social sciences in their home countries, and visa policies and regulations that control the entry of people from these countries into the United States. Although these (and other) factors can explain the low proportion of people from African and South Asian countries in TESOL in the global North, they do not explain the extremely low proportion of African Americans and people of other U.S.-based racial minorities in the profession. It is here that race becomes relevant again. It is my understanding, based on my research on NNESTs (nonnative English speakers in TESOL; e.g., see Mahboob, Uhrig, Newman, & Hartford, 2004), that part of this has to do with hiring practices and administrators' perceptions of what the students want. There is a widely held perception that EAL (English as an Additional Language) students want native speakers as their teachers (Braine, 1999; Cook, 1999; Mahboob et al., 2004, Medgyes, 1992), and that a native speaker is of an Anglo (White) origin (Amin, 1999, 2004; Paikeday, 1985). This perception results in a hiring bias that, in turn, translates into a lack of enthusiasm of non-Anglos to enter this profession.

These critical conditions have now persisted over such a length of time that people who are victims of these conditions themselves reflect and emulate them. Lambert, Hodgson, Gardner, and Fillenbaum (1960) have termed such acceptance of low status by members of a minority group as "minority group reaction." This minority group reaction subdues the minorities and helps them accept their unprivileged status. However, the recent critical movement in applied linguistics and TESOL has questioned these power dynamics (this book being an example of such work) and is raising our awareness of the issues.

Narrative 1 is, in many ways, a benign narrative. It is one in which I was enraced not as much through what other people said or did, but rather through what I felt they did or did not do. It was partly, I believe, due to my own heightened sensitivity of being different. Most students in the room might not even have looked at me, but I felt that they were all staring at me. This suggests that enracement may happen in absence of any specific actions and can be a consequence of one's own sensitivities. However, not all narratives of enracement are benign. Let me share another story in which I felt that race was of central concern.

Narrative 3: Where Race Matters

A person I know quite well and who in 1996 earned her master's degree in applied linguistics with straight As wanted to go on for a doctorate. However, being an international student (who is not allowed to work off campus in the United States) from a middle-class background, she could not afford to pay her way through the program. Her only hope of pursuing her dreams was to be given a job at the affiliated English language program (ELP) as an ESL teacher. She set up an appointment to see the program director. During the interview, the program administrator said:

> While I have no problems with your grades or language skills or letters of support, I do have concerns about how you look. Now don't get me wrong, dear, but as you know our students pay a lot of money to come and study with Americans. Although I would like to hire you, how will I be able to justify this to our students? They will not be happy to see a person with your appearance as their teacher.

These were words that neither my friend nor I have ever been able to forget. Needless to say, she did not get this job—it was offered instead to an Anglo American graduate student who was not as qualified as my friend was (his GPA was not as high and he did not have any previous teaching experience). With this refusal, my friend lost all faith in being accepted as an equal in a profession in which she had invested so much (money and time). Her dreams shattered and she returned to her country.

Every time I recall this story, it makes me really angry and frustrated: angry because the director of the ELP was so overtly racist about their hiring policies, and frustrated because there is not much that we can realistically do about such behavior.

Narrative 3 supports the claim that hiring decisions are made based on administrators' perceptions of who students want or do not want as their teachers (Braine, 1999). It is interesting to note that current research suggests that administrators' perceptions of students' beliefs are not always accurate (Mahboob, 2003, 2004). We also know that even if some students have biases, exposure to trained professionals of different races/accents educate and change these perceptions. In addition, we cannot be sure if the administrator in Narrative 3 referred to the issue of students' beliefs because she truly believed in it or because using students' beliefs was an easy excuse for not hiring my friend, a person of color. Regardless, this incident not only enraced my friend, but also greatly affected me. It is coincidental (or maybe not, because it occurred in the same critical conditions that I described earlier) that I had a very similar experience shortly after my friend went through this rejection.

Narrative 4: Accent and Race

When my friend was going through these difficult times, I had only been in the United States for about a year. I was nearly finished working on my master's degree in applied linguistics and was transitioning into the doctoral program. I considered myself, in some ways, very lucky, because I was one of the few international students in the master's program (in fact, if I remember correctly, I was the only one) who had an AI position (associate instructor, for which the department covered my tuition and gave me a small allowance to apply to my living expenses). I was (and still am) very appreciative of this support, because without it I would not have been able to pursue my doctoral education. However, my particular AIship setup was also a dilemma for me. Whereas all other AIs in the department taught ESL at an affiliated ELP, I was given the task by one of the ELP directors to help out the office staff. Thus, while my colleagues were gaining valuable experience (and training) in teaching ESL, I—who was studying for the same degree in the same program—was not considered good enough to teach. I can't help but to view this through the lens of my colonized (South Asian) history and see a reflection of the White officers walking freely and the dark coolies (luggage carriers) carrying their luggage for them.

Although I learnt a lot working in the office and made some good friends amongst the office staff, I was never satisfied with my position. I wanted to teach. I wanted to get the same experience and training as my colleagues were getting. When I approached one of the directors of the ELP, I was told that they could not let me teach unless I "changed my accent." And, once again (this time in person), I heard the now eerily familiar structure "You know we would love to have you join the teaching team, but ..." The director followed the "but" with a reference to students' desires. She said something like; "... the students come here to study with Americans and will complain." As she said this, I kept thinking of my friend who was given an almost identical response—the difference being that with her the issue was not her language but instead her race. I left the office sad, but not as devastated as my friend. I still had an AIship that supported my doctoral work, unlike my friend and many other people I knew. Before ending this narrative, I should mention that, over time, I was allowed to teach in this ELP. Once given an opportunity to prove myself, I was asked to teach every session until I left to take up my first tenure-track position.

What I did not include in Narrative 4 is that after I left the office and thought about what had happened, I realized that the administrator was being less than totally honest: There were at least two British speakers of English and one nonnative speaker of English with a European background. Thus, it was not true that they hired only Americans or speakers of American English. However, one thing that was terribly true about this was that the three non-Americans were all White. I wonder if it was my skin color rather than my accent that was really the issue. Race was definitely an issue in Narrative 3—it was clearly articulated as such. In my case however, it was camouflaged and couched in terms of "accent." To me, this episode implied that although non-American White accents were acceptable, non-American non-White accents were not. It wasn't so much that I had an accent that I refuse(d) to give up (it is who I am, it is part of my identity), as it was that even if I did not have that accent, I would be marked by the color of my skin. Narratives 3 and 4 have made me realize that race and accent in TESOL are closely tied together.

So far, I have shared narratives that I experienced/witnessed. However, the real-life consequences of the relationship among race, nativeness (accent), and TESOL are quite widespread. One good way of evaluating the scope of this relationship is to look at job advertisements that explicitly ask for "White native speakers." These ads exemplify the relationship that is raised in literature on NNESTs (e.g., Amin, 2004; Braine, 1999; Paikeday, 1985). Although there has been a decrease in the number of ads that state this openly, it is not uncommon to find them (and ads that specify the need for "native speakers" are still very common). A quick google search with the key terms *White native ESL teacher job* will lead you to some very interesting posts. Although there are a larger number of employers who specify race as a factor in their hiring policies, there are also some prospective teachers who market themselves as "White." Three ads that specifically request "White native speakers" are reproduced in Appendixes A, B, and C, and one ad placed by a prospective "White" teacher is shown in Appendix D. In addition to these ads, there are numerous Web sites that document first-hand experiences of people who found themselves victims of this racism in TESOL (Appendix E). The following quote is taken from one such Web site http://www.eslteachersboard.com/cgibin/forum/index.pl?noframes;read=2662&expand=1; accessed on April 15, 2005) and shares the lament of one non-White, nonnative ESL teacher who wanted to find a teaching position in China:

> I have tried for five months to contact the schools directly, but the only replies I got so far were "Sorry, your qualifications are great, but the school headmaster wants white native speakers." I am getting depressed.

This posting clearly articulated the discrimination that he or she had experienced in multiple attempts to find suitable employment. Browsing through this and other similar Web pages situates Narrative 3 and 4 in a larger critical context—where White native speakers are preferred over non-White nonnative professionals. They show that these narratives, although personally relevant to me because they enraced me, are not uncommon.

In this section, I focused on two overlapping (in terms of time) critical incidences that enraced me in terms of my skin color and my "non-White" accent (and situated them in a larger critical context). However, I must sadly acknowledge that while I was being enraced, I was simultaneously enracing others. These narratives are the focus of the following section.

ON ENRACING OTHERS IN TESOL

As I stated in Narrative 4, I was a privileged international graduate student in that I was offered an AIship soon after I began my master's program. None of the other international students in the MA program at that time had this opportunity. Maybe, as a result of this privileged status, or maybe simply because I was insensitive, I sometimes, uncritically, behaved in ways that I cannot justify—and, in doing so, enraced others. I offer the following unpleasant narrative to exemplify one such instance.

Narrative 5

It was during my second semester as a graduate student and an AI that I was working with a group of students on a set of questions in our language testing class. During the course of the discussion, I wanted to make my voice heard and therefore said something to the effect that "I know this better because I have studied English all my life and people from 'your' background do not know this." Although I won the argument that day and our group presentation went really well, I have often reflected on this episode and I feel that there were better ways of getting my point across.

This short episode has stuck with me. Although I'm not sure if people in my group found my comment racist or discriminatory, or if they accepted it as being a statement that described and compared our two backgrounds, to me, in retrospect, it was a racist comment. It was racist in the sense that I considered myself to be better than others because of my background/status (which the others in my group did not share). In a very ironic way, I was using my country's British colonial history to elevate my status and inferring that those whose countries had not been colonized by English speakers were somehow inferior. By making them conscious of their non-English-based background, I was enracing them—whether they were conscious of it or not. Although I am ashamed of what I said, in one way I am glad that it did happen. The incidence foregrounded what I must have been feeling for a long time—it brought to the surface and exposed the stereotypes and prejudices under which I was functioning.

Narrative 6

I have been actively involved in the NNEST Caucus in TESOL for several years. As part of our vision, the NNEST caucus wants to foster an environment in which nativeness and race are taken out of the equation in TESOL. Therefore, it came as a blow to me when one of the presenters at the 2005 TESOL convention said that she felt that she did not really belong in the NNEST community. She said that when she attended the NNEST Caucus meetings, she was the only Black professional and felt isolated and left out. She said that the caucus was dominated by people from an Asian background who did not always welcome her amongst them. Her presentation really moved me, and afterward I went up to her and, as the chair of the Caucus, formally apologized and told her that I would take active steps to reduce such unintended alienation.

As I noted earlier, I was shocked to hear these comments because we actively encourage diversity in the Caucus. However, regardless of our attempts, it appears that our members are enraced within the Caucus. This was extremely revealing to me. On reflection, I was able to appreciate the woman's comments and was able to see that this member's experience of being enraced by another member of a minority group was similar to those related in Narratives 2 and 5. In their attempt to gain equal status and recognition, members of one minority group at times fail to recognize their power of enracing members of another minority group. This is seen in Narrative 6, when the presenter felt that she was not included in the NNEST discourse at the various Caucus meetings (here the enracement occurred not because of a specific action by the members of the community, but rather the lack of any action). In order to redress this situation, I brought up her presentation/feelings at the Caucus open meeting and led a discussion on ways of integrating all voices into the Caucus. This episode showed to me that it is not only an individual, but also an organization/institution (even those that are designed to counter discrimination), that can enrace people. As members of these organizations, we need to monitor our actions (and nonactions) to reduce any negative enracement that may occur within them.

These narratives reflect how we need to continuously examine our own behavior and how it might contribute to the enracement of others. It is through this critically reflective journey that we can better understand the construct of enracement and how we (both individually and collectively) at once enrace and are enraced through our interactions with others. This journey, although painful and difficult at times, reveals that there is yet some hope in focusing on enracement.

CONCLUDING REMARKS: ON HOPE IN ENRACEMENT

This chapter has been a reflective journey in which I shared several narratives to show how race is not just a noun, but also a verb. My goal was to show how, through our actions (and sometimes nonactions), we enrace and are enraced by others. In this concluding section of the chapter, I would like to expand the scope of this discussion and address how we can use the notion of enracement in other work in TESOL. I would specifically like to do two things:

1. Consider how this notion of enracement may be used to study different aspects of race and TESOL.
2. Talk about how we can use this notion of enracement to begin a dialogue with ourselves and with others to create a more informed and tolerant society.

So far in this chapter, I have focused on how enracement is a result of our interactions with other individuals. Although this is still a ripe area for future research/reflection, the notion of enracement can also be used in other areas of interest to professionals in TESOL and applied linguistics. For example, we could look at how various EAL textbooks and material represent people of different races. We can ask questions like: Is there a pattern in which people of different races are identified as being native or nonnative speakers of English (e.g., through pictures in textbooks, etc.), and is there a pattern in the various social and/or professional roles assigned to people of different races in the textbooks? If such patterns are discovered, we could continue our research into how such patterns are developed/represented. This research will suit the critical discourse framework (Fairclough, 1995) and lend itself to multimodal discourse analysis (Baldry & Thibault, 2006).

In addition to applying the notion of enracement to future research, we could also use it to educate ourselves and others. Throughout this chapter, I have attempted to encourage us to reflect on the various processes of enracement and to consider not only how other peoples' behavior enraces

14. CONFESSIONS OF AN *ENRACED* PROFESSIONAL 185

us, but also to monitor how our behavior might enrace others. We could use this understanding of enracement to educate (ourselves and) others and to sensitize people to how their actions might affect others. It is through such reflection on enracement that we can find hope for a more equitable future.

QUESTIONS

1. Mahboob writes about using English at school but a mixture of languages at home. If you grew up in such an environment, how have such experiences impacted on your work as a TESOL professional?
2. Mahboob writes, of his first time in the Unites States, "I soon learnt that I had to retool myself to survive in this society." If you are living and working or studying in a place far from where you grew up, have you had to "retool" yourself? If so, what new tools have you had to acquire?
3. Mahboob has created the word *enraced* and given it his own definition. Do you agree with the definition? If so, do you think it is a helpful/useful word and notion? If not, could you create an alternative word or notion?
4. In his second narrative, Mahboob identifies the point at which he realized that he was letting his own racial stereotypes influence his behavior with others in the class. Have you been in such a situation, when you became aware of you or someone else exhibiting this kind of behavior? If so, what did you do about it, if anything?
5. Mahboob states his belief that "a claim that race is intrinsically tied to the TESOL profession is not really accurate." Do you agree with this position? If so, why? If not, can you offer an alternative position?
6. In his third narrative, Mahboob recalls an incident in which a program administrator said to a colleague and friend of Mahboob's, "While I have no problems with your grades or language skills or letters of support, I do have concerns about how you look …. They will not be happy to see a person with your appearance as their teacher." How would you respond if you were told this in an interview?
7. In his fourth narrative, Mahboob reports on being told by a program administrator that he would have to change his accent before being allowed to teach on the university's English language program. How would you respond if you were told this?
8. Mahboob suggests that "we could look at how various EAL textbooks and material represent people of different races" and that we can ask questions such as: "Is there a pattern in which people of different races are identified as being native or nonnative speakers of English (e.g., through pictures in textbooks, etc.), and is there a pattern in the various social and/or professional roles assigned to people of different races in the textbooks?" If you were to ask these questions about the textbooks/materials you use in your classes, what would be some of your answers?

REFERENCES

Amin, N. (1999). Minority women teachers of ESL: Negotiating White English. In G. Braine (Ed.), *Non-native educators in English language teaching* (pp. 93–104). Mahwah, NJ: Lawrence Erlbaum Associates.
Amin, N. (2004). Nativism, the native speaker construct, and minority immigrant women teachers of English as a second language. In L. Kamhi-Stein (Ed.), *Learning and teaching from experience: Perspectives on nonnative English-speaking professionals* (pp. 61–80). Ann Arbor: University of Michigan Press.
Baldry, A., & Thibault, P. (2006). *Multimodal transcription and text analysis*. London: Equinox.
Braine, G. (Ed.). (1999). *Non-native educators in English language teaching*. Mahwah, NJ: Lawrence Erlbaum Associates.
Cook, V. (1999). Going beyond the native speaker in language teaching. *TESOL Quarterly, 33*(2), 185–210.
Cowie, A. P. (Ed.). (1989). *Oxford advanced learner's dictionary* (4th ed.). Oxford, UK: Oxford University Press.
Fairclough, N. (1995). *Critical discourse*. London: Longman.
Kamhi-Stein, L. (Ed.). (2004). *Learning and teaching from experience: Perspectives on nonnative English-speaking professionals*. Ann Arbor: University of Michigan Press.
Lambert, W. W., Hodgson, R., Gardner, R. C., & Fillenbaum, S. (1960). Evaluational reactions to spoken languages. *Journal of Abnormal and Social Psychology, 60,* 44–51.
Mahboob, A. (2003). *Status of nonnative English speaking teachers in the United States*. Unpublished doctoral dissertation, Indian University, Bloomington.
Mahboob, A. (2004). Native or nonnative: What do the students think? In L. Kamhi-Stein (Ed.), *Learning and teaching from experience: Perspectives on nonnative English-speaking professionals* (pp. 121–147). Ann Arbor: University of Michigan Press.
Mahboob, A., Uhrig, K., Newman, K., & Hartford, B. (2004). Children of a lesser English: Nonnative English speakers as ESL teachers in English language programs in the United States. In L. Kamhi-Stein (Ed.), *Learning and teaching from experience: Perspectives on nonnative English-speaking professionals* (pp. 100–120). Ann Arbor: University of Michigan Press.
Medgyes, P. (1992). Native or non-native: Who's worth more? *ELT Journal, 46*(4), 340–349.
Paikeday, T. M. (1985). *The native speaker is dead!* Toronto: Paikeday Publications.

APPENDIX A[1]

We urgent want 2 white native English teachers in our Xi'an Kingdergartin ,we will offer rmb 3500–4500 a month and one year round ticket,rmb 2000 summer holiday travel allowance,free accommodation,health insurance,etc.

You're freely welcomed to contact us soon!

---

[1]Source: http://marksesl.com/china_jobs/webbbs_files/index.cgi?read=200712
[2]Source: http://www.esljunction.com/jobs/about5520.html

APPENDIX B[2]

If you are a responsible, creative, hardworking, punctual, organized and easygoing individual, than we may have the right opportunity for you. We are one of the fastest growing schools in Indonesia. We are currently hiring for the 2005/2006 school year. We have immediate openings for pre-school, kindergarten, elementary and high school teachers.

Position requirements:

1. Due to new government policies, we can only accept resumes from applicants from Canada, United States, Australia, New Zealand, and the United Kingdom.
2. Be under the age of 35 years old.
3. Have a TEFL or TESOL certificate from an accredited education institution.
4. Have a college or university degree from an accredited institution (any field of study).
5. Have a minimum of six months to one-year actual teaching experience.
6. Have a proven track record of success and contract completion.
7. Applicants cannot have facial hair (men), i.e. mustaches or beards, visible tattoos, or piercing other than the ears (women only and only one hole).
8. No history of drug or substance abuse (all teachers will be tested).
9. No history of mental illness.

All utilities and other expenses are the personal responsibility of the employee.

Application procedure:

1. Please email all relevant documents in JPEG or PDF format.
2. CV/resume
3. A recent color photo
4. University/college degree
5. TEFL or TESOL certificate
6. Two letters of references from previous employers (all references will be contacted)

Please do not apply, if you do not meet the requirements stated on job posting. Only a short list of applicants will be contacted. Thank you.

Email address: XXX

Deadline to submit all documents: June 15, 2005.

APPENDIX C[3]

White Native English Teacher Available in Shanghai

ESL-EFL Teaching Job Wanted

Experienced business teacher capable of lecturing on management, e-commerce, finance, accounting, sales & marketing, communication.

Looking for position to begin in September some where in Asia. I have a degree, TEFL certificate and 15 years of international business experience. Email me at: XYZ.

APPENDIX D[4]

I'm an Australian born chinese and I have been applying for a few jobs teaching english in Hong Kong. I have a degree and a teaching diploma. However, when I applied for a job I got an email from a prospective employer who told me they were interested in my application. When he found out that I was asian (my surname) he told me that even though I had an Aussie accent it didn't matter because it was the fact that I was asian that stopped him from employing me. He also told me that it was going to be very difficult to become employed because of my 'face'. Has this happened to anyone else? And is it really that difficult for Western born asians to become employed as Teachers of english?

APPENDIX E[5]

Post: ... but would anyone on this list be familiar with how an Asian-American or Asian-Canadian or ANY female with obviously Asian ethnic blood (but who grew up in the West) would be treated in the Middle East? Would I be at a disadvantage in the hiring process (since we're required to send photos) because I don't have the Western "look" despite my Western credentials and upbringing?

Response: In almost all of the top TESL jobs in the UAE, recruitment decisions are taken by Western expats .... Without the luxury of anti-racist legislation in the West, you may very soon become appalled by attitudes of fellow Western expats.

Response: As for getting a teaching job, well let me put it like this: it would be perfectly normal for a white Brit with mediocre experience and qualifications to be preferred over a non-white native-speaker of English with excellent qualifications and extensive experience. Sad, but unfortunately very true. Sadder still: it's normally Westerners making these decisions NOT locals!

---

[3]Source: http://www.englishschoolwatch.org
[4]Source: http://hongkong.asiaxpat.com/forums/speakerscorner/threads/59469.asp
[5]Source: http://www.eslcafe.com/forums/job/viewtopic.php?t=3461

Chapter 15

Conclusion

Mary Romney
Quinebaug Valley Community College

RECURRING THEMES EMERGING FROM THE NARRATIVES

This collection of narratives has captured and presented some of the formative personal-professional experiences of TESOL professionals of color. But before looking back at the narratives, assessing the realities of English as a world language, and then suggesting some ways of moving forward, it might be helpful to provide a definition of the term *TESOL professional of color*. Generally, the term refers to non-White or non-Caucasian people in the TESOL professional, and that is how it is used in most of the chapters of this volume. The TESOL professionals of color who have written the narratives in this volume are of African, East Asian, South Asian, and Latin American descent.

However, other than the definition of TESOL professionals of color, what are the major commonalities that have emerged through these narratives? There are at least six recurring themes:

1. Mistaken identity based on race and assumed relationship to the English language.
2. Challenges to nationality and/or English nativeness.
3. The influence of popular culture on perceptions of people of color.
4. Compounding of English nonnativeness with race.

5. The dearth of TESOL professionals of color in certain contexts and in positions of influence and authority.
6. A shared responsibility for the struggle for equality with all TESOL professionals.

The issue of mistaken identity highlights what we have on occasion referred to as people "listening with their eyes." This group sometimes includes qualified, experienced professionals who should be expected to have to have a greater sensory self-awareness. The question of what it means to be a native speaker (in this case, of English) was also a recurring theme in a number of the narratives, including who makes this decision and what parameters are being employed as its basis. In many of the narratives, the impact of the media, music, television, and other aspects of popular culture came through as a significant set of forces that mold and shape our experiences and expectations of race, color, and nativeness. For a number of the contributors, they were among the few—and sometimes the only—TESOL professionals of color in their particular teaching and learning organization, and thus the issue of "conspicuous by its absence" was also noticed and noted. Although all minorities, visible and invisible, almost by definition face the challenges of striving for terms and treatment comparable with their dominant-culture or dominant-race counterparts, another important theme that emerged from these narratives was the need for a sense of a shared responsibility in moving all of us forward.

WHAT WE CAN LEARN ABOUT THE TESOL PROFESSION AND ABOUT TESOL PROFESSIONALS FROM THESE NARRATIVES

It seems clear that the profession needs to move toward an increased awareness of the demographic complexities and realities of the English language worldwide. One lesson that can be learned from the experiences of the TESOL professionals of color in this collection is that there is a disconnect between the realities of the English language and its perception by some students, employers, and others, and that this disconnect is closely related to race. Furthermore, based on the narratives in this collection, the treatment of TESOL professionals of color is often based on this disconnect. Nonnativeness can also be a factor, but it is the race of these professionals that has been the principal determining factor in several areas, from the conditions they work under and their treatment by classmates, students, employers, and colleagues, to society at large. This disconnect, disjunction, or misalignment is related to issues that are addressed in the next section of this chapter.

15. CONCLUSION

ISSUES IN THE TESOL PROFESSION THAT NEED TO BE ADDRESSED

Who Speaks English Worldwide? Perception Versus Reality

The experiences articulated by TESOL professionals of color in the preceding chapters reveal several important aspects of the TESOL profession and the English language, some of which are best illustrated (some might even claim that they can only be illustrated) through such narrative inquiry. One of the most significant among these is the egregious disjunction between the reality of the English language in terms of its speakers worldwide on the one hand, and generally held perceptions of the language on the other.

Since at least the last decade of the 20th century, English has been referred to as a "world language" (Graddol, 1997) or a "global language" (Crystal, 1998). This is not only because of its widespread use, but also because of the unique cultural, socioeconomic, and sociopolitical position of the language. As Crystal (1998) observed, "Why a language becomes a global language has little to do with the number of people who speak it. It is much more to do with who those speakers are.... Without a strong power-base, whether political, military or economic, no language can make progress as an international medium of communication" (p. 5). Crystal's observation reiterates the long-accepted relationship among language, power, and perception that was addressed in a number of the narratives in this collection.

Approximately one quarter of the world population speaks English to some degree. Although there is a great variety between the two ends of this continuum of degree, there is also an enormous diversity of speakers of English worldwide. The Kachru construct for the use and users of English throughout the world (Kachru, 1985) has been a widely accepted, although increasingly challenged (Higgins, 2003; Yano, 2001), paradigm. It consists of three concentric circles, in which the "inner circle" is where English originated, was first disseminated, and is the predominant language, the national language or the official language (or one of only two official languages; i.e., the United Kingdom, the United States, Canada, Australia, and New Zealand). The "outer circle" is where English shares official status with indigenous languages, having been disseminated through a later period of colonialism (e.g., Nigeria, India, and Singapore). Finally, the "expanding circle" is where English has no official status and is a foreign language (e.g., Spain, Brazil, and China). As the narratives in this collection clearly illustrated, despite the vast multiplicity of Englishes, many students and members of the educational professions (inside and outside of the field of TESOL) only include White native-speaking members of the inner circle in their consideration of legitimate speakers and qualified teachers of English. This excludes most speakers of English. Even when there is awareness of the diversity of native speakers, the preference for White native speakers from the inner circle is still prevalent. White native speakers from the inner circle are generally also perceived as the owners of the language, so English is perceived as an inner-circle language, rather than as a language whose ownership is shared with the majority of its speakers, who are a combination of people of color, nonnatives, and World English speakers.

As the contributors to this collection have observed, inner-circle native speakers often feel that they own the language, but, in his study on the future of the language, Graddol issued a cautionary note: "Native speakers may feel the language 'belongs' to them, but it will be those who speak English as a second or foreign language who will determine its world future" (p. 5). Widdowson (1994) put it this way:

> The very fact that English is an international language means that no nation can have custody over it. To grant such custody of the language, is necessarily to arrest its development and so undermine its international status. It is a matter of considerable pride and satisfaction for native speakers of English that their language is an international means of communication. But the point is that it is only international to the extent that it is not their language.... *Other people actually own it.* (p. 385; emphasis added)

According to Crystal (1998), "Within ten years, there will certainly be more L2 speakers [of English] than L1 speakers. Within fifty years, there could be up to 50 per cent more. By that time, the only possible concept of ownership will be a global one" (p. 130).

Understanding Some Basic Demographics of the English Language

There are approximately 375 million native speakers of English (British Council, n.d.). English is spoken by more than one fourth of the world population, or over 1.5 billion people, and is the national language or an official language of about 75 countries (British Council, n.d.). A comparison of native speakers in the inner circle with the English-speaking populations in only three countries in the outer and expanding circles can be instructive. As of 1995, China had between 200 million and 300 million users and learners of English (Yong & Campbell, 1995). India is estimated to have 350 million English speakers, not counting the 15 million Indians in the diaspora, most of whom live in the English-speaking countries of the Americas, Africa, and Europe. China alone could have more English speakers than the total population of the United States, and India already has more. Crystal (1998) estimated that the combined populations of the outer circle and the expanding circle could be at 1.3 billion, whereas the inner circle is estimated to be between 375 and 380 million (British Council, n.d.; Crystal, 1998). India, in the outer circle, is the world's largest English-speaking country. Also in the outer circle is Nigeria, the largest country in Africa, with a population of over 130 million and English as its official language. It is said to have more English speakers than does the United Kingdom (Emeagwali, 2005).

Commenting on shifting patterns of English use in the future, Graddol (1997) observed that "India and Nigeria may experience substantial increase in numbers of first language speakers of English ... and it is worth remembering that even a small percentage change in these countries would greatly increase the global number of native English speakers" (p. 58). These limited demographics do not include the majority of countries where English is spoken, or even the fact that there are English-speaking countries on every continent, but they can help contextualize the population of native speakers in the rest of the world, and perhaps, contribute to an understanding of the extent to which English is truly a world language. Yet, based on the personal-professional accounts in this collection of narratives, the notion of inner-circle ownership of English appears to persist.

How Perceptions of the English Language Influence Perceptions of TESOL Professionals of Color

The majority of English speakers worldwide are people of color (Center for Immigration Studies, 1996). In addition, Canagarajah (1999) pointed out that "more than 80% of the ELT professionals internationally are non-native speakers" (p. 91). As stated earlier, English is a language spoken mainly by nonnatives, World English speakers, people of color, and any combination of these. This has nothing to do with how many of them are qualified to teach ESOL, but there are qualified TESOL professionals in all of these categories. However, if the ownership of English is still perceived—in spite of all the evidence to the contrary—to be largely held by White native speakers in the inner circle, then TESOL professionals of color, even if they are members of the inner circle, will not usually be perceived as members. Because of this, they may experience anything from mistaken identity to discrimination by employers and students, as we have seen in the narratives in this volume. How perceptions of the English language can influence perceptions of TESOL professionals of color can be summarized by the research of Amin (1999) in Canada: "The findings of the study indicated that some ESL students make two major assumptions. This first is that only White people can be native speakers of English and the second is that only native speakers know 'real,' 'proper,' 'Canadian' English" (p. 94).

ESL students in Canada are not the only ones with these perceptions; in Amin's quote, "Canadian English" could be substituted with the English of any inner-circle country. And, as we have seen, there are countries in the other two circles where these perceptions are also held.

One of the most important recurring themes of the experience articulated by the contributors to this collection is that the field of TESOL needs to move away from the Eurocentric, native-speaker-dominated notion of the English language, because it is erroneous and anachronistic. Although it may represent a historical artifact, which was perhaps partially true at one time, it does not reflect present and future realities, it has a deleterious effect on the profession, and it disproportionately and negatively effects on the lives of TESOL professionals of color.

ACCEPTANCE OF ENGLISH AS A WORLD LANGUAGE

It appears that a few (mis) conceptions and (mis) perceptions must be at least challenged, and preferably counteracted, if TESOL professionals of color are to be fully accepted worldwide, no matter which of the three circles they come from or inhabit, and no matter which of the Englishes in those circles they speak. One persistent misunderstanding is that the only (legitimate) English is that of the inner circle. Another is that this English is spoken only by inner-circle White people. Two other misconceptions are that English is an "owned" language and that the inner-circle members are the owners.

Acceptance of all Englishes (i.e., Creole, native, nonnative, and World English) is acceptance of all English speakers. And acceptance of all Englishes as equally legitimate is acceptance of English as a world language. The historical, political, social, racial, economic, and other factors that separate people worldwide and keep them from living in equality and harmony are largely the same factors that inhibit the acceptance of all Englishes as equal. Until all English speakers are accepted as being of equal relevance and equal worth, and until English is generally perceived as a world language in terms of all its speakers, TESOL professionals of color will continue to experience the kinds of events described in this volume. One forum in which equal acceptance of all Englishes would be evident would be at the curricular level. Not only would speakers of diverse Englishes find greater acceptance as teachers, but ESOL materials would also reflect this diversity. Matsuda (2003) addressed the incorporation of World Englishes in ELT in a Japanese context:

> The international scope of learners' English learning agenda should logically be matched by pedagogical approaches that teach English as an international language (EIL), in part through inclusion of variants of world Englishes. However, examination of English language teaching (ELT) practices in Japan reveals that English is still being taught as an inner-circle language, based almost exclusively on American or British English, and textbooks with characters and cultural topics from the English-speaking countries of the inner circle.... (p. 719)

Matsuda further warned of the "problem of inner-circle English only":

15. CONCLUSION

> Moreover, teaching inner-circle English in Japan neglects the real linguistic needs of the learners, eclipses their education about the history and politics of English, and fails to empower them with ownership of English. (p. 721)
>
> The assumption of native-speaker authority that underlies teaching inner-circle varieties of English puts the other circles in an inferior position to the NSs [native speakers] and threatens to undermine Japanese learners' agency as EIL users. (p. 722)

Japan is not alone in endowing inner-circle English with this power; it shares this attitude toward the language with many other countries. However, as long as ESOL learners—especially those in the two outer circles—perceive English as an inner-circle language, they will not perceive themselves as sharing in its ownership. This does not serve to empower them, but rather disenfranchises them in an age of globalization, when a world language seems increasingly essential.

SOLUTIONS AND IMPLEMENTATION

Solutions

Collections of narratives like this one can be enlightening in terms of raising consciousness of the complexities and realities of the TESOL profession that have previously received little or no attention. However, their usefulness is limited if they do not include suggestions on some of the directions in which this consciousness should lead the profession.

One direction in which the profession needs to move is toward an acknowledgment of the demographics of the English language worldwide. At least in the inner-circle or inner-circle-controlled environments (e.g., EFL programs that use materials and teachers from the inner circle), there should be more inclusion of the English of the other two circles. The contention here is that English should be taught within the context of its worldwide use rather than within the context of its inner-circle native speakers. An awareness of its worldwide use and its role as a world language needs to be added to ESOL and teacher education curricula, in combination with exposure to a wide variety of Englishes represented in ESOL materials and teachers.

Full acceptance of nonnative English speakers as owners of the English language needs to be incorporated into all aspects of the profession. This has implications for both nonnative English-speaking teachers (NNESTs) and for ESOL students. The literature on NNESTs is extensive (see http://nnest.moussu.net/bibliography.html for a bibliography), so there is no need for an in-depth treatment of the rationalization for this position here. Suffice it to say that nativeness should no longer be the standard by which teachers are judged, because it neglects and invalidates many qualifications and much of the experience of competent professionals. Also, students need to feel empowered as members of the worldwide English-speaking community rather than feeling like imitators, spectators, and guests of the inner-circle—politely tolerated, but never completely accepted. Inclusion of the full spectrum of Englishes worldwide—Creole, native, nonnative, World English, and so on—and their speakers must become a part of the TESOL profession, rather than the privilege of only the inner circle and some of its speakers.

Implementation

In order to implement the suggestions that have been made, every area of the TESOL profession would have to support efforts to recognize, study, value, respect, accept, and include all Englishes and their speakers. This might be done in at least three ways, as discussed next.

Development and Publication of ESOL Materials Reflecting the Diversity of the English Language and Its Speakers. Powerful messages about English are conveyed through ESOL materials, independent of the actual subject matter. Among these messages is the notion of which English is legitimate and worth learning. If ESOL materials are inclusive of a wider variety of Englishes, students are more likely to become aware of who its users are and thus develop a sense of English as a world language. In addition, students are more likely to feel empowered if they see others like themselves portrayed in the materials they are using.

Materials development is also a forum in which to counteract stereotypical images of people of color in dominant popular cultures. Popular culture is a principal export of the United States, and is perhaps a significant export of other inner-circle countries. In the case of the United States, it is largely through the popular culture that people all over the world form impressions of the United States and its people. Practically every element of the popular culture is replete with stereotypical images of people of color from the United States itself and from other countries. Many, if not most, of these images are harmful and create negative impressions of people of color, especially those in the inner circle. When students find that people of color from the inner circle (and elsewhere) are their teachers, they often may transfer their negative impressions to the classroom.

Professional Development Organizations That Reflect the Demographics of the English Language Worldwide. No organization can accurately or fairly represent the profession without a membership that reflects both the professional population and the (users of the) language. With current membership mainly belonging to the inner circle, the two major organizations,

15. CONCLUSION

TESOL and IATEFL, perpetuate the privileging of inner-circle English and its users. This has implications for the development of materials, for hiring practices, and for other areas of the profession. Although, as we have seen, most TESOL professionals are nonnative speakers, this fact is not reflected in the membership of these organizations, nor is the World English population. A truly global membership would support greater awareness of the worldwide diversity of English.

Teacher Education. A professional workforce that more closely reflects the demographics of the English language in all three circles must be developed, including the education of more TESOL professionals of color in the inner circle. This means recruiting and mentoring students of color from the inner circle. Teacher education must include both curricula that raise awareness of the diversity and legitimacy of Englishes worldwide, and materials that represent them. In a world where there are more nonnative and World English speakers than inner-circle native speakers of English, preservice educators must learn that it is pedagogically healthy for their students to be exposed to a variety of Englishes, through materials and teachers, because they will probably interact with speakers in all three circles.

Although this is not meant to be a comprehensive list of what is necessary to create a more inclusive professional environment, if various areas of the TESOL profession implemented some of these recommendations, the result would be less marginalization of the types described in this collection of personal-professional narratives from the field.

REFERENCES

Amin, N. (1999). Minority women teachers of ESL. In G. Braine (Ed.), *Non-native educators in English language teaching* (pp. 93–104). Mahwah, NJ: Lawrence Erlbaum Associates.
British Council. (n.d.). Retrieved June 7, 2005, from http://www.britishcouncil.org/english/engfaqs.htm
Canagarajah, A. S. (1999). Interrogating the "native speaker fallacy": Non-linguistic roots, non-pedagogical result. In G. Braine (Ed.), *Non-native educators in English language teaching* (pp. 77–92). Mahwah, NJ: Lawrence Erlbaum Associates.
Center for Immigration Studies. (1996). *Are immigration preferences for English-speakers racist?* Washington, DC: Author.
Crystal, D. (1998). *English as a global language.* Cambridge, UK: Cambridge University Press.
Emeagwali, P. (2005). *Globalization not new: Look at slave trade.* Retrieved July 7, 2005, from http://www.nigeriansinamerica.com/articles/539/1/Globalization-Not-New%3B-Look-at-Slave-Trade/print/539
Graddol, D. (1997). *The future of English?* London: British Council.
Higgins, C. (2003). "Ownership" of English in the outer circle: An alternative to the NS–NNS Dichotomy. *TESOL Quarterly, 37,* 615–644.
Kachru, B. (1985). Standards, codification and sociolinguistic realism: The English language in the outer circle. In R. Quirk & H. G. Widdowson (Eds.), *English in the*

world: Teaching and learning the language and literatures (pp. 11–30). Cambridge, UK: Cambridge University Press.

Matsuda, A. (2003). Incorporating world Englishes in teaching English as an international language. *TESOL Quarterly, 37,* 719–729.

Widdowson, H. G. (1994). The ownership of English. *TESOL Quarterly, 28,* 377–389.

Yano, Y. (2001). World Englishes in 2000 and beyond. *World Englishes, 20,* 119–131.

Yong, Z., & Campbell, K. P. (1995). English in China. *World Englishes, 14,* 377–390.

Author Index

A

Abraham, C., 2, *9*
Aguirre, A., 5, *9*
Akamatsu, A., 67, *79*
Alderfer, C. P., 113, *120*
Alvarez, L., 59, 61, *63*
Amanti, C., 90, *92*
Amin, N., 29, *35*, 55, *62*, 111, 116, *120*, 178, 181, *186*, 193, *197*
Ang, I., 76, *78*

B

Baldry, A., 184, *186*
Bannerji, H., 161, *172*
Befu, H., 45, *48*
Belcher, D., xi, xii, *xvi*
Bernal, D., 4, 5, *10*
Blake, W., 11, *22*
Bonilla Silva, E., 169, *172*
Bourdieu, P., 65, 68, 69, 70, *78*, 89, 90, *92*
Bragg, B., 93, *106*
Braine, G., 29, *35*, 55, *62,120*, 178, 179, 181, *186*, *197*
Brayboy, B., 4, *9*
Brockhart, J., 52, *63*
Brutt-Griffler, J., 28, 29, *35*, 59, *63*

C

Cain, C., 51, *63*
Campbell, K. P., 192, *198*
Canagarajah, S., xii, 31, *35*, 193, *197*
Canton, C., xii, *xvi*
Carty, L., 161, 168, *172*
Chacón, C., 59, 61, *63*
Cintron, J., xii, *xvi*
Clandinin, D. J., 7, *9*
Cook, V., 178, *186*
Connelly, F. M., 7, *9*
Connor, U., xii, *xvi*
Cowie, A. P., 175, *186*
Crenshaw, K., 4, *9*
Cresse, G., 8, *9*
Crystal, D., 28, *35*, 152, *160*, 191, 192, *197*
Curtis, A., xi, 4, xvi, *10*

D

Davidson, M., 31, *35*
Dehli, K., 161, *172*
Dehn, R., 25, *35*
Delgado, R., 3, 4, 5, 6, *9,10*
Delpit, L. D., 65, *78*
Deyhle, D., 3, *10*
DuBois, 2, 85, *92,162*, *172*

199

AUTHOR INDEX

E

Emeagwali, P., 193, *197*

F

Fairclough, N., 184, *186*
Fels, D., 111, 119, *120*
Fillenbaum, S., 178, *186*
Foster-Johnson, L., 31, *35*
Freire, P., 126, 167, *172*
Fricker, M., 76, *78*
Fujimoto, D., xi, *xvi*

G

Gardner, R. C., 178, *186*
Gee, J. P., 71, *78*
Gillborn, D., 3, *9*
González, N., 90, *92*
Gotanda, N., 4, *9*
Graddol, D., 191, 193, *197*
Grant, R., 121, 124, *172*
Gudmunsdottir, S., 7, *9*
Gutierrez, G., 4, *9*

H

Harding, S., 74,*78*
Harris, R., 31, *35*
Hartford, B., 178, *186*
Heald, S., 161, *172*
Helms, J. E., 110, 111, *120*
Henig, J., 3, *9*
Hernstein, R., 25, *35*
Higgins, C., 191, *197*
Hill, J., 88, *92*
Hodgson, R., 178, *186*
Holland, D., 51, 56, *63*
Hornig, L., 171, *172*
Hooks, b., 171, *172*
Hornsby, J., *78*
Hula, R., 3, *9*

J

Jacobs, L., xii, *xvi*

K

Kachru, B., 53, 55, 60, 61, *63*, 191, *197*

Kamhi-Stein, L., 179, *186*
Kambere, E. N., 8, *9*
Kubota, R., 124, 165, 169, *172*

L

Lachiotte, W., 51, *63*
Ladson-Billings, G., 4, 5, *9*
Lambert, W. W., 178, *186*
Lave, J., 66, *79*
Lee, C., 2, *9*
Leung, C., 31, *35*
Levins, H., 114, *120*
Lin, A., 79, 124, *172*
Lippi-Green, R., 59, *63*, 86, *92*, 111, *120*
Liu, J., 29, 30, *35*,73, *79*
Lopez, G. R., 3, *9*
Luk, J., 67, 76, *79*

M

Mahboob, A., 178, 181, *186*
Matsuda, A., 194, *198*
Matsuda, M. J., 111, *120*
McIntosh, P., 166, *172*
McKenna, K., 161, *172*
Medgyes, P., 178, *186*
Moll, L.C., 90, *92*
Montañez, L., 57, *63*
Moses, Y., 168, *172*
Murray, C., 25, *35*

N

Neff, D., 90, *92*
Nero, S., 29, 34, *35*, 111, 116, *120*, 123, 152, *160*
Newman, K., 178, *186*
Ng, R., 4, 8, *9, 172*
Norment, L., 115, *120*
Norton, B., 170, *172*
Nussbaum, M., 164, *172*

O

Olson, M., 7, *10*
Orr, M., 3, *9*

P

Paikeday, T. M., 178, 181, *186*
Parker, L., 3, *10*
Pedescleaux, D., 3, *9*

AUTHOR INDEX

Peller, G., 4, *9*
Pennycook, A., 55, 57, 59, 60, *63*
Phillipson, R., 52, 55, 58, 59, *63*
Piper, R.E., 110, *120*
Pollock, M., 2, *10*, 27, *35*

R

Rampton, B., 31, *35*
Rasool, J., 4, *10*
Riazi, M., 67, *79*
Rockhill, K., 60, *63*
Romney, M., xi, xv, *xvi*, 111, *120*
Rosiek, J., 3, *10*
Rowley, L. R., 2, *10*

S

Samimy, K. K., 59, *63*
Scane, J., 4, *9*
Schecter, S., xi, xii, *xvi*
Schockman, H. E., *120*
Shamdasani, R., *135*
Simon, T. W., 6, *10*
Skinner, D., 51, *63*
Sleeter, C., 3, 4, 5, *10*
Smith, D., 72, *79*
Staton, P., 4, *9*
Stefanic, J., 3, 5, *9*
Stephan, M. H., 110, 113, 115, *120*

T

Takaki, R., 82, *92*
Tang, C., 55, *63*
Tate, W., 3, 4, *9, 10*
Tatum, B., 3, *10*
Taylor, C., 74, *79*
Thibault, P., 184, *186*
Thomas, K., 4, *9*
Tinker Sachs, G., xi, xv, *xvi*, 124, 127, 129, 130, *172*
Tobash, L., 111, 116, *120*
Tomic, P., 60, *63*
Totten, G. O. ,III *120*
Trinh, T. M. H., 75, *79*

U

Uhrig, K., 178, *186*

V

Van de Weyer, R., 1, *10*
Van Manen, M., 5, *10*
Vandrick, S., 124, *172*
Velez, D. L., 77, *79*
Villena, S., 3, *10*
Vygotsky, L., 52, *63*

W

Wang, W., 67, *79*
Weedon, C., 54, 55, 58, *63*
Wehrman, J., 25, *36*
Wenger, E., 66, *79*
Widdowson, H., 28, 31, *36*, 192, *197, 198*
Wong, S., xi, xvi, 76, *79*, 124, *172*
Wu, E., *135*

Y

Yano, Y., 191, *198*
Yong, Z., 192, *198*
Young, M. D., 3, *10*

Z

Zentella, A., 88, *92*
Zia, H., 89, *92*

Subject Index

A

Accent, 56, 69, 102, 180–181
  English, 162–163
Advertisements for teaching positions, 186–188
African Americans, 153, 156
Americans, 82
  becoming, 90
  real, 155, 157
Antiracism, 166–167
Asian Americans, 40

B

Bahamas, 123–124, 125–126
Bias, racial, 116
Black professionals, 24–28
British Asians, 95–96, 103
  colonialism, 162
  Commonwealth, 140
  India, 173
  Whiteness, 162
Bullying, 98

C

Canada, 121–122
Cantonese, 129
Caribbean Creole English, 34
Cartoon American, 111, 117
Chaptas/Chinkas, 177
Chinese Americans, 81–82
Color, 2–3
Colorblindness, 50
Communities of practice, 66
Counterstorytelling, 5
Critical legal studies, 4
Critical race theory, 3–10
Cultural brokers, 128
Cultural capital, 162

D

Darkie, 121, 126
Dolls, Bratz, 131–132
Double consciousness, 85–86

E

Ebonics, 156
England, 94, 97
Englishness, 101, 103, 105
English
  as gate-keeper, 76
  as linguistic capital, 68
  as an international language, 52, 59
  as a world language, 151, 152, 194–195
  for expressing selves, 67
English language demographics, 192–193, 195, 196–197

203

Enracement, 175–176
research into, 184
ESL students' instructor preference, 115–116
Exclusion, 87–88

F

Fairytales, 132

G

Guyana, 19, 26, 32–33
Gaigin, 41–42, 43

H

Hong Kong, 14–16, 21, 65, 86–87, 121, 126–134
  local classroom persons, 70–71
  population, 127
  school system, 66

I

Indian, 137–138
  English spoken in India, 138–139
International Black Professionals and Friends in TESOL (IBPFT) caucus, 32, 111, 118
Invisible minorities, 40–41

J

Japanese Americans, 38, 45

K

Martin Luther King, Jr., 150

M

Madrid, 154
Media, influence of, 53, 61, 86, 114–115, 190
  American, 95, 153
  British, 95
Mentors/mentoring, 170–171
Minority group reaction, 178
Mistaken identity, 190

N

Narrative inquiry, 5–8
Native/Non-native speakers of English, 28–30, 54–55, 58, 101, 142, 145, 118, 195
  hiring bias, 178
  inner circle, 191, 194–195
  White, 181–182, 192
Native speaker fallacy, 58–60
Nigeria, 141
Non-Native English Speakers (NNEST) in TESOL caucus, 183

O

Otherness, 75, 76, 176

P

Poetry, 11–12
Perceptual frames, 41–43
Professional discrimination, 43–45
Paki(stani), 97, 98, 99, 101, 103
Persons of color, 110
Professors of color, 145
Popular culture, 155, 156
Pakistan, 174

R

Race, 2–3, 163, 175
Racial profiling, 17–19, 88–89, 107, 152, 157
  linguistic, 152, 157
Racism, denial of, 165, 169
Racial identity, 177
Racial prejudice, 177
Race talk, 27
Race in TESOL, 178–179

S

Safety zones, 168–169
Severe Acute Respiratory Syndrome (SARS), 133–134
Shades, color of skin, 57
Social (in)justice, 169
Spain, 151, 158
Sri Lanka, 161, 162
Standard English, 59, 156
Stereotyping
  in the media, 53

… in school textbooks, 130
negative, 155
using language, 51–53
St. Maarten/St. Martin, 149
Students, Japanese, 46–47
Subjectivity, 53–54, 61
Suriname, 107, 108, 109, 114
    Institute for Language Research and Development, 109
Symbolic market, 69–70, 73

T

TESOL professionals of color, 24, 28–30, 89–90, 159, 163, 164, 193
TESOL professional of color, a definition, 110–114, 119, 189
Theory-practice divide, gender and race 73–75
Teacher education, 168–169, 197
Teaching materials, 196

U

United Arab Emirates (UAE), 174
United States, 24–25, 53, 103–104, 143–145, 158
United Nations, 104

V

Venezuela, 49–51

W

White
    people, 110
    privilege, 77, 112
    teachers, 164
    TESOL professionals, 112, 113
Women faculty of color, 72–73, 77
Women of color, 168